Chewy the Wo

Based on a true story, it begins on the next page. Yeah!!!

Digital illustrations & edit by Peter S. Vinal

Story & illustration by Joan B. Vinal

Based on a true story seen by the author in 1957

PSV Holdings, Inc
5741 Oak Bluff Ln
Wilmington, NC 28409
www.drinkgenies.com
www.whitemencantdance.com
noannie11@gmail.com

First published by PSV Holdings, Inc 2012

ISBN; 9780615737614

Printed in the United States of America

This book is printed on acid-free paper
Dedicated to Joan B Vinal

A ray of golden sunshine seeped into the long underground tunnel of a fat little woodchuck named Chewy.

It was Springtime, and Mr. Sunshine knew it was way beyond the proper hour for nice animals to be sleeping Slowly Chewy's eyes opened and he woke up.

"Hello Mr. Sunshine!" yawned Chewy. "Why do you have to wake me up so early in the morning!"

"It is Springtime, and I have made you a beautiful new day, Chewy," said Mr. Sunshine. "Come outside and nibble on some nice nice juicy apples and the delicious green leaves."

"OK," said Chewy.
"I'll get up in a minute ...
But gee, my bed feels
so warm and comfy
and ...(yawn) ...
I'm still
so very
sleepy,"

"You are
the laziest animal
I have ever known," said
Mr. Sunshine. "All you ever
do is eat and sleep." Just then,
Mr. Sunshine was gone, and Chewy's
hole was dark and cold once again.

"Oh dear," yawned Chewy. "I guess Mr.
Sunshine is punishing me for being so
lazy. I must hurry and get out of bed!"

So Chewy hustled out of his snug little bed.
But just as he was about to leave, a beam of
bright warm sunshine flooded back into his tunnel.

"Oh, goody!" cried Chewy, "Mr. Sunshine
has decided not to be angry with me.
He has made the day all beautiful
and sunny again and ..."

But just then, everything grew
dark and dreary again. That's
strange, thought Chewy.
Suddenly Chewy noticed
that something was
blocking the entrance
to his hole. Something
big, brown and hairy
with lots and lots
of TEETH!

Chewy scrambled back to his little bed and jumped into it as quick as a wink.

"Some horrible monster is trying to get into my home and eat me up! Oh dear, what will I do?" Chewy heard the monster growling outside his hole, and he didn't make a sound. Then, suddenly, the monster was gone and Mr. Sunshine came back into Chewy's tunnel.

"Oh, Mr. Sunshine," Chewy cried out in a trembling voice. "What was that horrible thing that was trying to get into my house? I was so frightened. It made such horrible noises."

That's just Rusty the Terrier, and he
is here with his family on summer vacation.
He just discovered your tunnel. I guess he
is angry because he couldn't fit in and
chase you. I shined very brightly when I
saw him trying to get in, because I knew
he would cast a shadow inside
to warn you.

"Oh, thank you Mr. Sunshine!" said Chewy. "I will have to be more careful from now on. Is it safe for me to go out now? I am very hungry!" "Yes, it is safe now Chewy," said Mr. Sunshine. "Follow me!"

So Chewy followed Mr. Sunshine out of the tunnel and into the bright beautiful day. The apples looked so red and tempting.

The leaves looked so green and tender. And Rusty the Terrier was nowhere to be seen.

So Chewy began to eat. He ate and ate until his little tummy bulged out like a balloon.

He was having such a wonderful time eating that he completely forgot about Rusty. But not for long ...

"Woof ... Arf ... Arf ... Woof" In a flash, Rusty the Terrier came bounding across the grass, lickety split, right after Chewy.

Chewy threw away the apple he was eating and dashed back to his tunnel. Rusty stuck his black nose right into Chewy's tunnel and started to huff and puff just like before.

Chewy wasn't as scared as before. He knew that if he waited quietly and patiently that Rusty the Terrier would get tired of waiting and go away. So Chewy waited and waited. Rusty huffed and puffed. But finally Rusty could wait no longer, and with a final huff, away he went.

Back into Chewy's house came the warm and friendly Mr. Sunshine. "Well, Chewy, I see you were enjoying the beautiful day so much that you nearly got caught by Rusty.

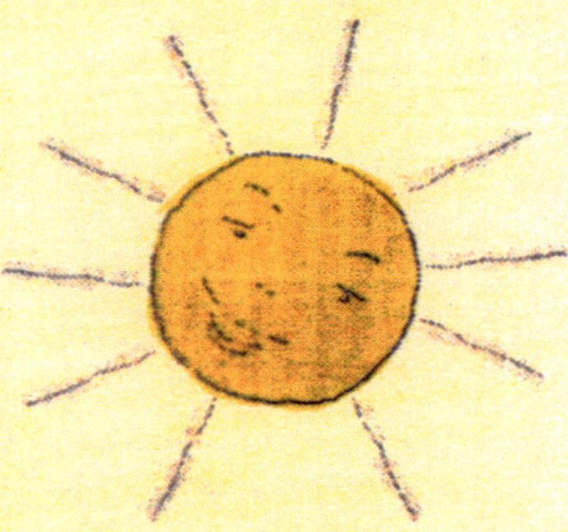

I don't think Rusty wants to hurt you though. If he did he wouldn't bark to warn you. I think you and Rusty the Terrier will have lots of fun this summer.

Over the summer, Chewy and Rusty did have a lot of fun together. It became a daily game.

Mr. Sunshine would give Chewy the signal that Rusty was coming, and then Chewy would run for his hole, with Rusty in close pursuit.

Chewy was always careful not to go too far from his hole, so Rusty never caught him.

Until one day, late in the fall. . .

The days were getting shorter and cooler, and Mr. Sunshine came earlier and left earlier every day. Chewy had strayed far from his hole to get some apples. Mr. Sunshine had drifted behind some trees, so he couldn't warn Chewy that Rusty was nearby.

Suddenly, Chewy looked up to find that Rusty was between him and his tunnel Chewy scrambled back to the hole but Rusty caught up with him, barking loudly, teeth glaring. In a panic, Chewy rolled on to his back.

But then Rusty stopped, sniffed Chewy a few times, and then trotted away, satisfied that he had finally caught up with the fat little woodchuck.

Just like Mr. Sunshine had said, Rusty didn't want to eat Chewy, he just wanted to catch him. Chewy rolled over and crawled back into his hole. He was shaking with fear from his close encounter, but happy that he now knew that Rusty the Terrier was his friend.

The next day, Mr. Sunshine did not peep into Chewy's hole until late in the morning, and Chewy woke up slowly.

"You better get up, Chewy, and say goodbye to your friend Rusty," said Mr. Sunshine. "Summer vacation is over, and his family is leaving."

Chewy scrambled out of bed and poked his head out of his hole, and sure enough, Rusty the Terrier was getting ready to climb into his family's car. Chewy walked over near the car and stood up on his hind legs to watch his friend Rusty leave. Just before he climbed into the car, Rusty looked back and saw Chewy.

"Woof Woof," Rusty said, and to Chewy it sounded like he said "See you next year." Chewy waved goodbye to Rusty, the big brown hairy thing with teeth that was now his friend.

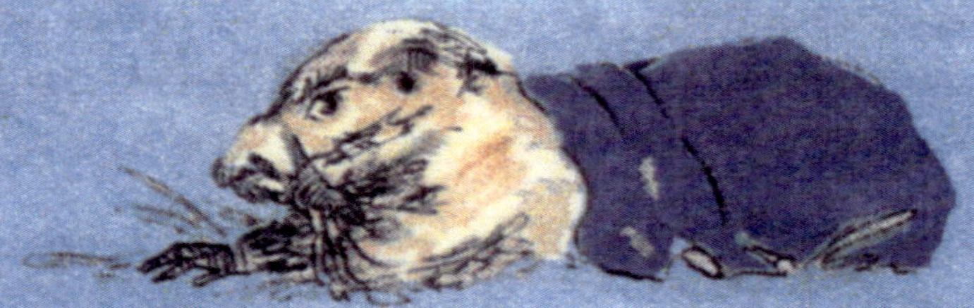

"I'm sad to see him go," said Chewy to Mr. Sunshine.

"Me too, but summer is gone," said Mr. Sunshine. "I can't warm the air as much as I did during the summer.

Soon it will be winter, and it will be time for you to curl up for your long winter nap."

Chewy yawned. He was getting sleepy. He waddled his brown, furry fat little body slowly back into his tunnel and then climbed into bed. One beautiful brown eye slowly closed, and then the other, and soon Chewy was fast asleep for the winter, dreaming of the wonderful fun he would have next summer with Mr. Sunshine and Rusty the Terrier.

NTER
PLAYHOUSE
EXI

Notes or write your own story

Notes or write your own story

Notes or write your own story

ISBN - 9780615737614

DOT TO DOT
TRAINS
FOR ADULTS

This book includes 30 Unique Dot Pages.

Start from 1st Number dot and continue all the way till you reach end of numbers, all the designs are continous lines and there are no jumps or breaks!

If you have any suggestions or ideas, please drop an email to info@coloringbooks101.com

TABLE OF CONTENTS

» Train 1 (601 dots) - Black 4
» Train 10 (520 dots) - Black 6
» Train 11 (515 dots) - Black 8
» Train 12 (427 dots) - Black 10
» Train 13 (400 dots) - Black 12
» Train 14 (528 dots) - Black 14
» Train 15 (512 dots) - Black 16
» Train 16 (675 dots) - Black 18
» Train 17 (651 dots) - Black 20
» Train 18 (540 dots) - Black 22
» Train 19 (702 dots) - Black 24
» Train 2 (657 dots) - Black 26
» Train 20 (468 dots) - Black 28
» Train 21 (504 dots) - Black 30
» Train 22 (545 dots) - Black 32
» Train 23 (600 dots) - Black 34
» Train 24 (630 dots) - Black 36
» Train 25 (708 dots) - Black 38
» Train 26 (745 dots) - Black 40
» Train 27 (671 dots) - Black 42
» Train 28 (570 dots) - Black 44
» Train 29 (515 dots) - Black 46
» Train 3 (558 dots) - Black 48
» Train 30 (505 dots) - Black 50
» Train 4 (557 dots) - Black 52
» Train 5 (588 dots) - Black 54
» Train 6 (516 dots) - Black 56
» Train 7 (525 dots) - Black 58
» Train 8 (500 dots) - Black 60
» Train 9 (531 dots) - Black 62
» Completed Dot to Dot Pages Previews 66

Train 1 (601 dots) - Black

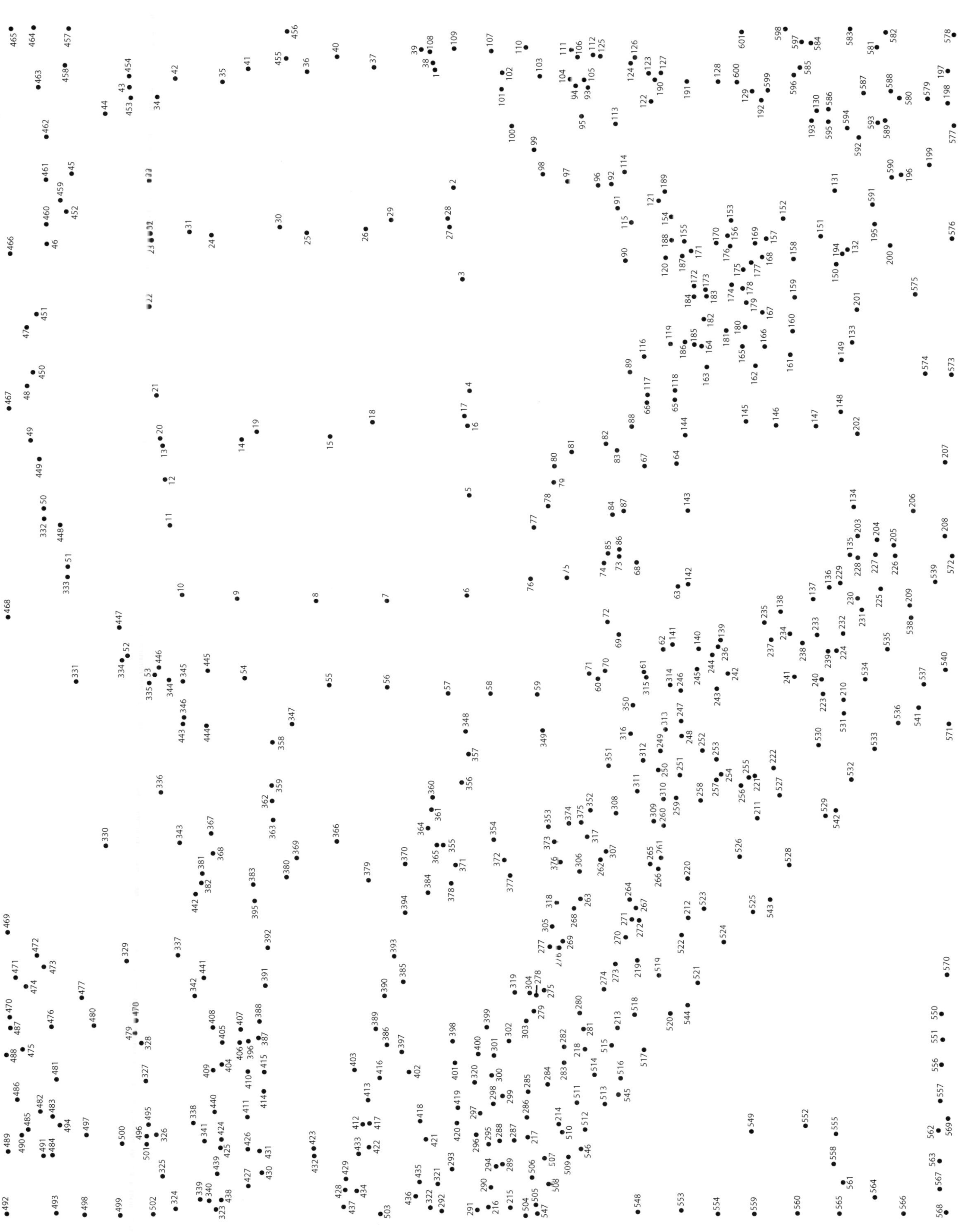

Train 10 (520 dots) - Black

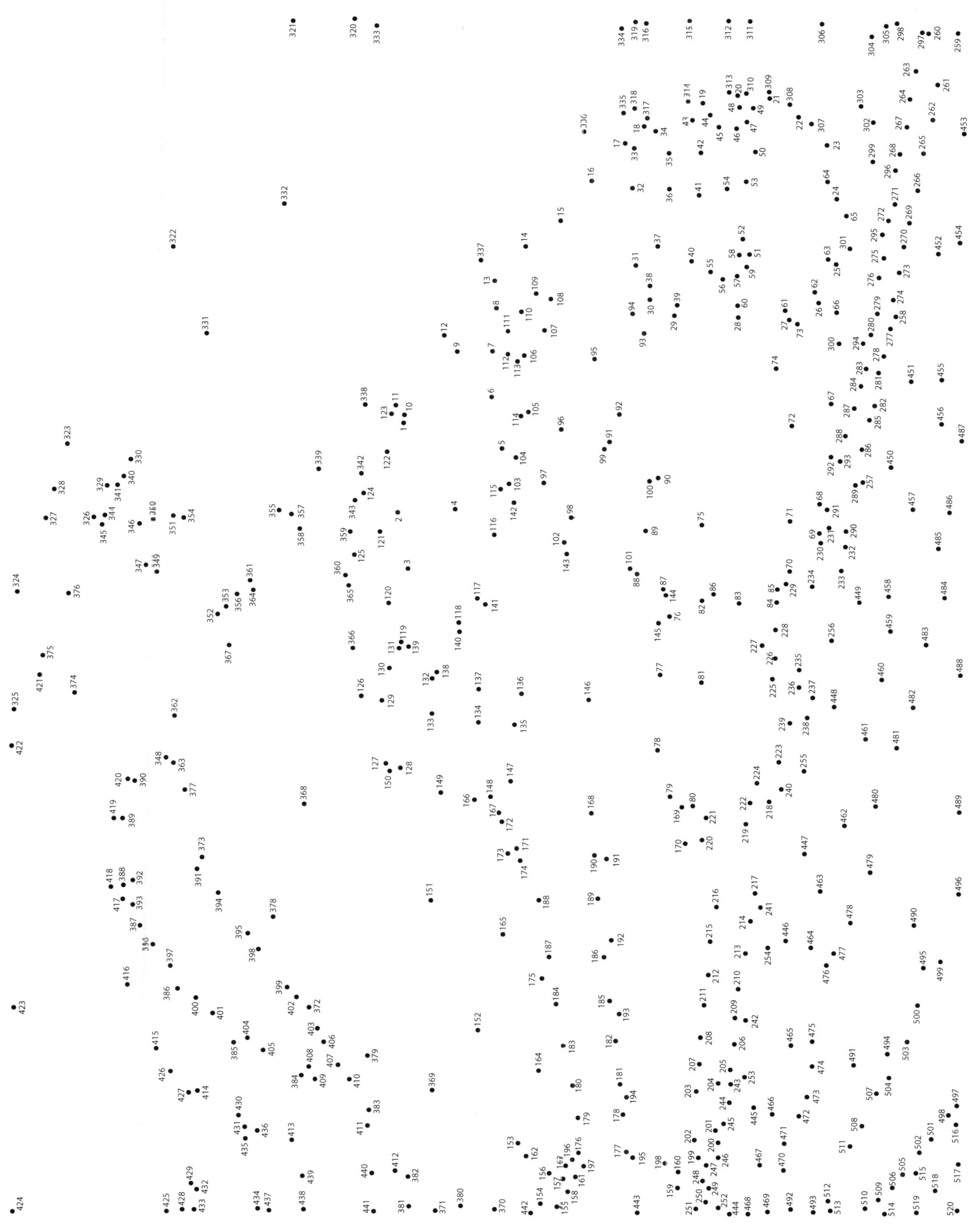

Train 11 (515 dots) - Black

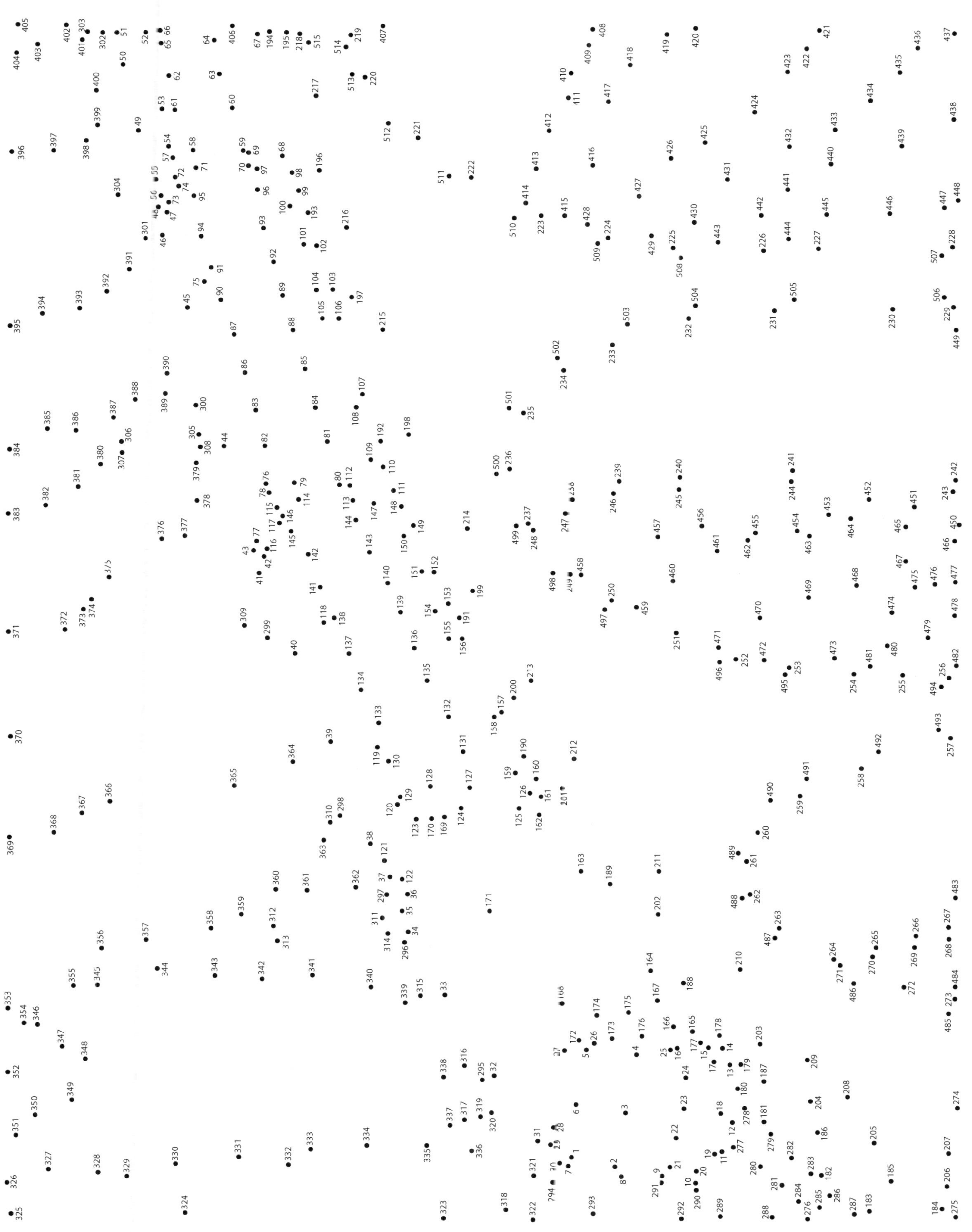

Train 12 (427 dots) - Black

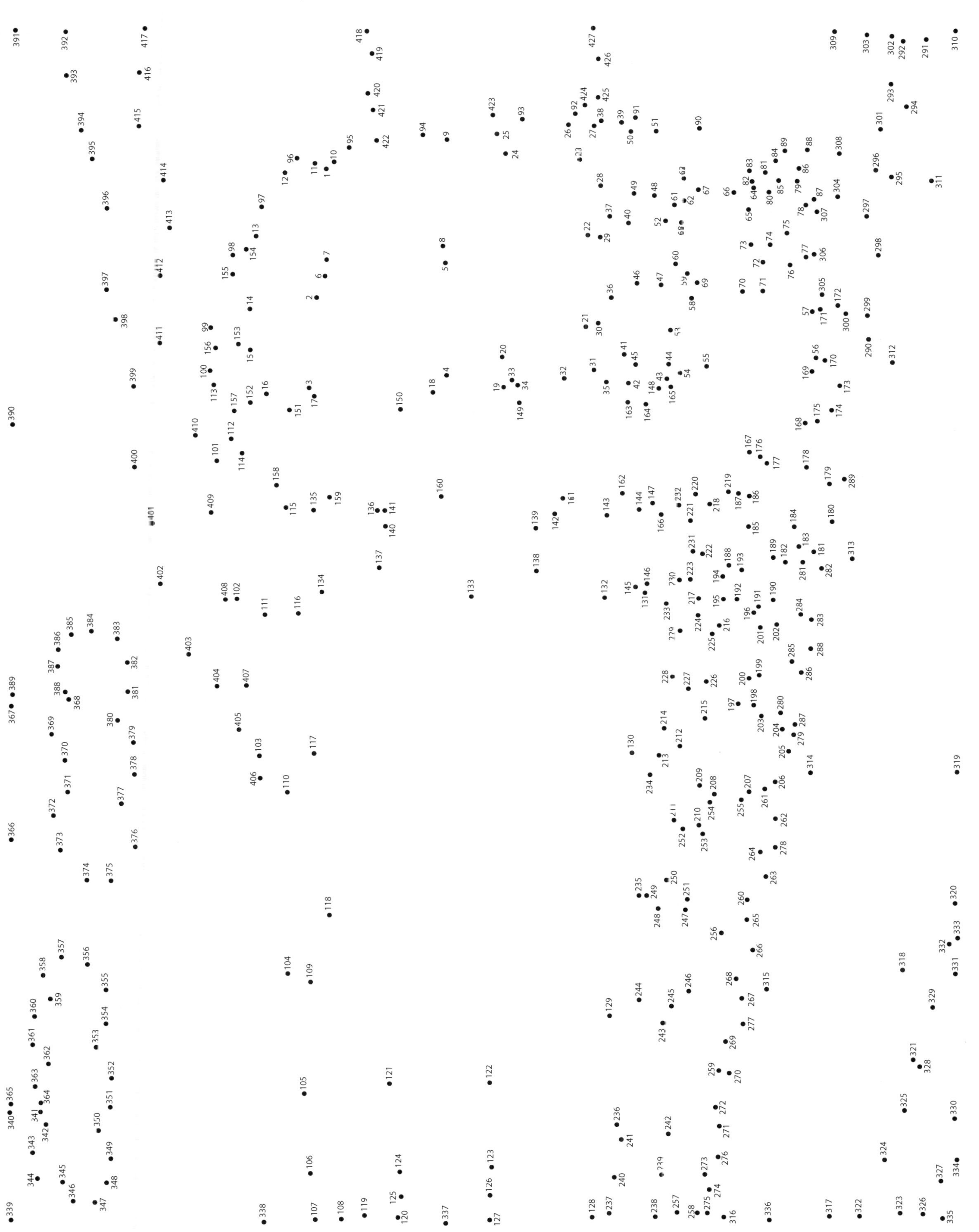

Train 13 (400 dots) - Black

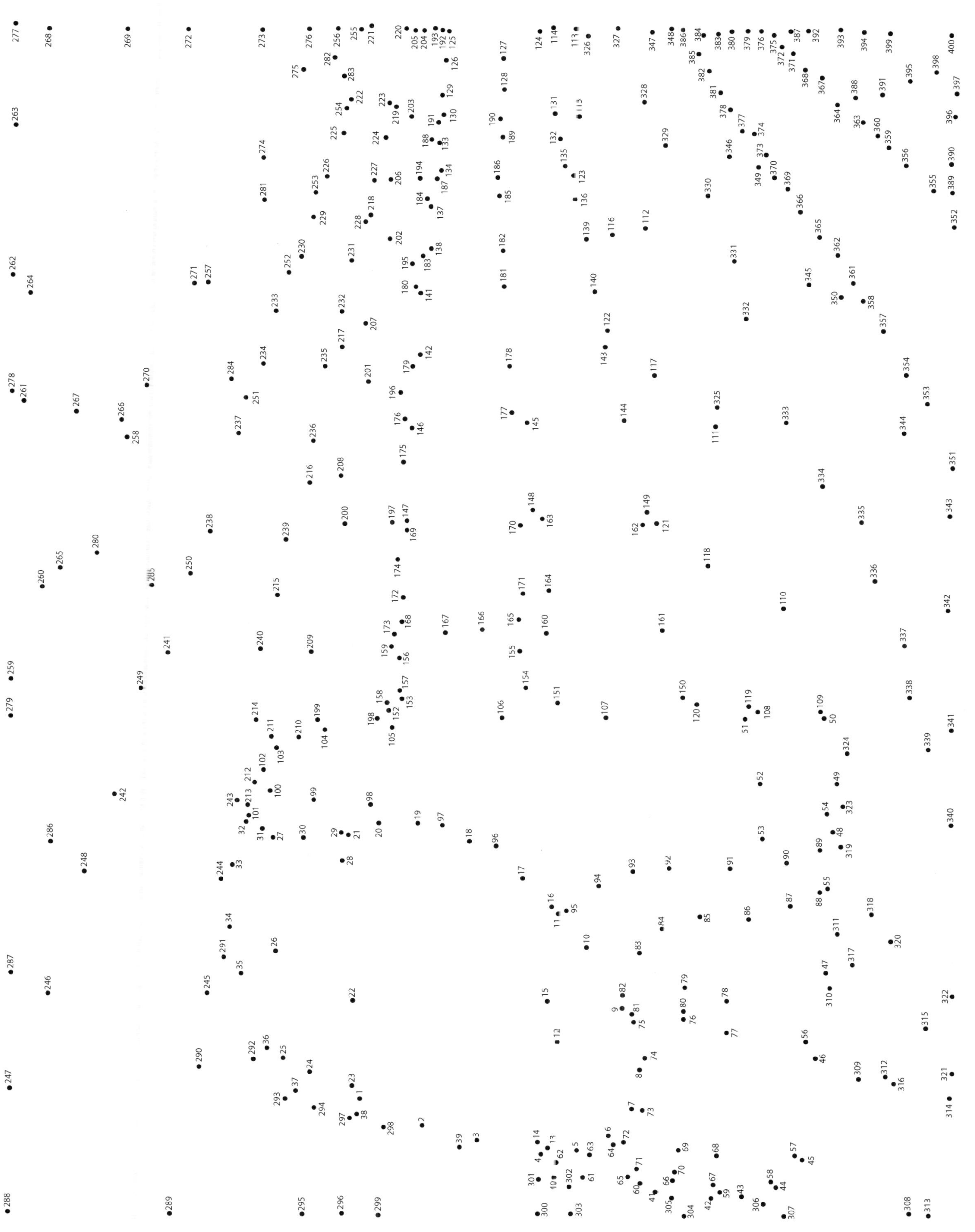

Train 14 (528 dots) - Black

Train 15 (512 dots) - Black

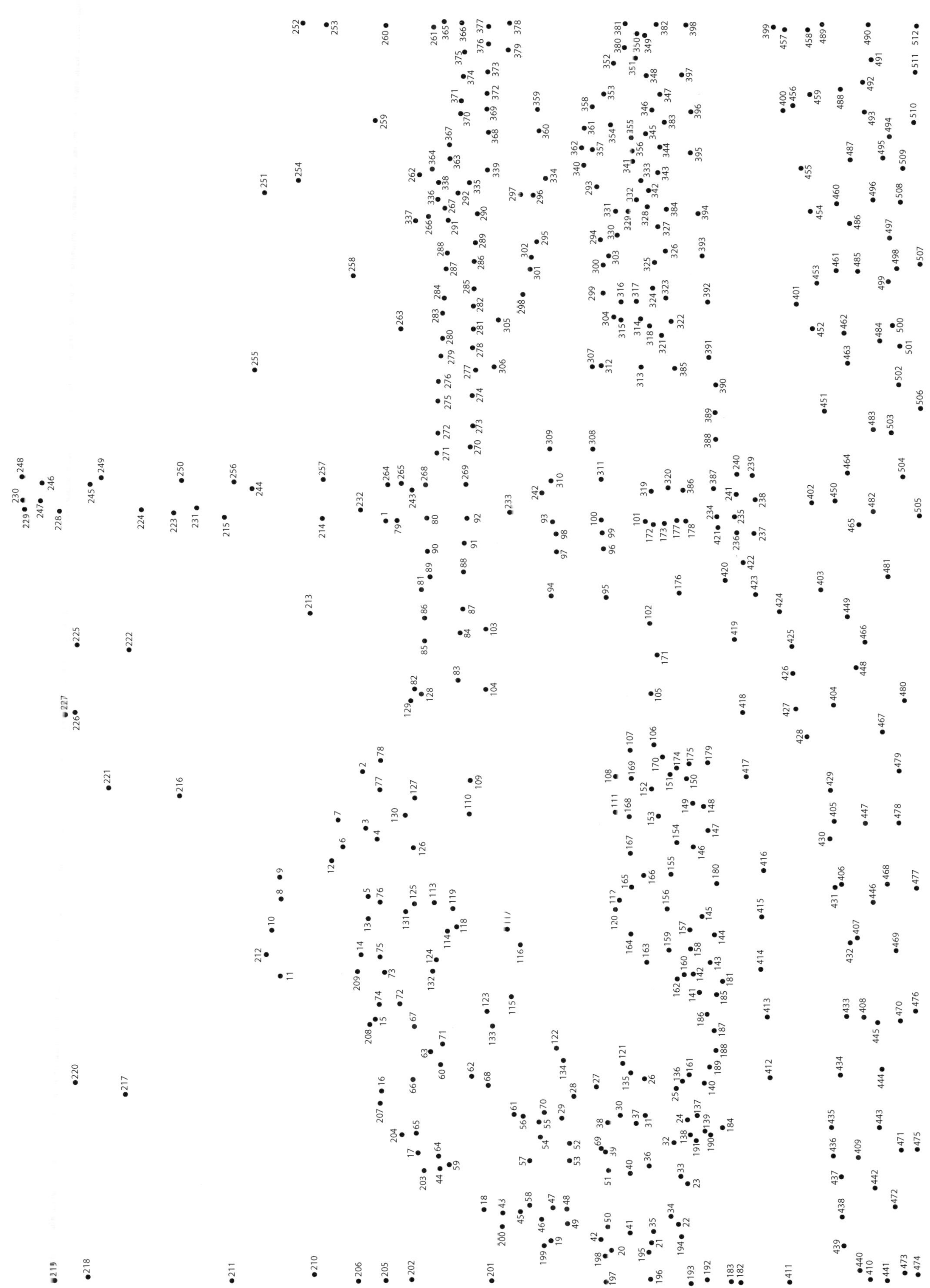

Train 16 (675 dots) - Black

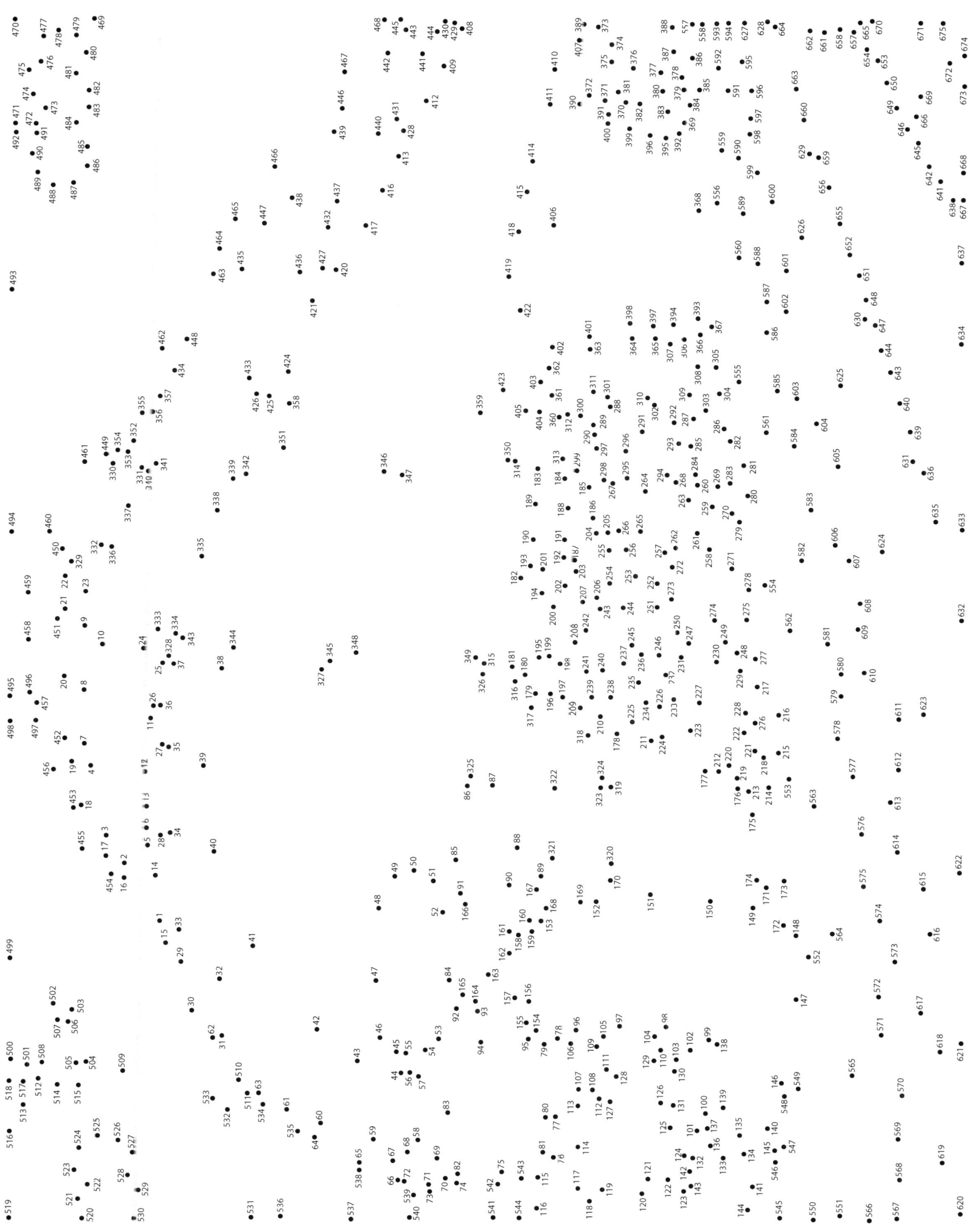

Train 17 (651 dots) - Black

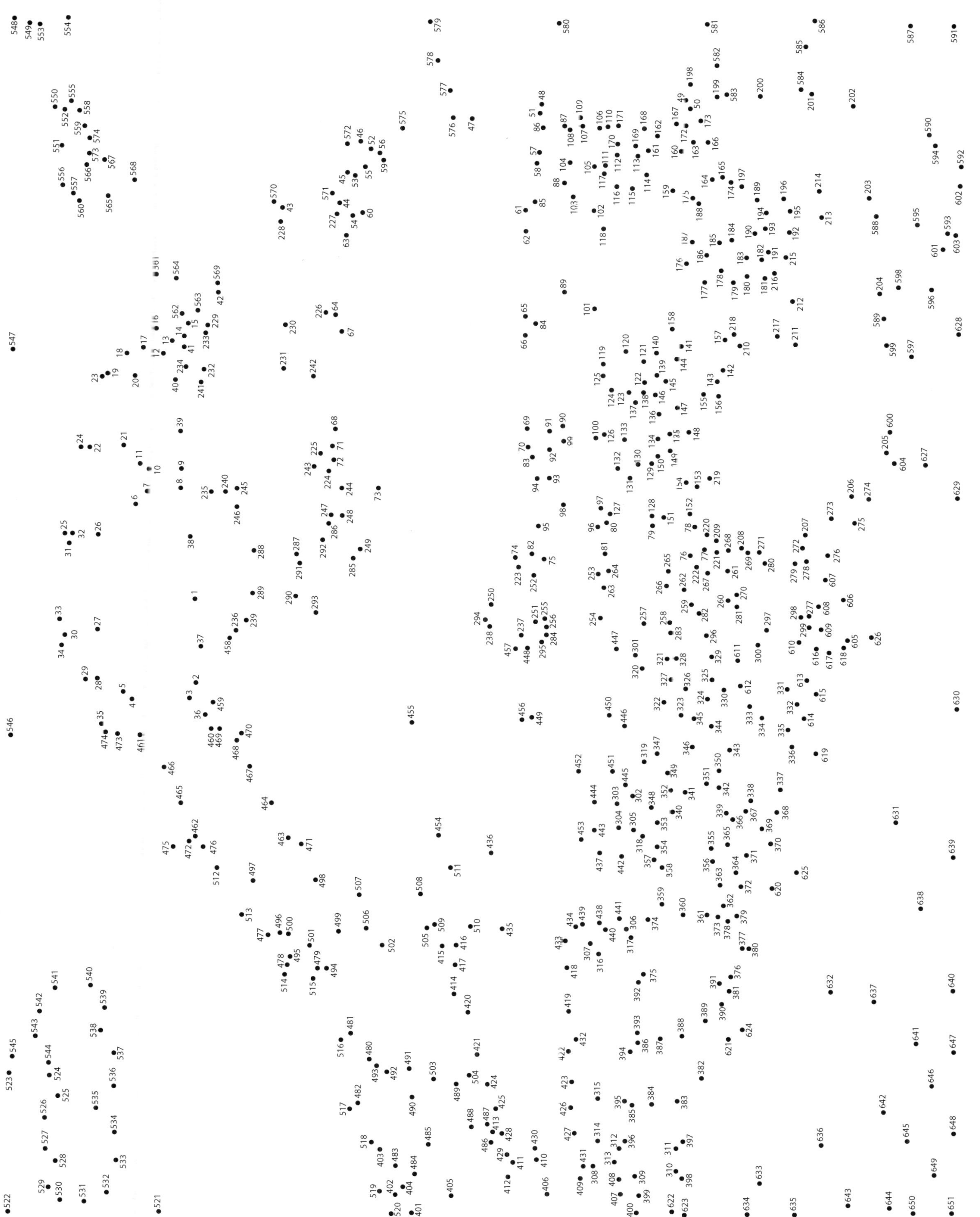

Train 18 (540 dots) - Black

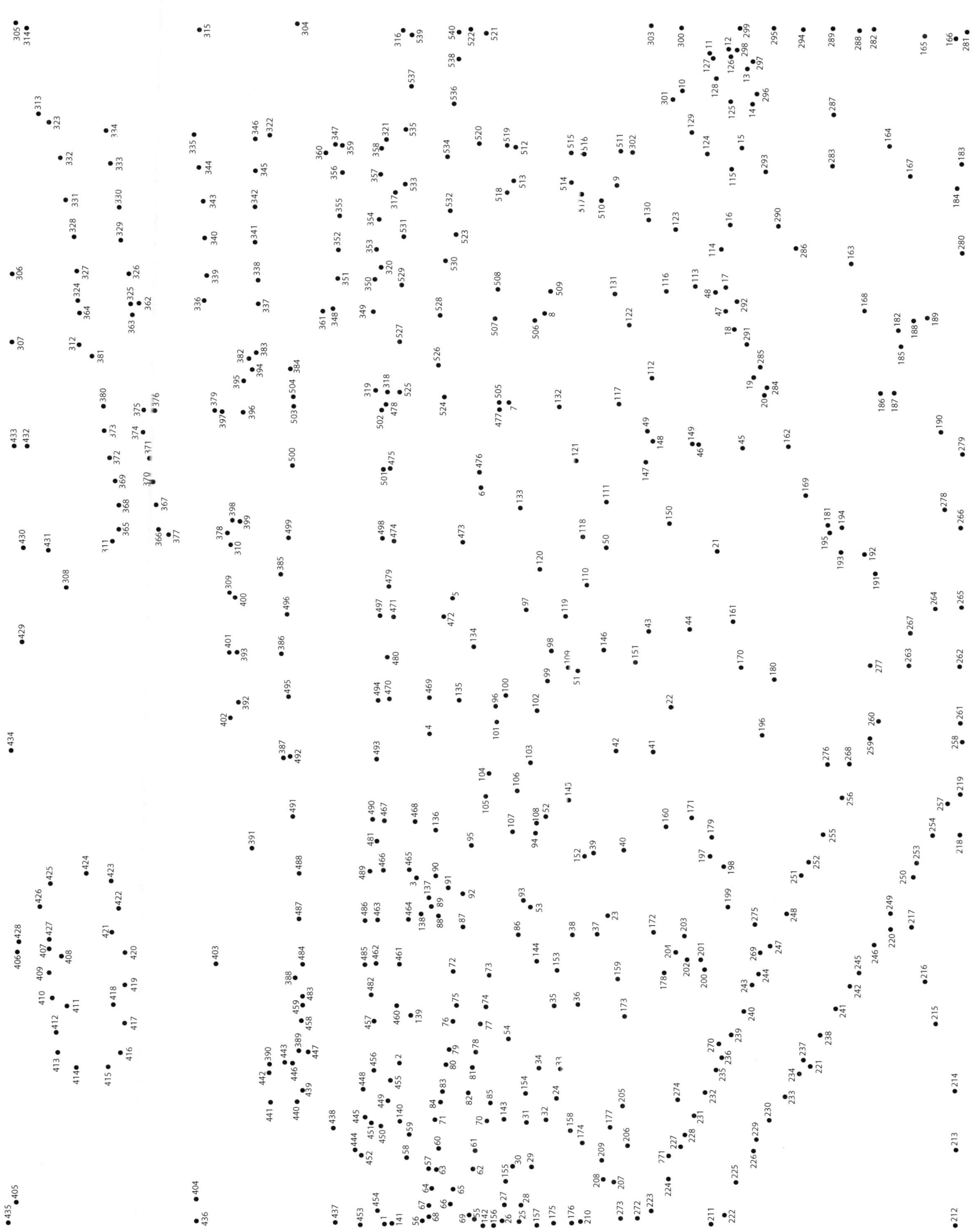

Train 19 (702 dots) - Black

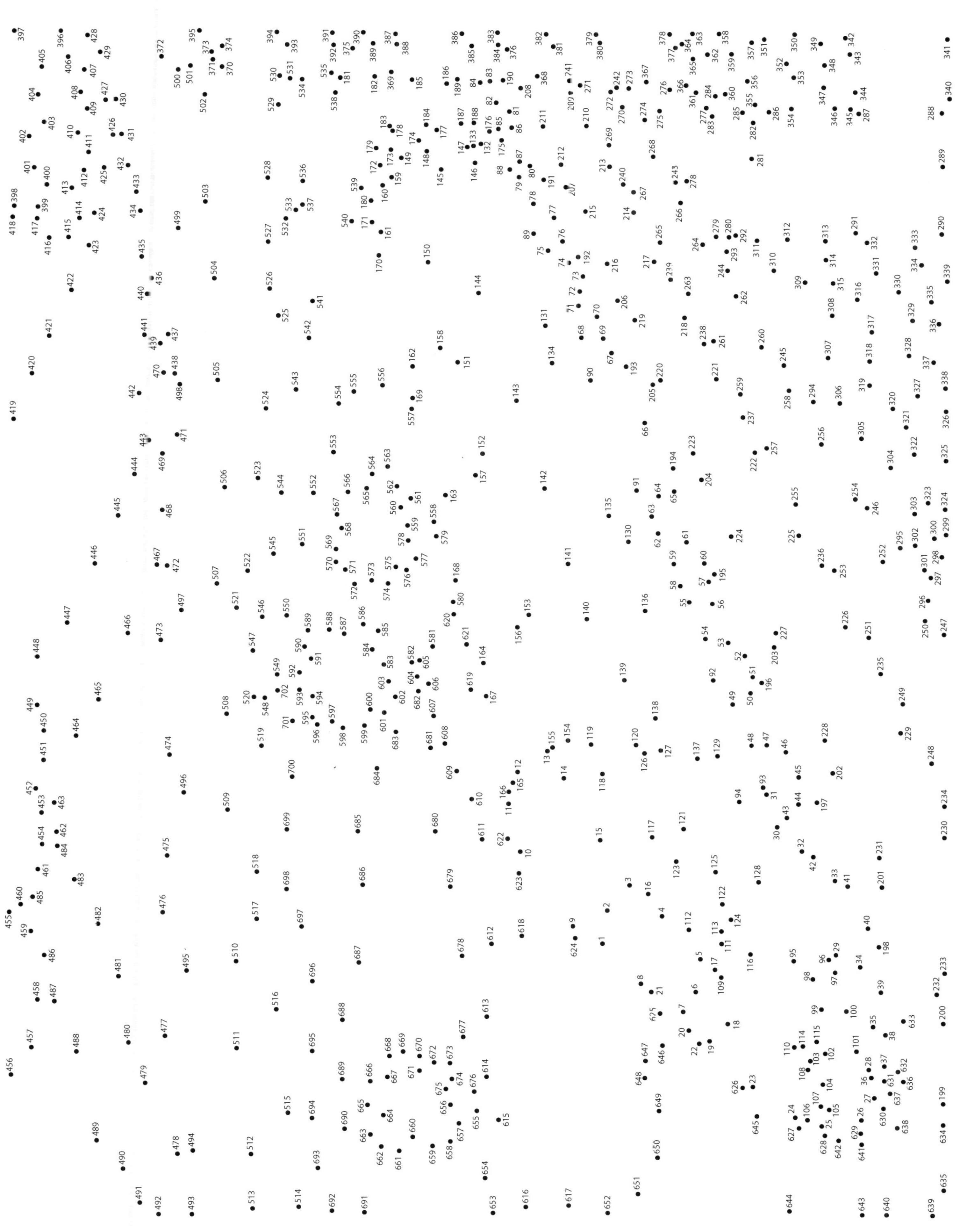

Train 2 (657 dots) - Black

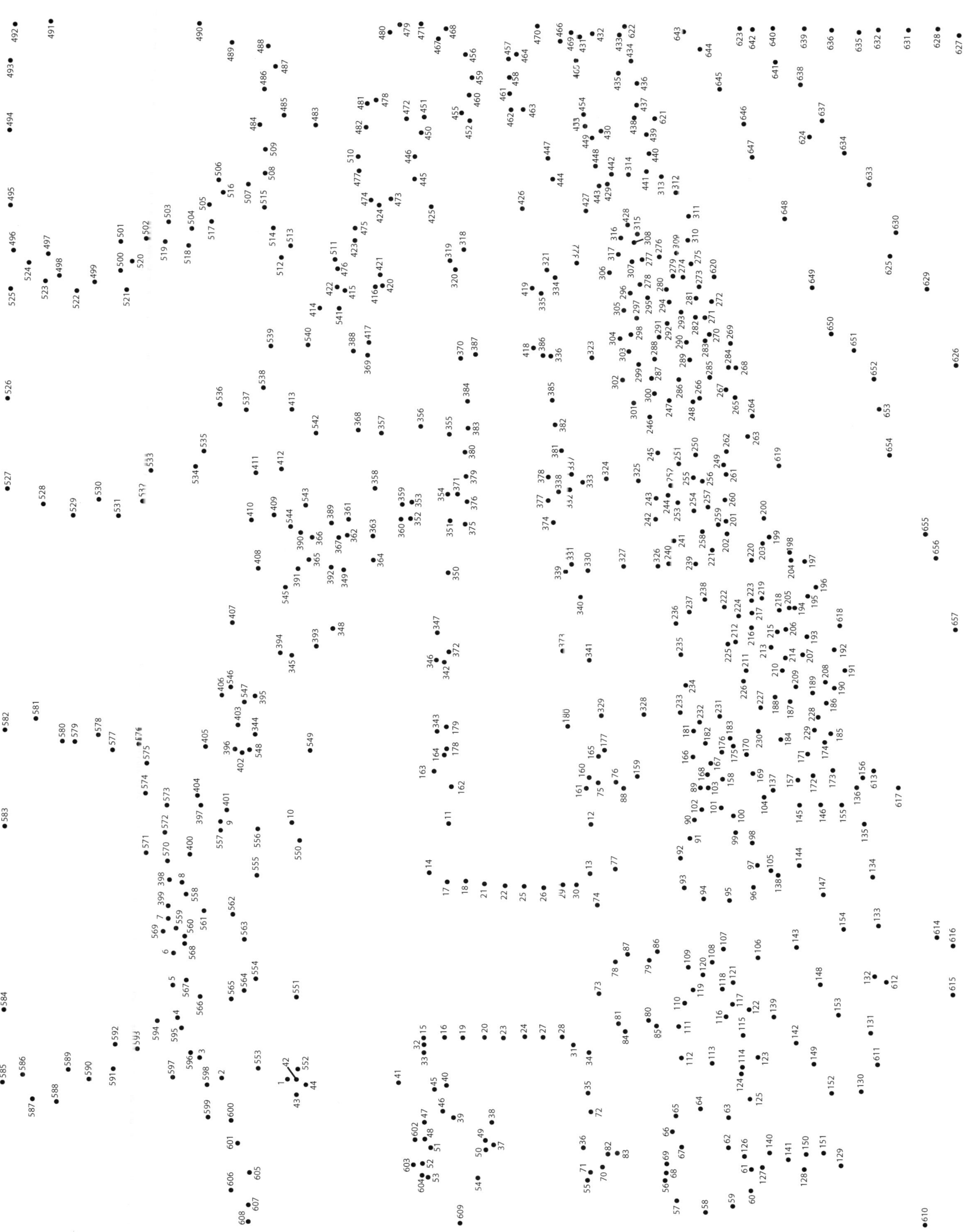

Train 20 (468 dots) - Black

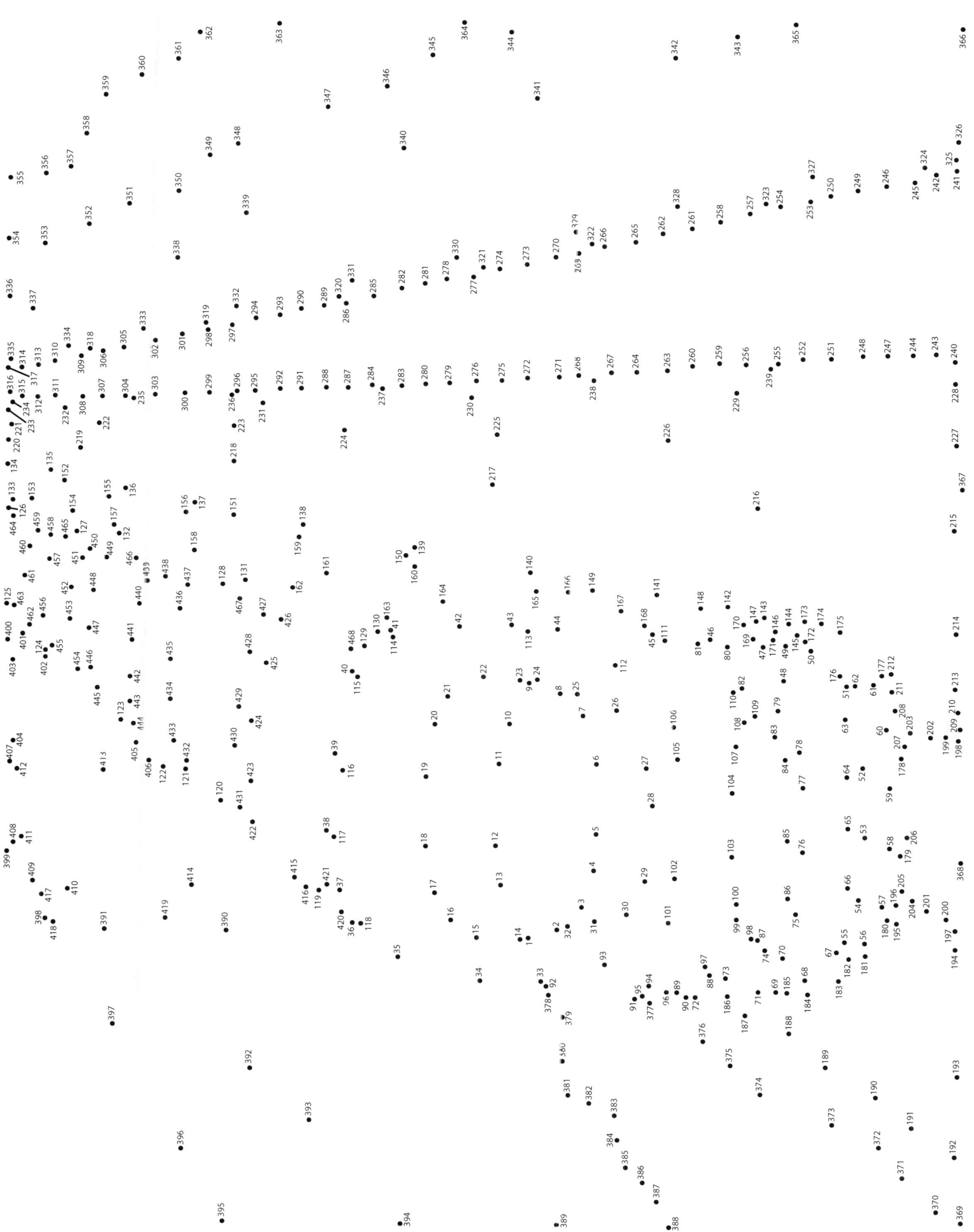

Train 21 (504 dots) - Black

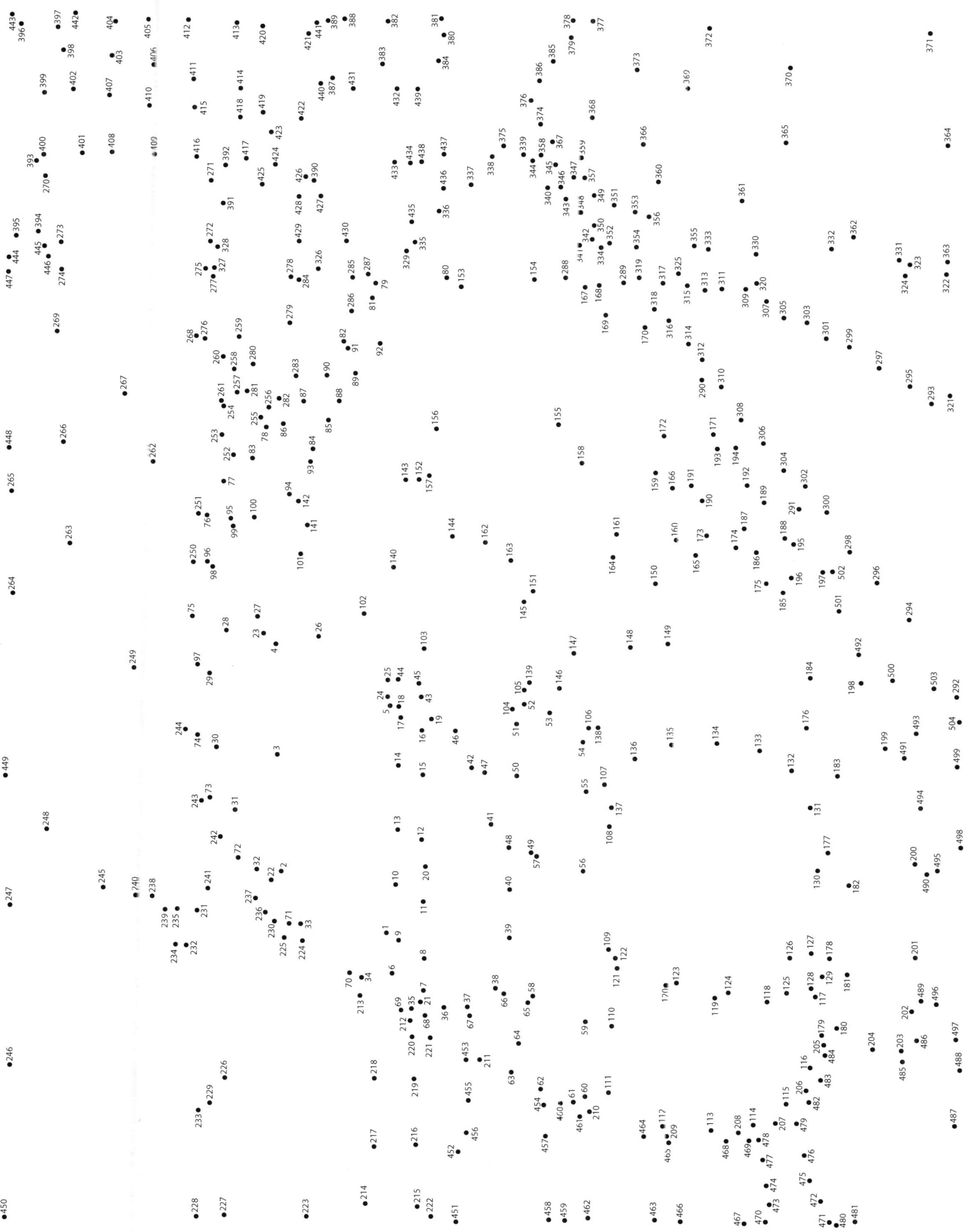

Train 22 (545 dots) - Black

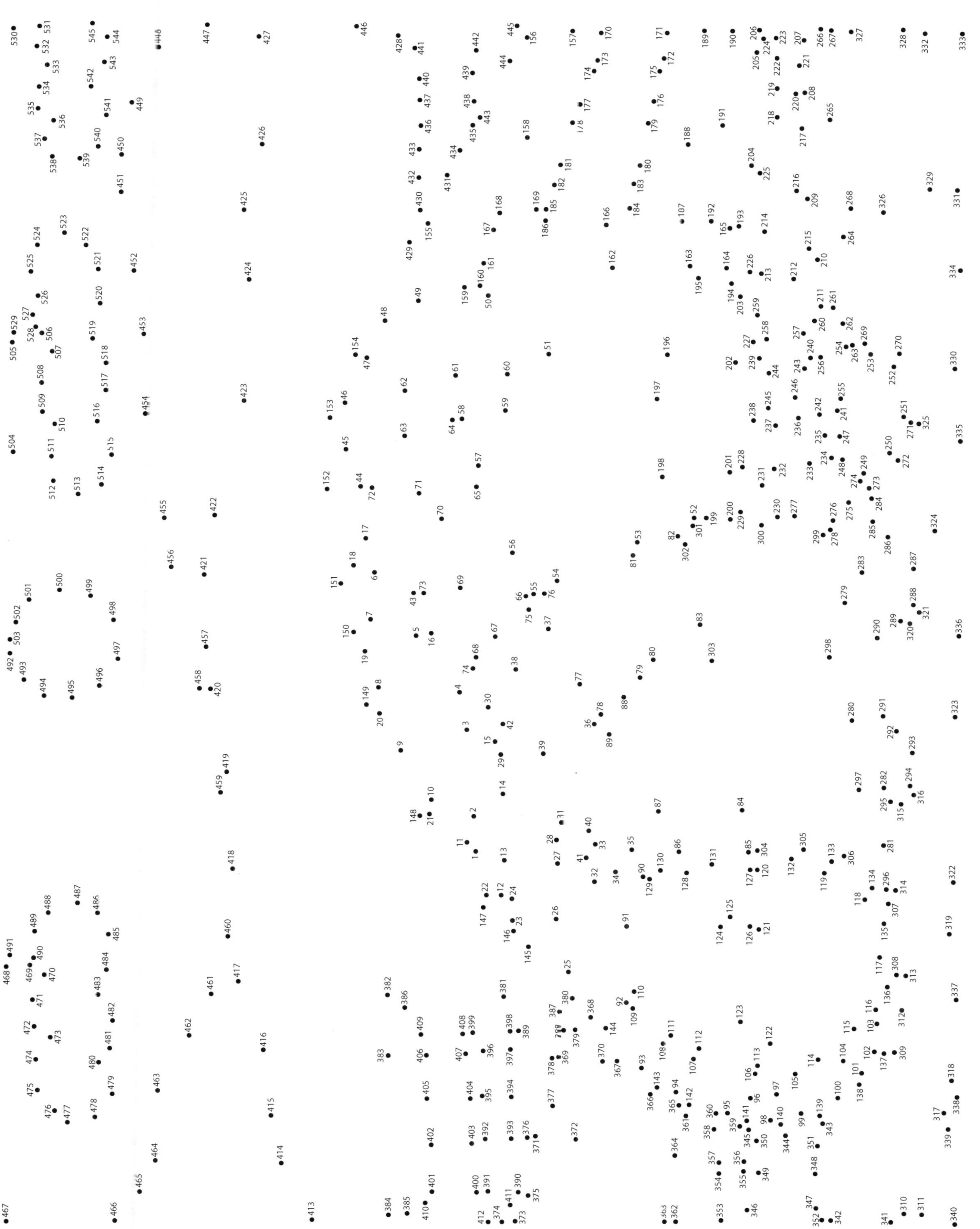

Train 23 (600 dots) - Black

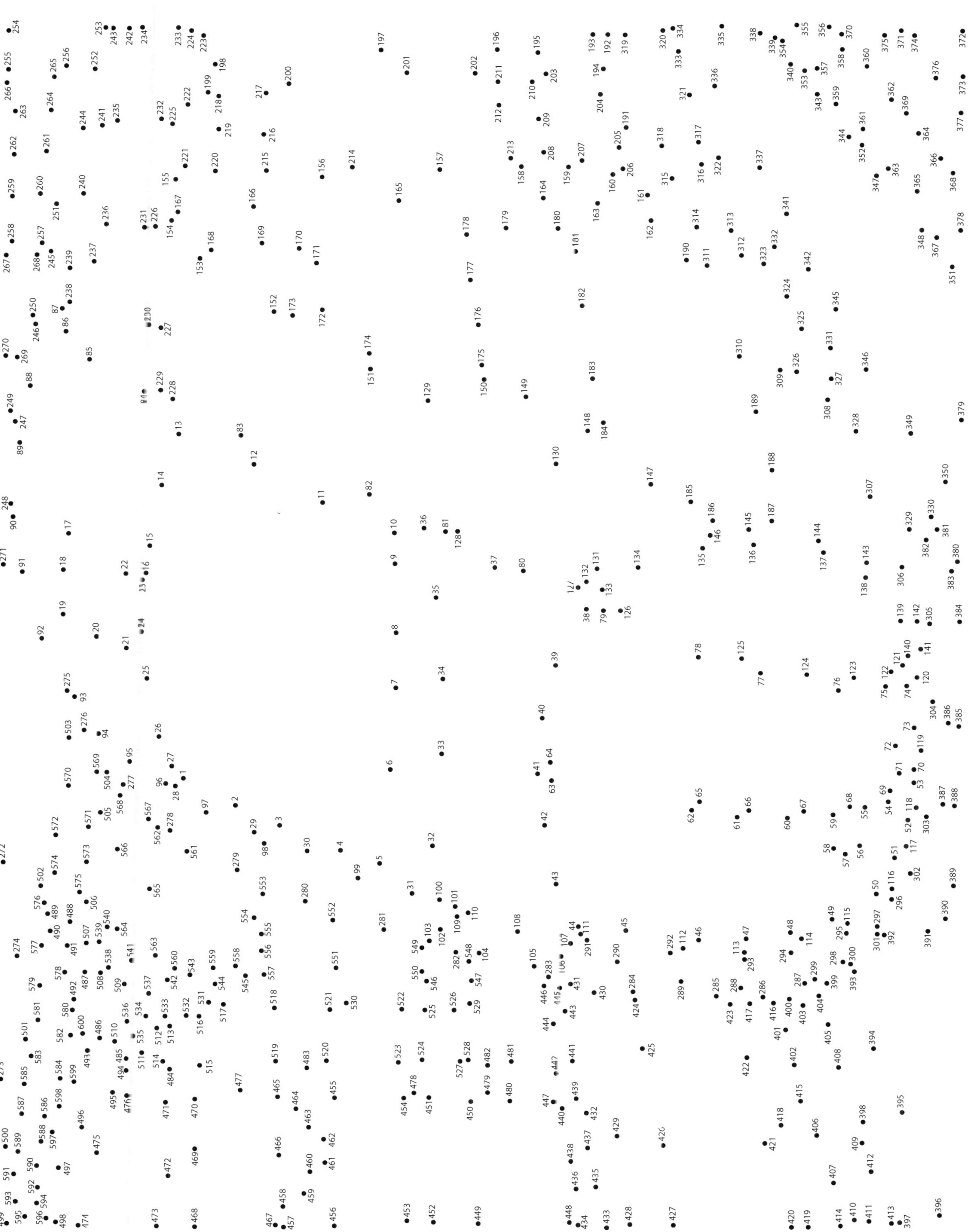

Train 24 (630 dots) - Black

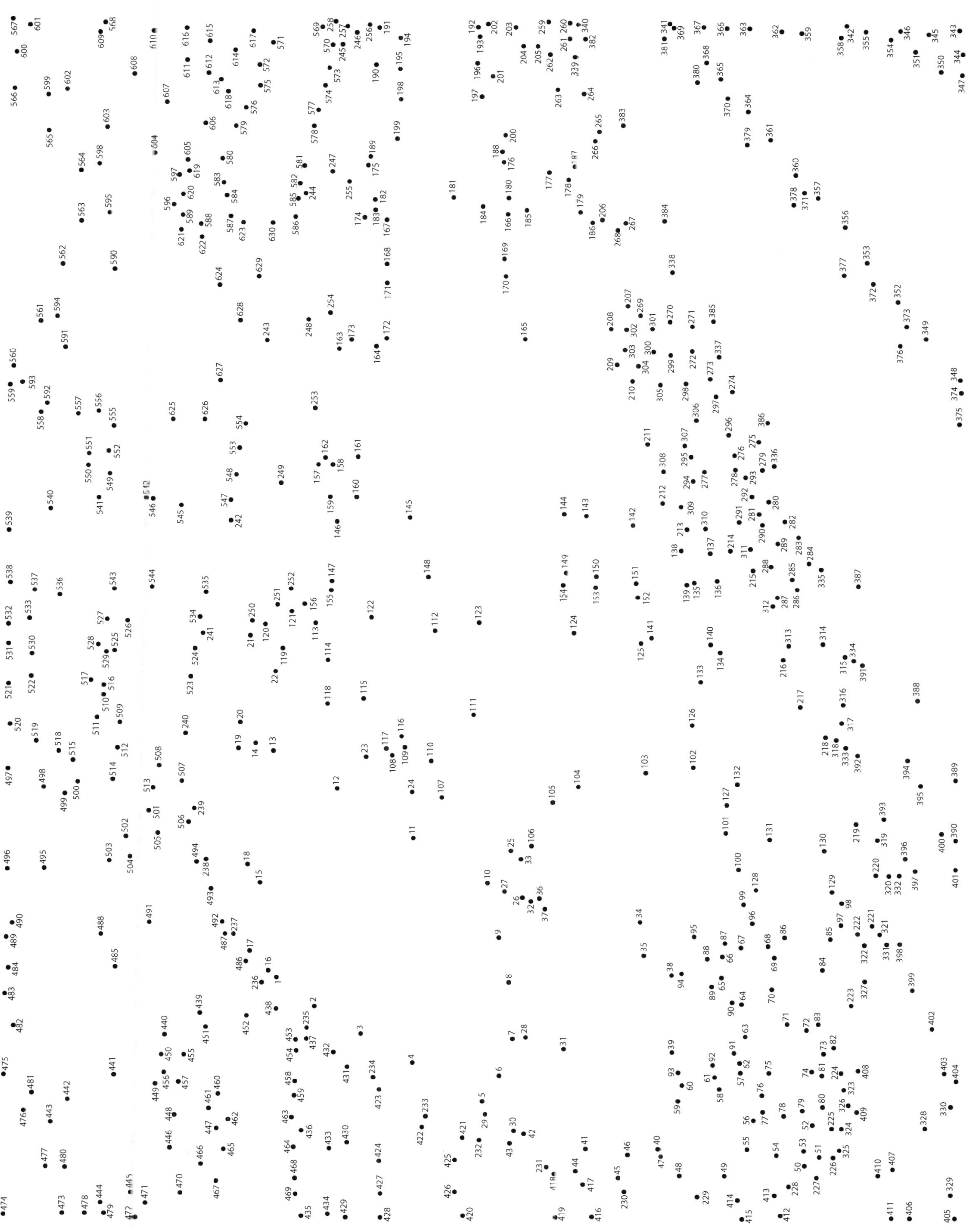

Train 25 (708 dots) - Black

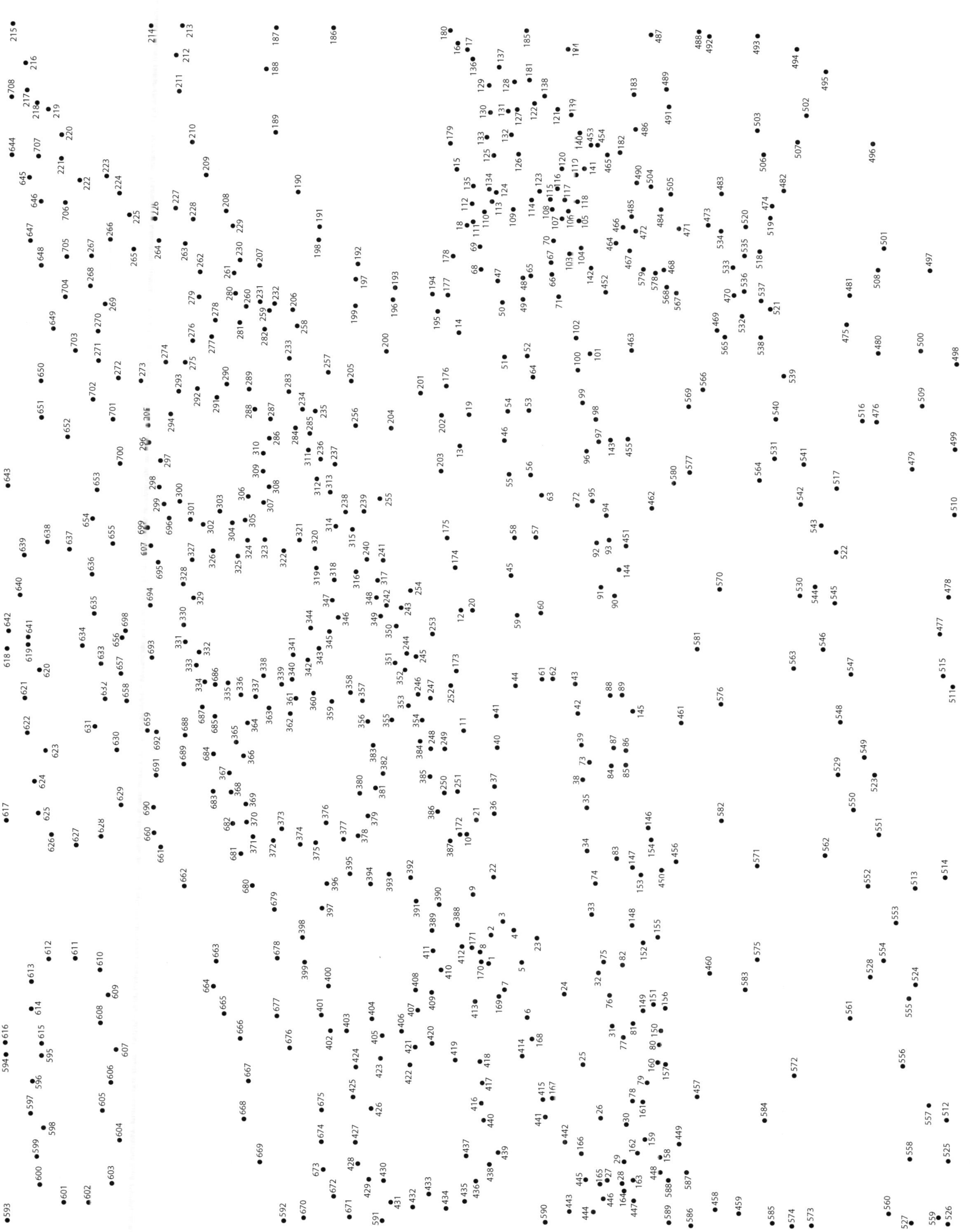

Train 26 (745 dots) - Black

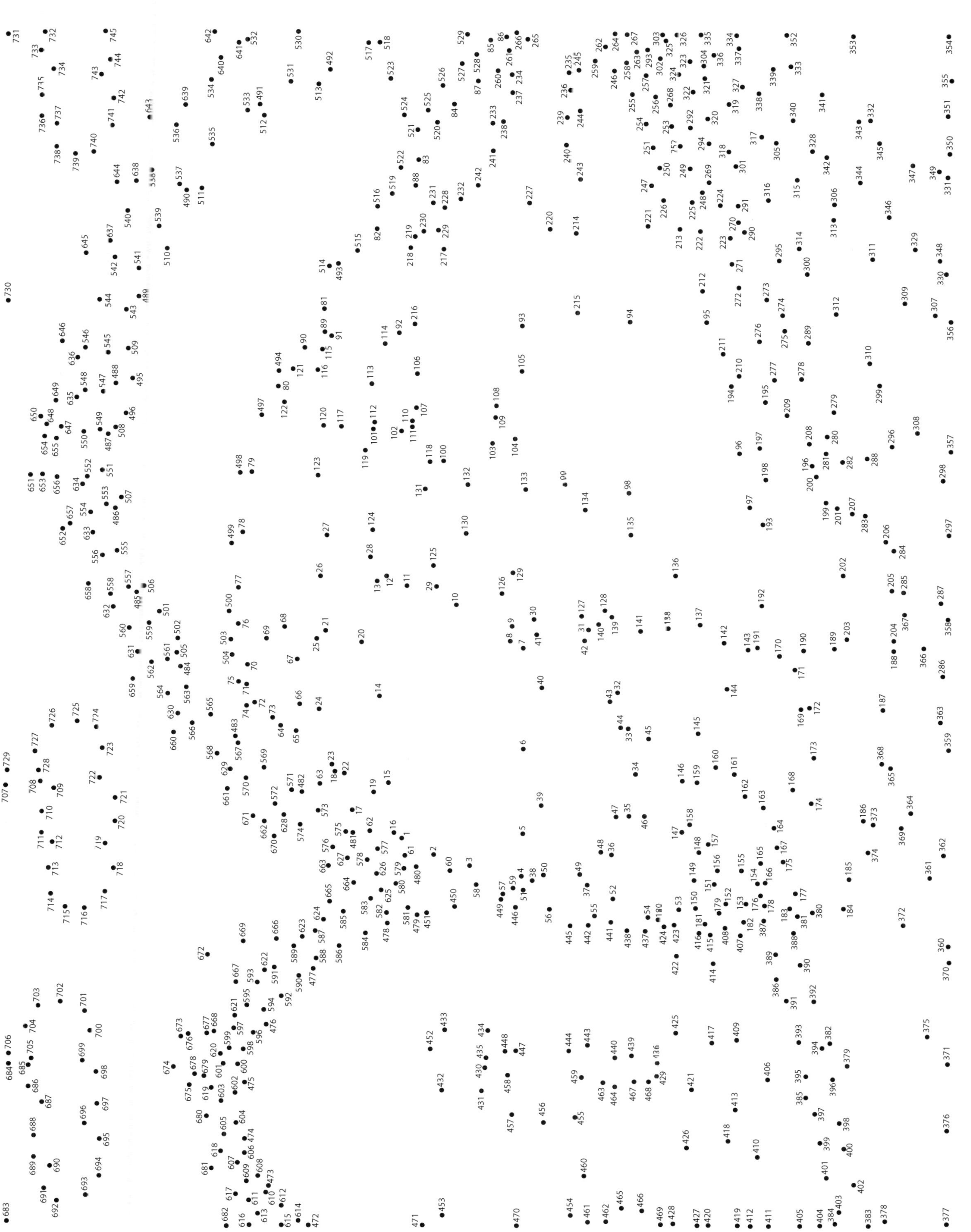

Train 27 (671 dots) - Black

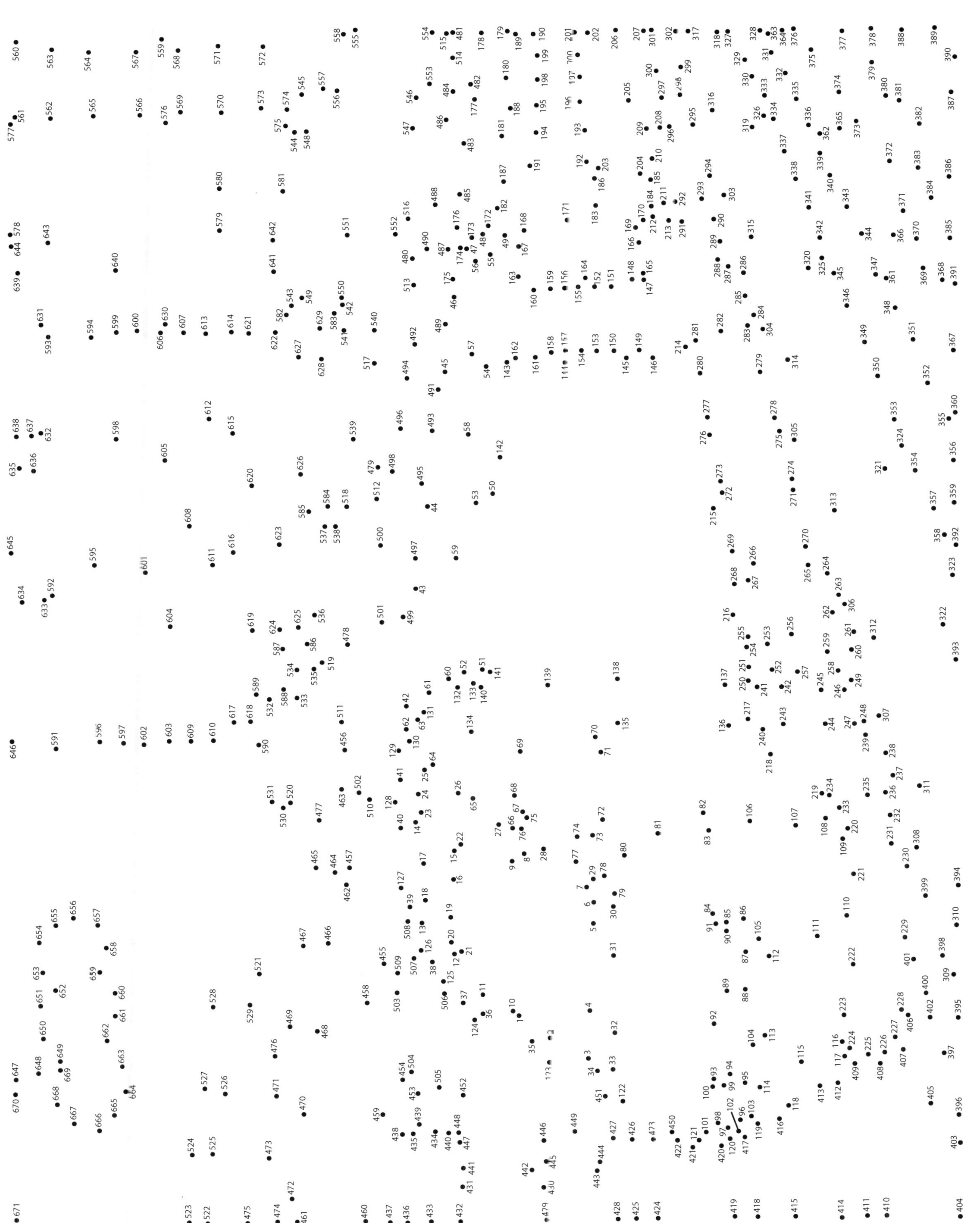

Train 28 (570 dots) - Black

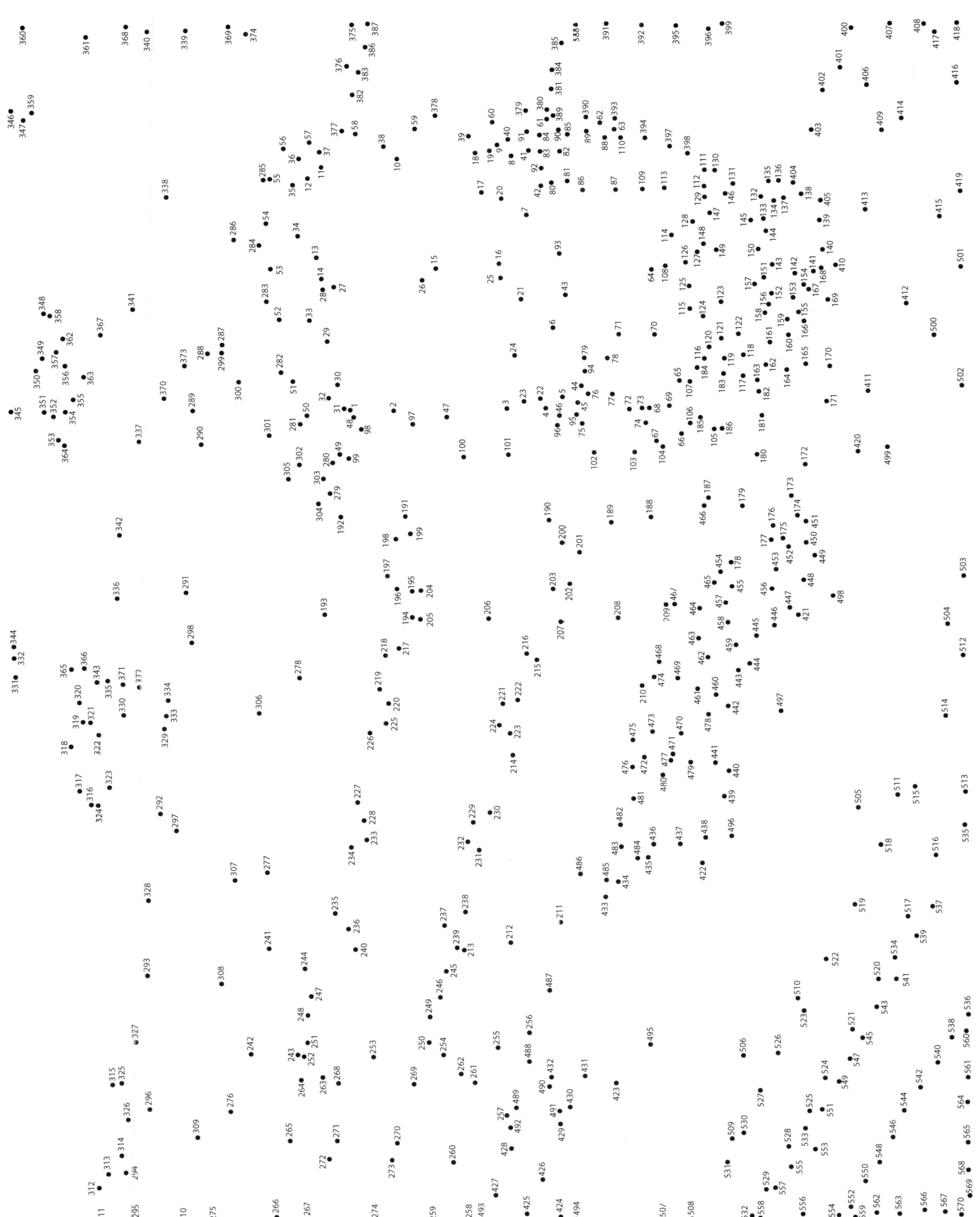

Train 29 (515 dots) - Black

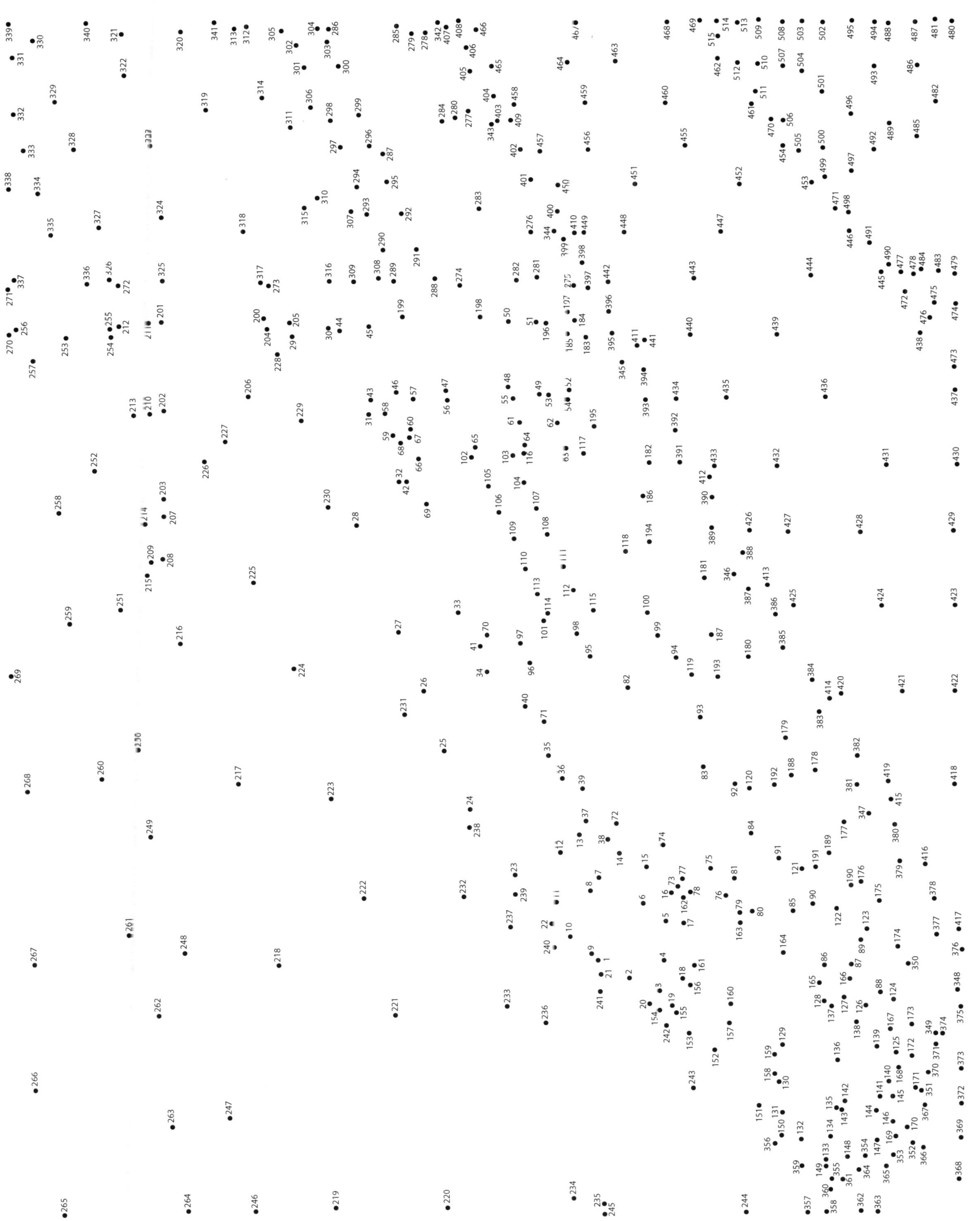

Train 3 (558 dots) - Black

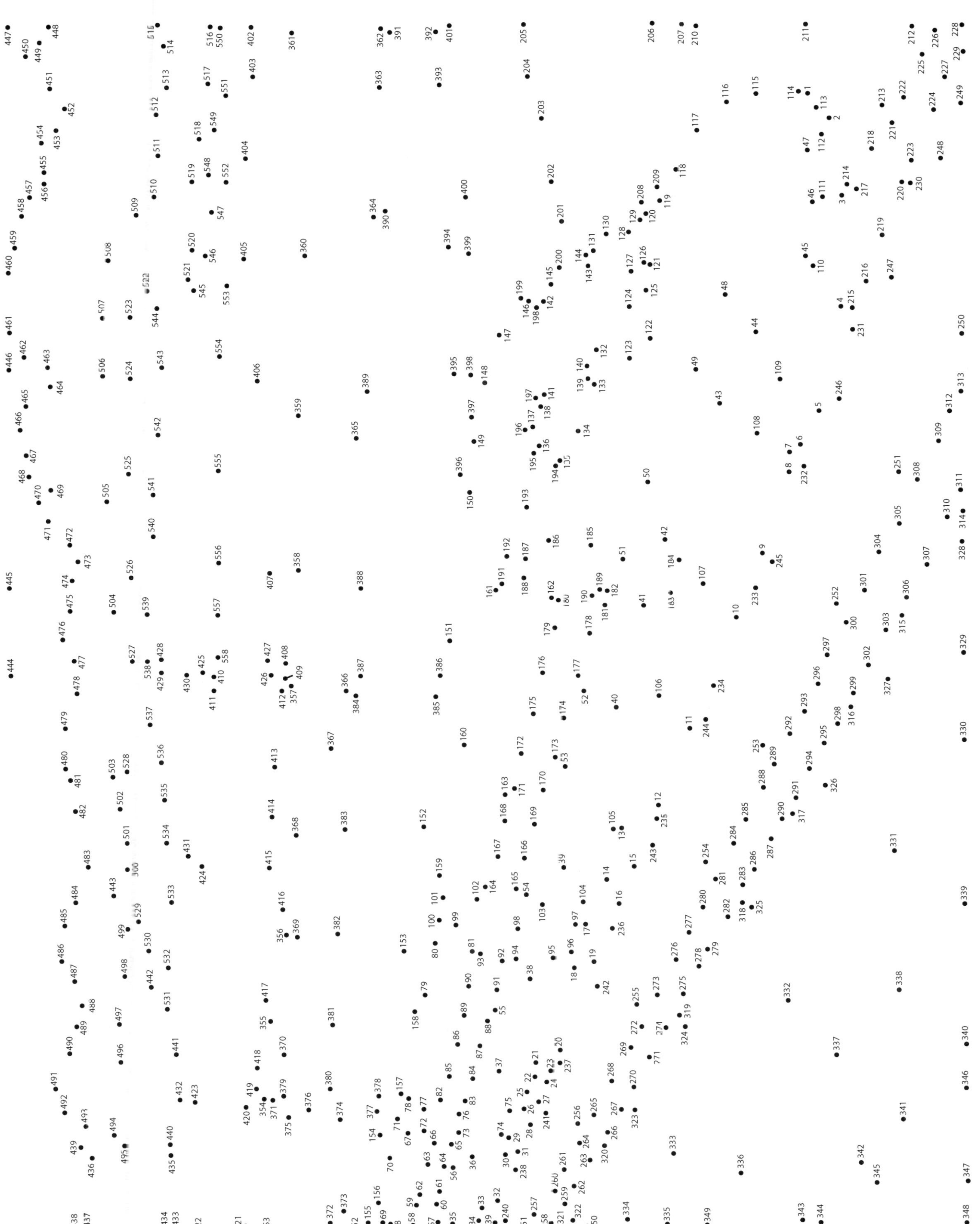

Train 30 (505 dots) - Black

Train 4 (557 dots) - Black

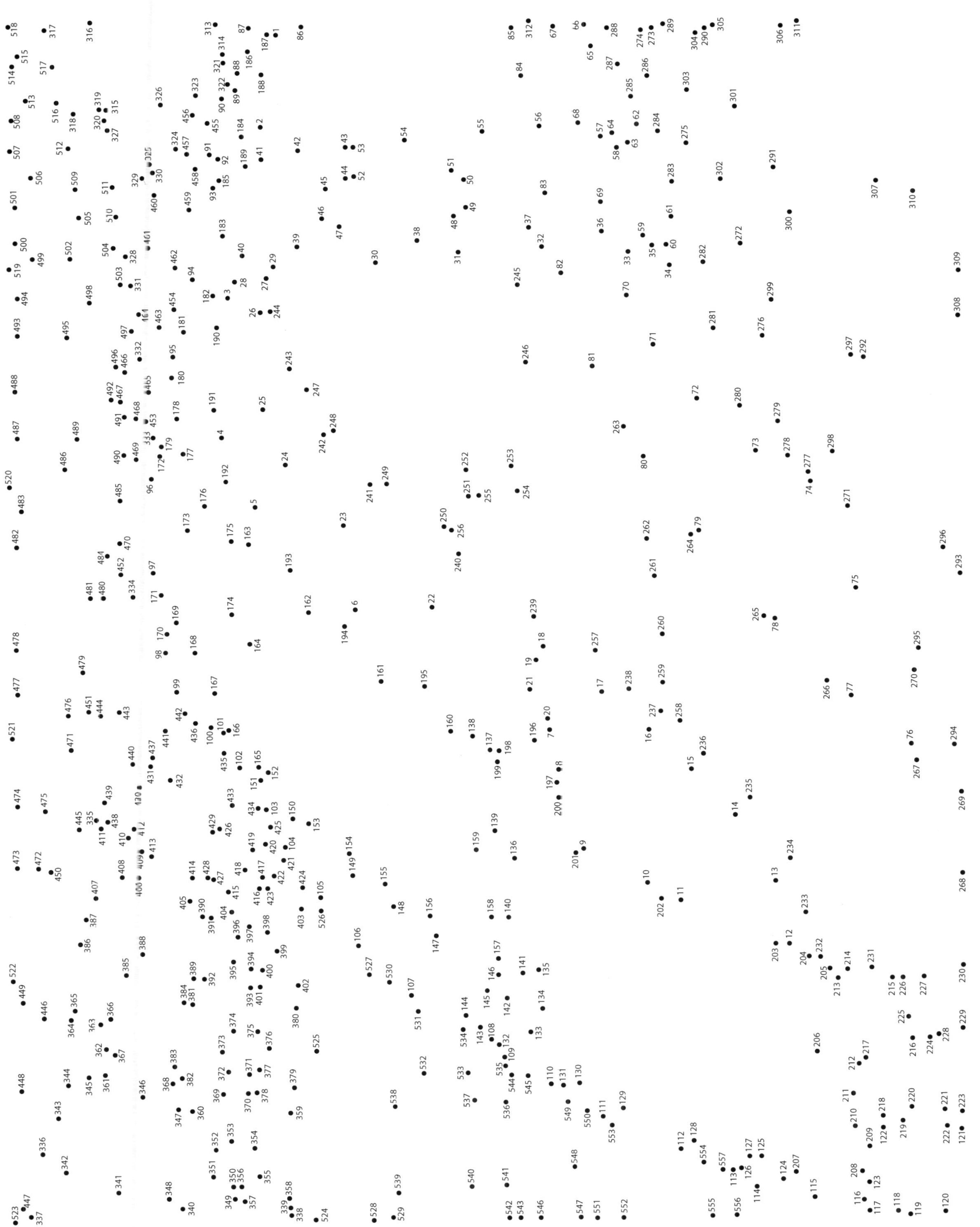

Train 5 (588 dots) - Black

1 2 3 4 5 6 7 8 9 10 11 12 13 14 15 16 17 18 19 20 21 22 23 24 25 26 27 28 29 30 31 32 33 34 35 36 37 38 39 40 41 42 43 44 45 46 47 48 49 50 51 52 53 54 55 56 57 58 59 60 61 62 63 64 65 66 67 68 69 70 71 72 73 74 75 76 77 78 79 80 81 82 83 84 85 86 87 88 89 90 91 92 93 94 95 96 97 98 99 100 101 102 103 104 105 106 107 108 109 110 111 112 113 114 115 116 117 118 119 120 121 122 123 124 125 126 127 128 129 130 131 132 133 134 135 136 137 138 139 140 141 142 143 144 145 146 147 148 149 150 151 152 153 154 155 156 157 158 159 160 161 162 163 164 165 166 167 168 169 170 171 172 173 174 175 176 177 178 179 180 181 182 183 184 185 186 187 188 189 190 191 192 193 194 195 196 197 198 199 200 201 202 203 204 205 206 207 208 209 210 211 212 213 214 215 216 217 218 219 220 221 222 223 224 225 226 227 228 229 230 231 232 233 234 235 236 237 238 239 240 241 242 243 244 245 246 247 248 249 250 251 252 253 254 255 256 257 258 259 260 261 262 263 264 265 266 267 268 269 270 271 272 273 274 275 276 277 278 279 280 281 282 283 284 285 286 287 288 289 290 291 292 293 294 295 296 297 298 299 300 301 302 303 304 305 306 307 308 309 310 311 312 313 314 315 316 317 318 319 320 321 322 323 324 325 326 327 328 329 330 331 332 333 334 335 336 337 338 339 340 341 342 343 344 345 346 347 348 349 350 351 352 353 354 355 356 357 358 359 360 361 362 363 364 365 366 367 368 369 370 371 372 373 374 375 376 377 378 379 380 381 382 383 384 385 386 387 388 389 390 391 392 393 394 395 396 397 398 399 400 401 402 403 404 405 406 407 408 409 410 411 412 413 414 415 416 417 418 419 420 421 422 423 424 425 426 427 428 429 430 431 432 433 434 435 436 437 438 439 440 441 442 443 444 445 446 447 448 449 450 451 452 453 454 455 456 457 458 459 460 461 462 463 464 465 466 467 468 469 470 471 472 473 474 475 476 477 478 479 480 481 482 483 484 485 486 487 488 489 490 491 492 493 494 495 496 497 498 499 500 501 502 503 504 505 506 507 508 509 510 511 512 513 514 515 516 517 518 519 520 521 522 523 524 525 526 527 528 529 530 531 532 533 534 535 536 537 538 539 540 541 542 543 544 545 546 547 548 549 550 551 552 553 554 555 556 557 558 559 560 561 562 563 564 565 566 567 568 569 570 571 572 573 574 575 576 577 578 579 580 581 582 583 584 585 586 587 588

Train 6 (516 dots) - Black

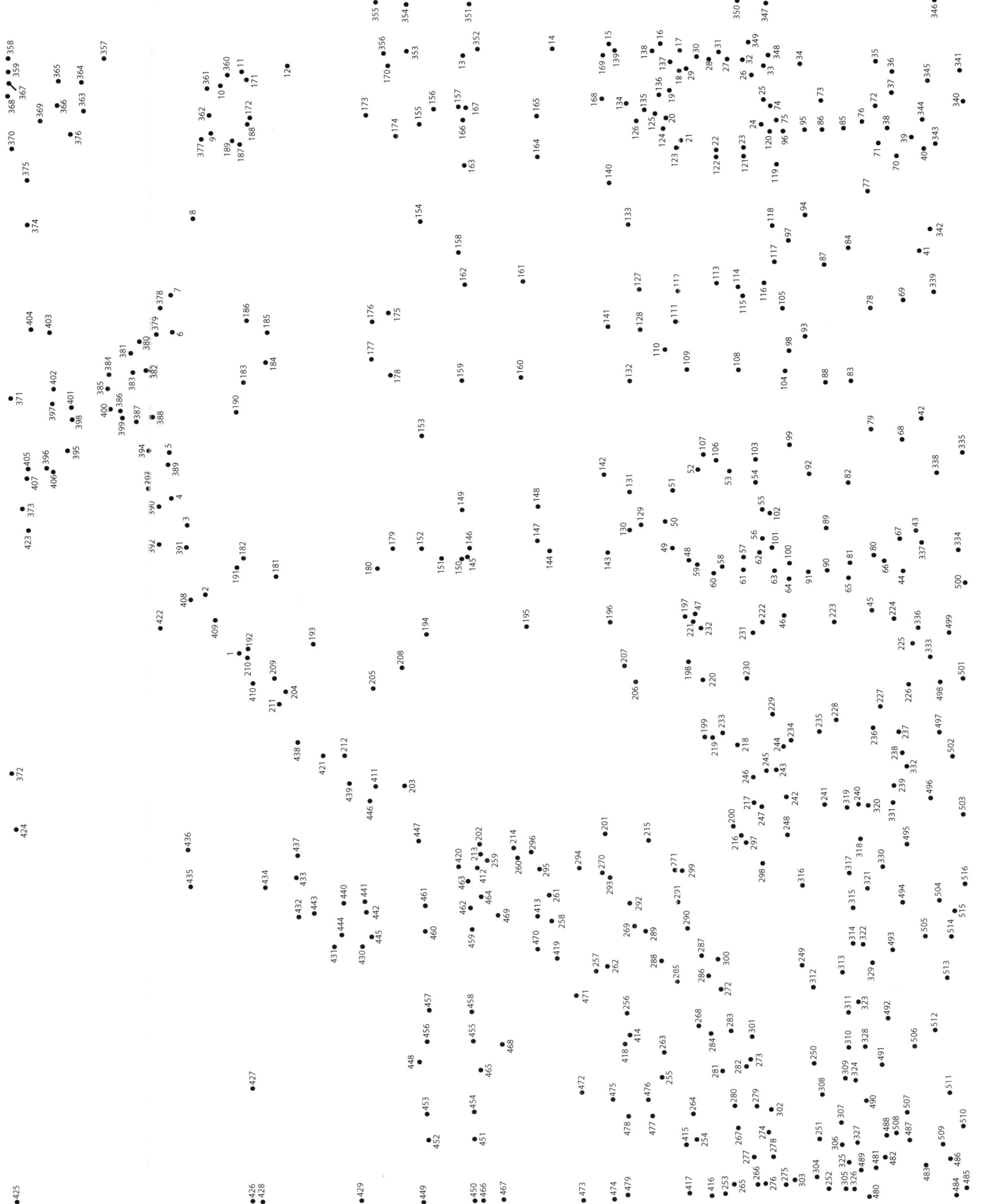

Train 7 (525 dots) - Black

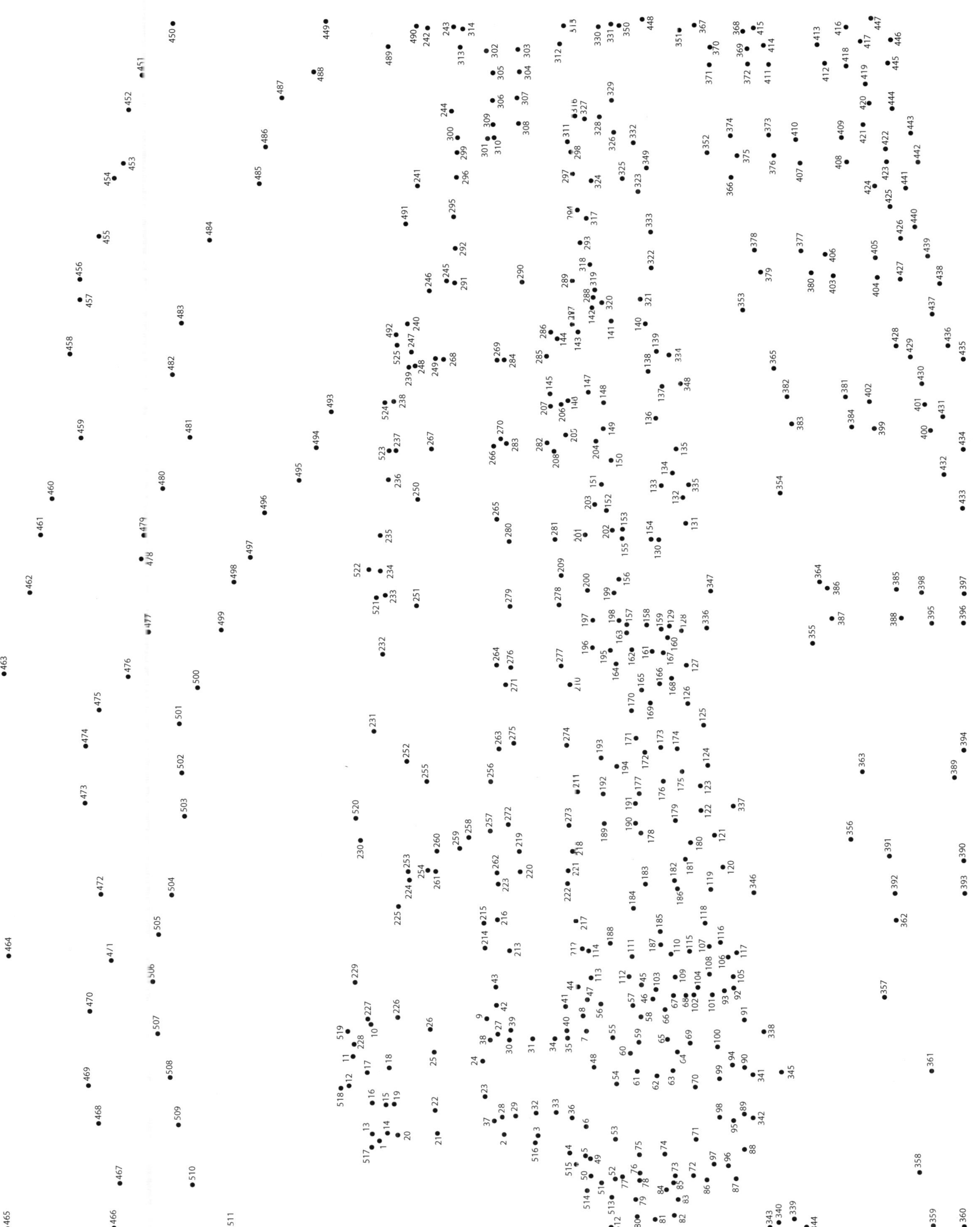

Train 8 (500 dots) - Black

Train 9 (531 dots) - Black

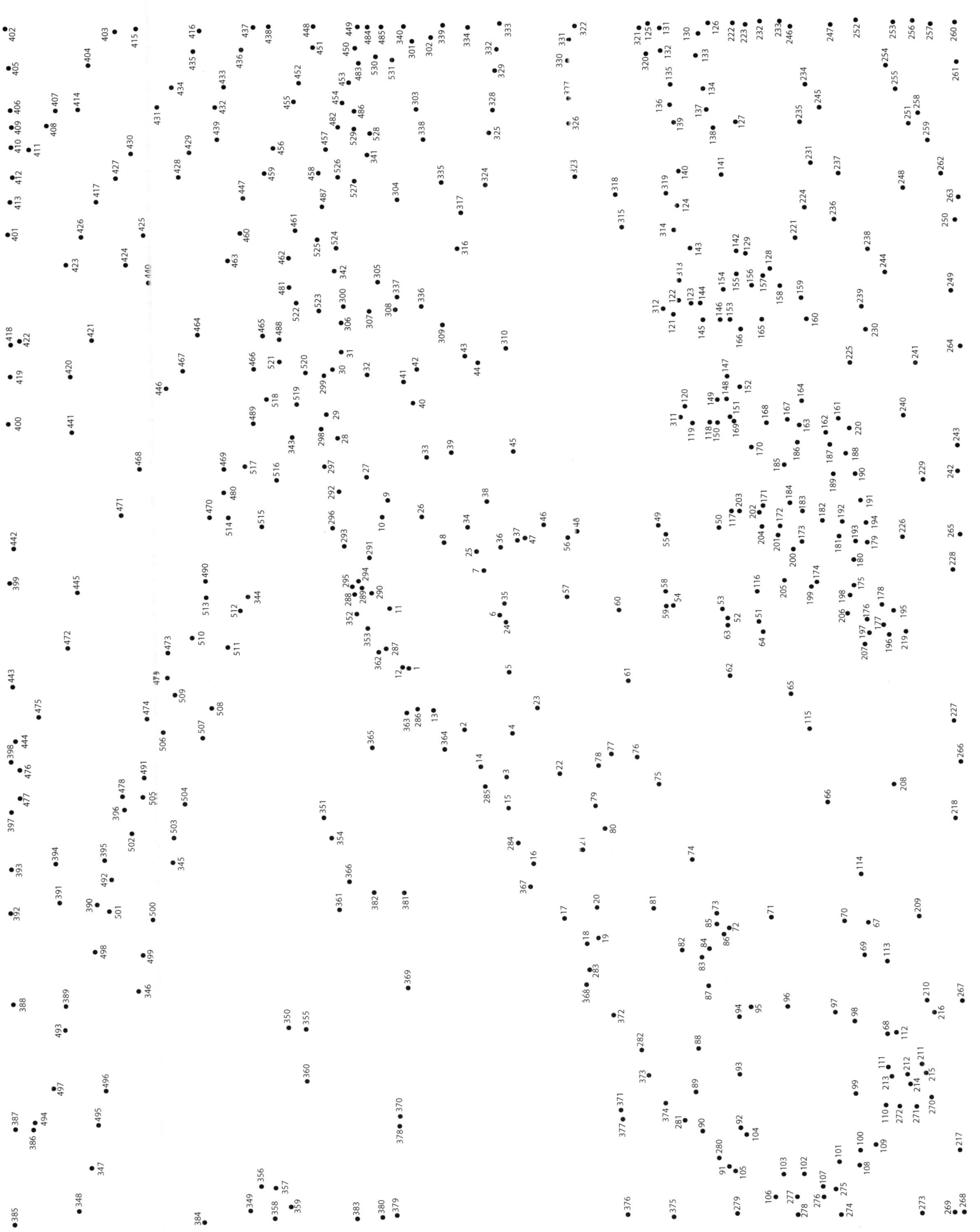

COMPELTED
DOT PAGES PREVIEWS

Completed Dot to Dot Pages Previews

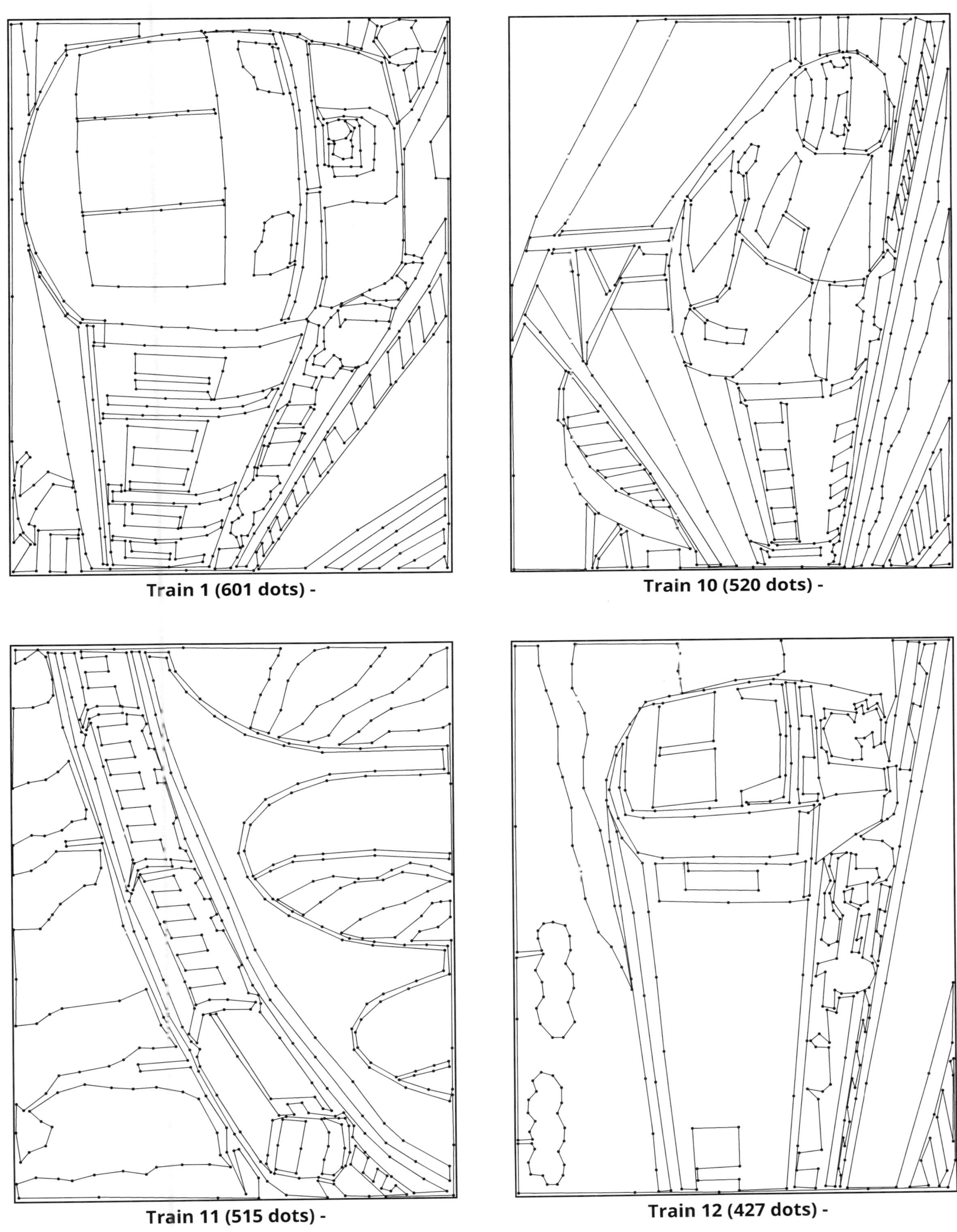

Train 1 (601 dots) -

Train 10 (520 dots) -

Train 11 (515 dots) -

Train 12 (427 dots) -

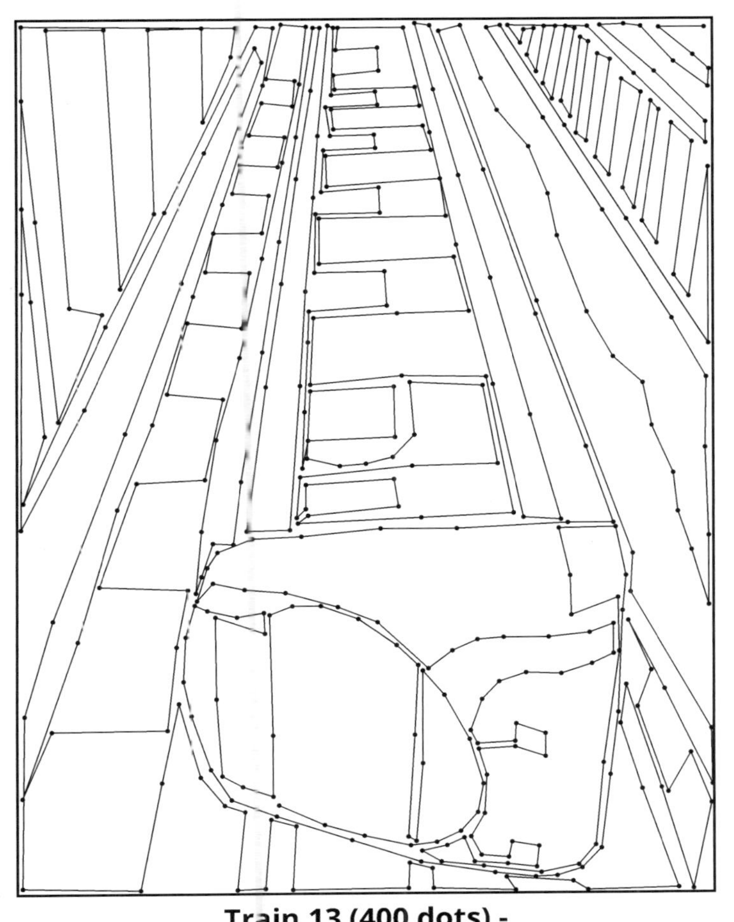
Train 13 (400 dots) -

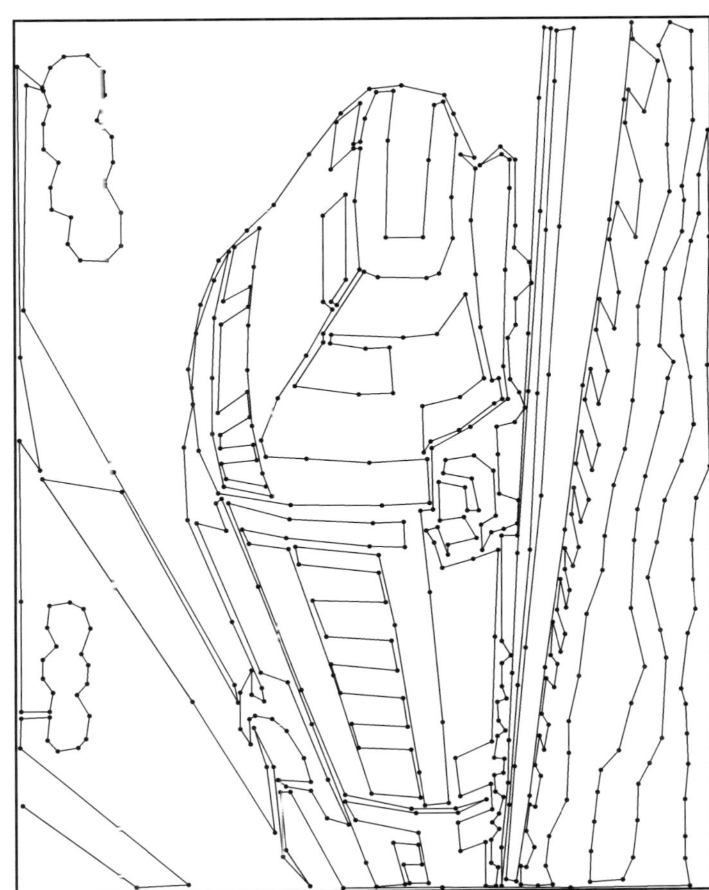
Train 14 (528 dots) -

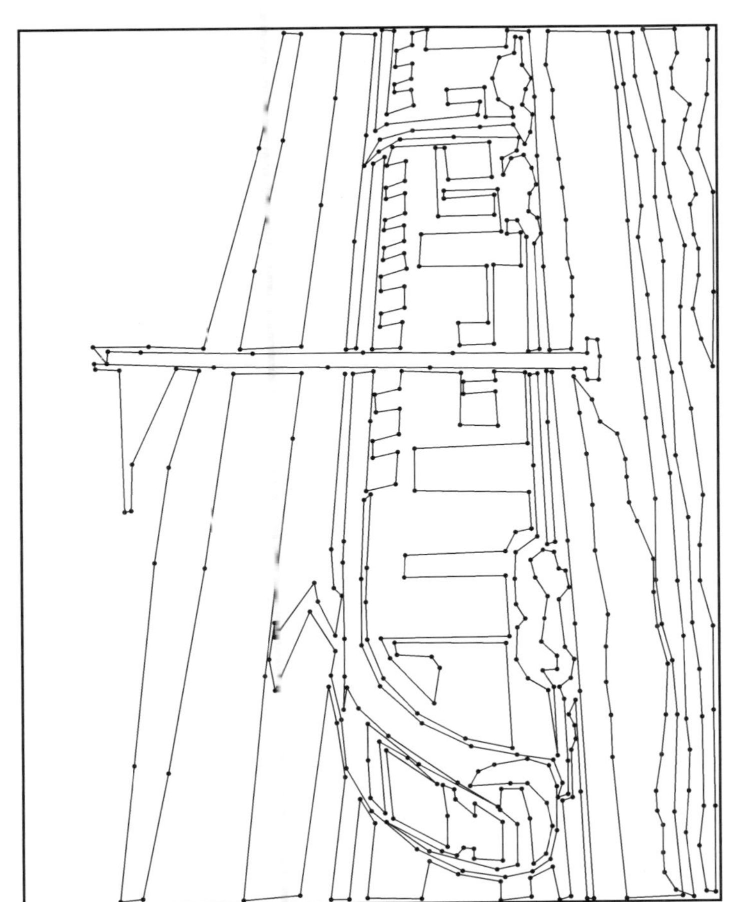
Train 15 (512 dots) -

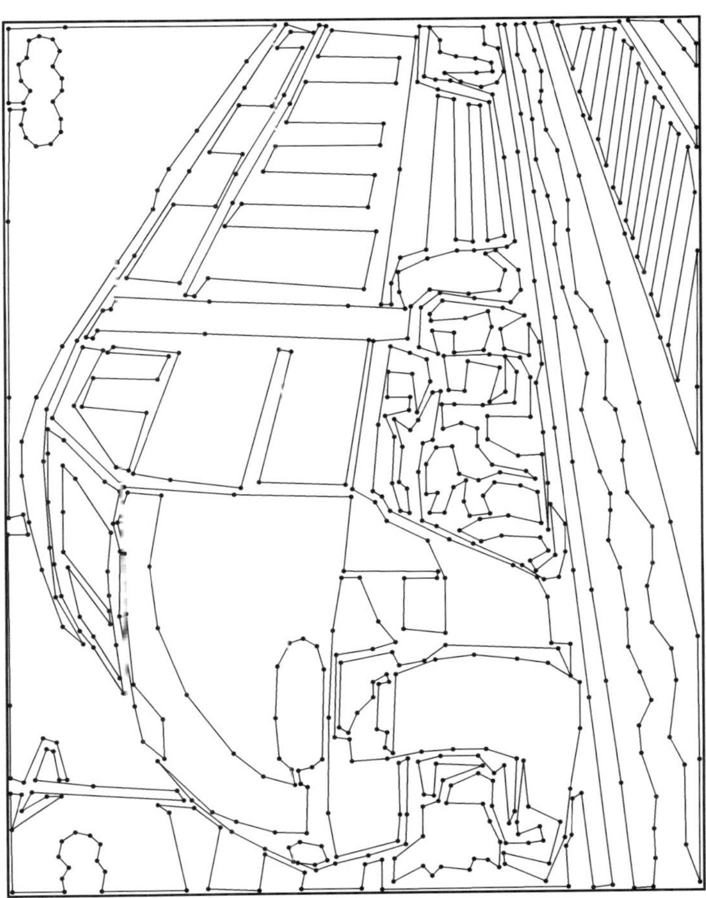
Train 16 (675 dots) -

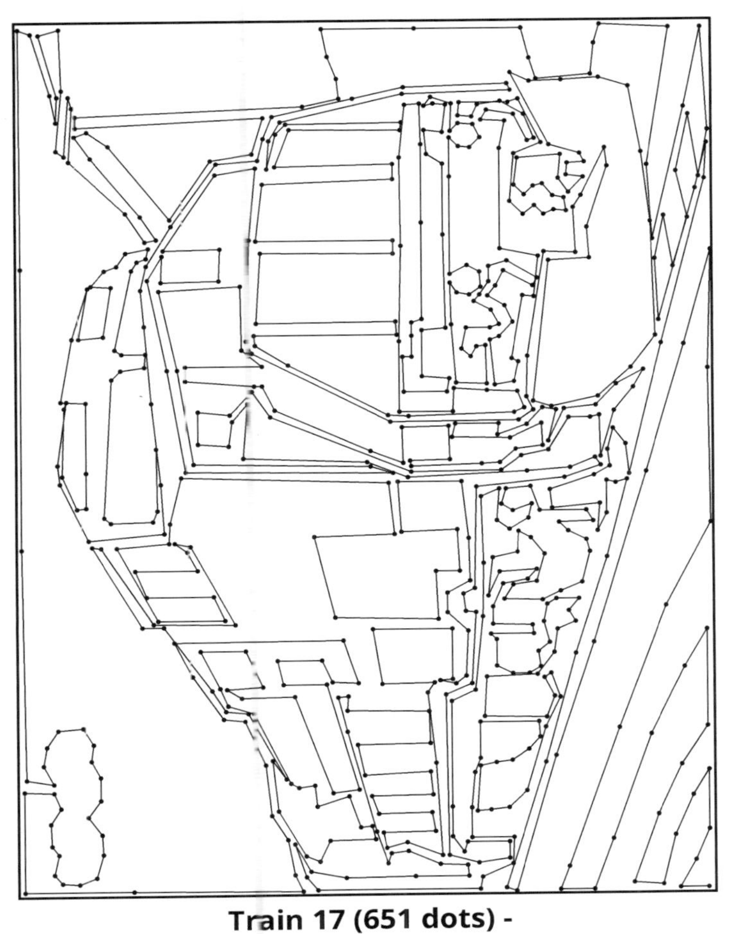

Train 17 (651 dots) -

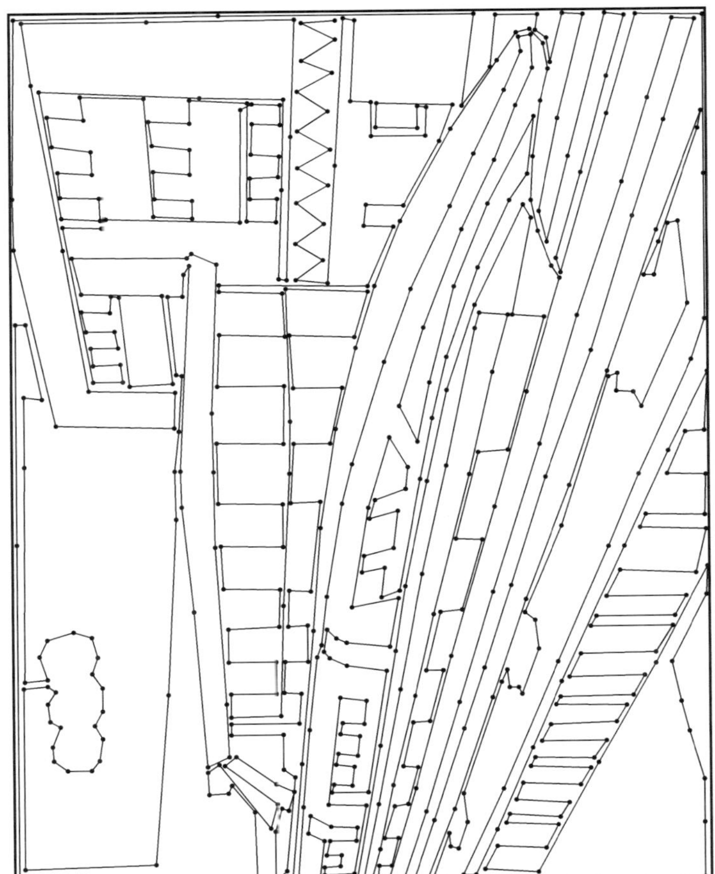

Train 18 (540 dots) -

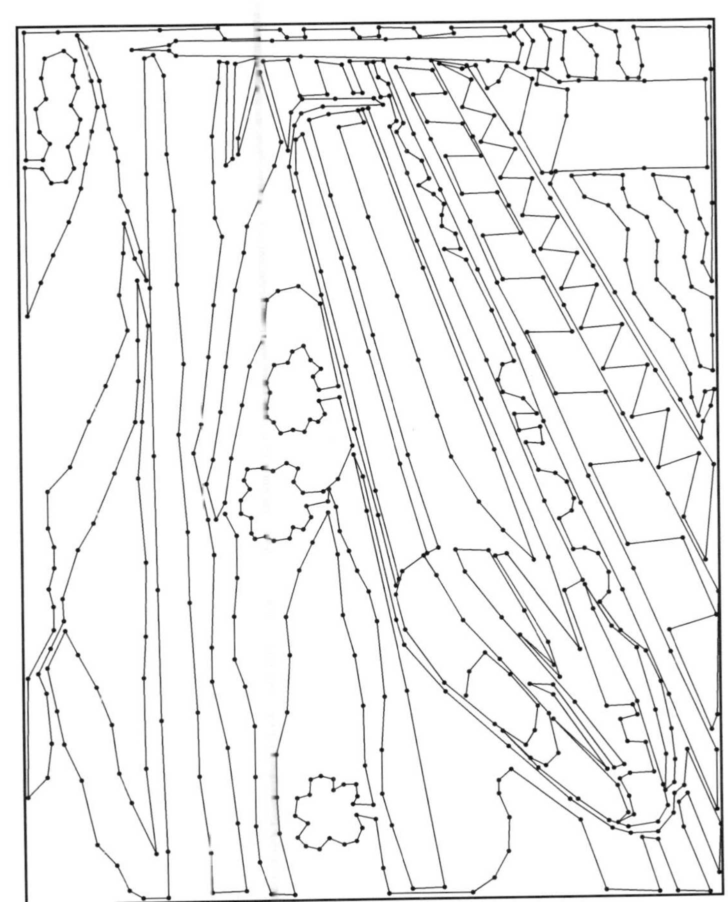

Train 19 (702 dots) -

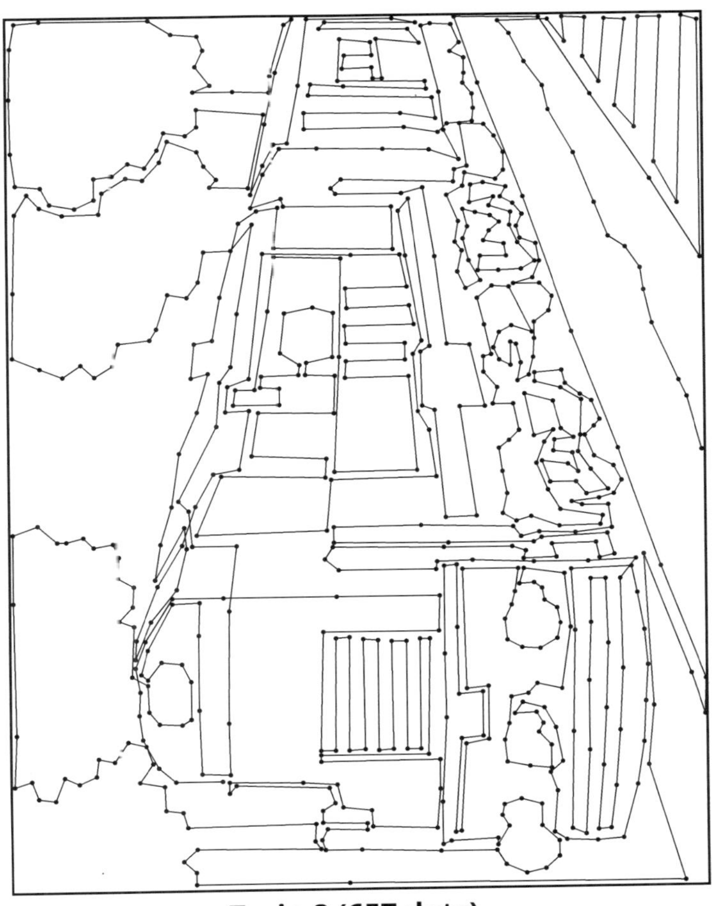

Train 2 (657 dots) -

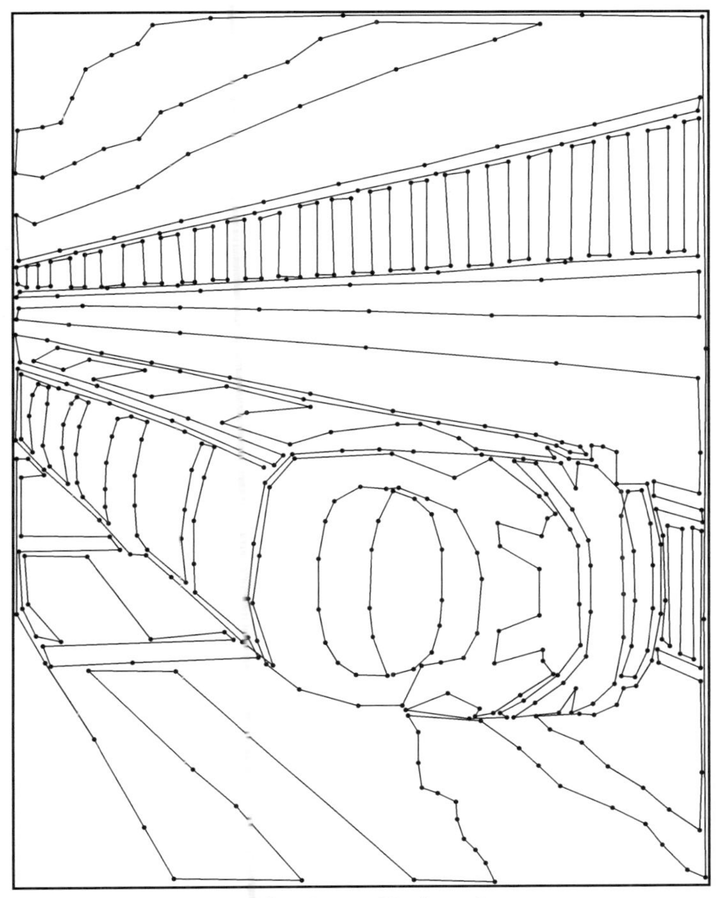

Train 20 (468 dots) -

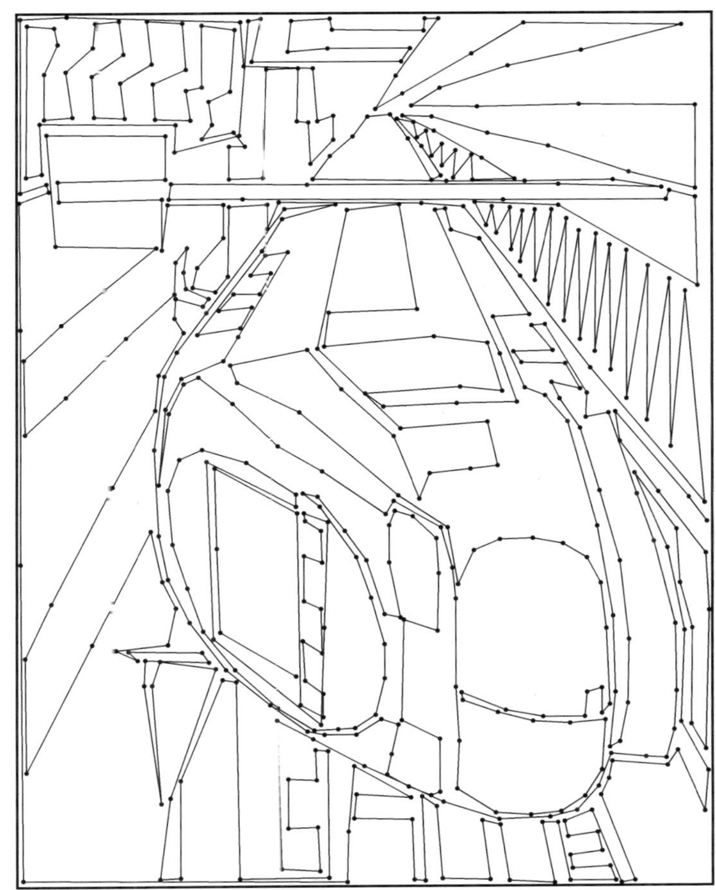

Train 21 (504 dots) -

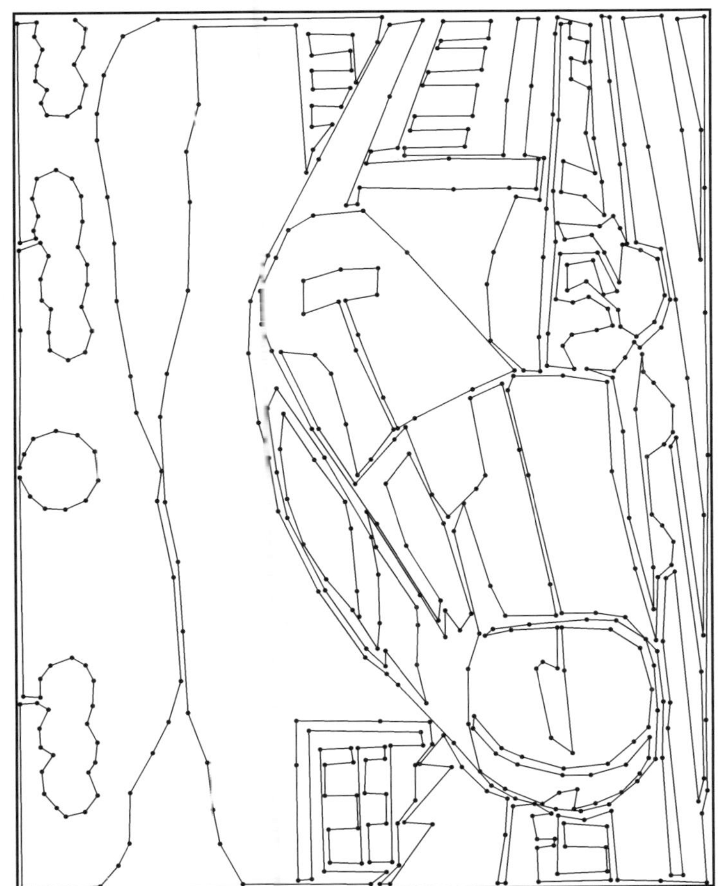

Train 22 (545 dots) -

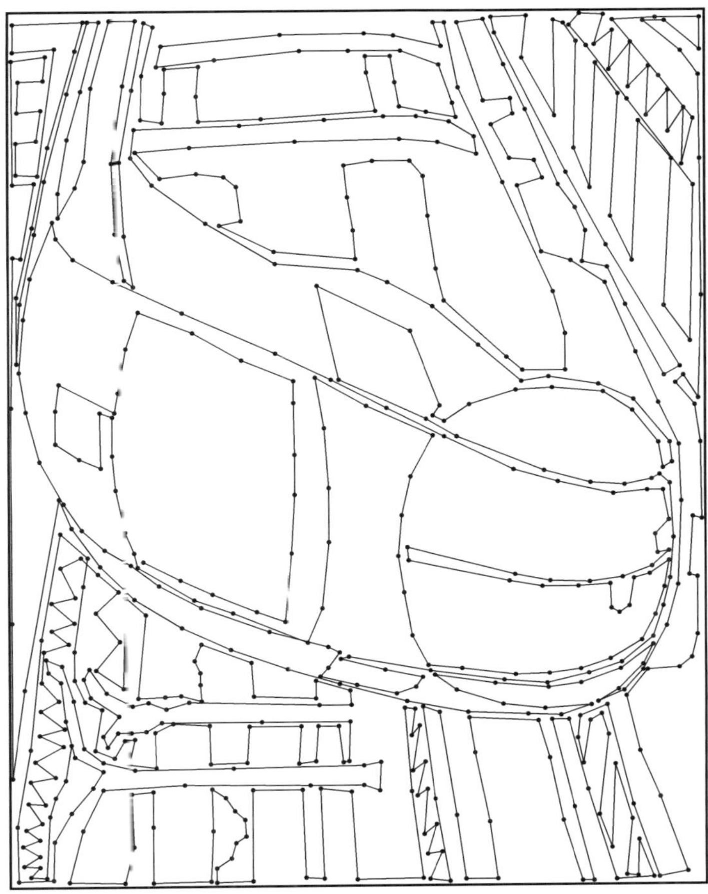

Train 23 (600 dots) -

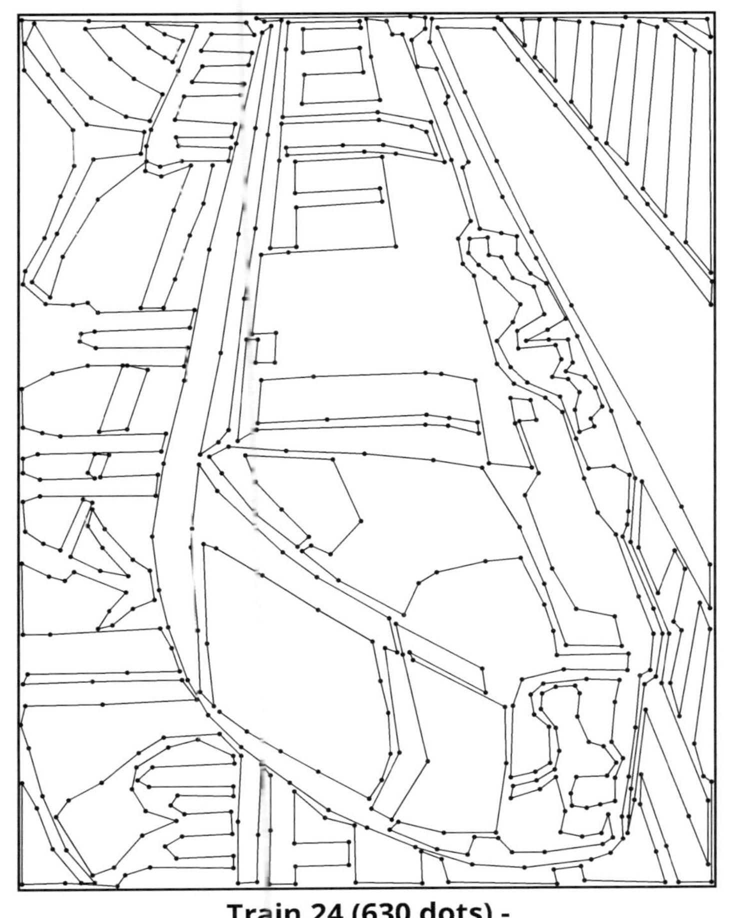

Train 24 (630 dots) -

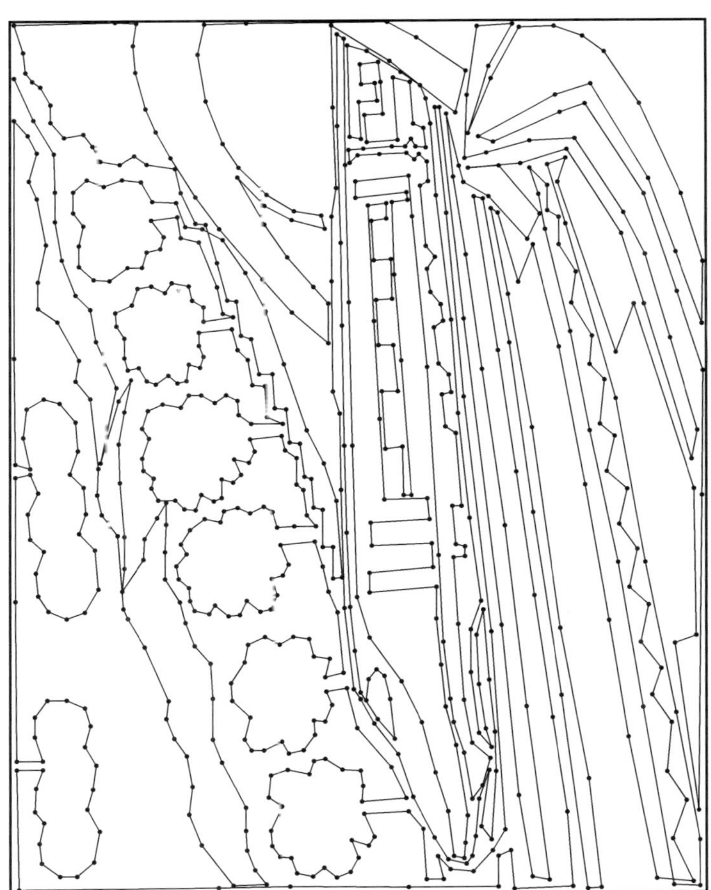

Train 25 (708 dots) -

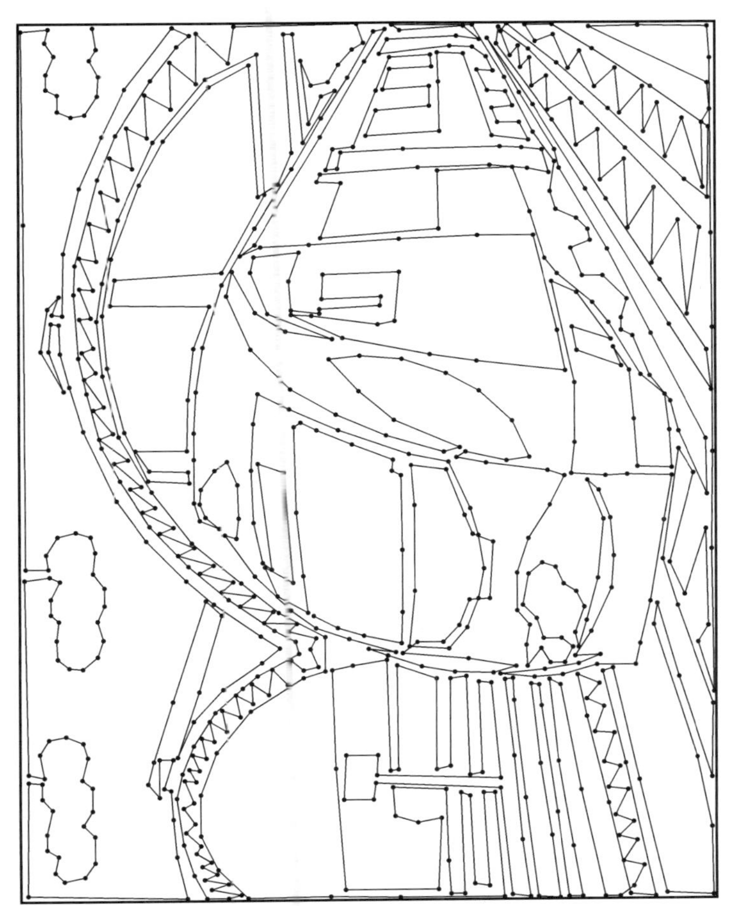

Train 26 (745 dots) -

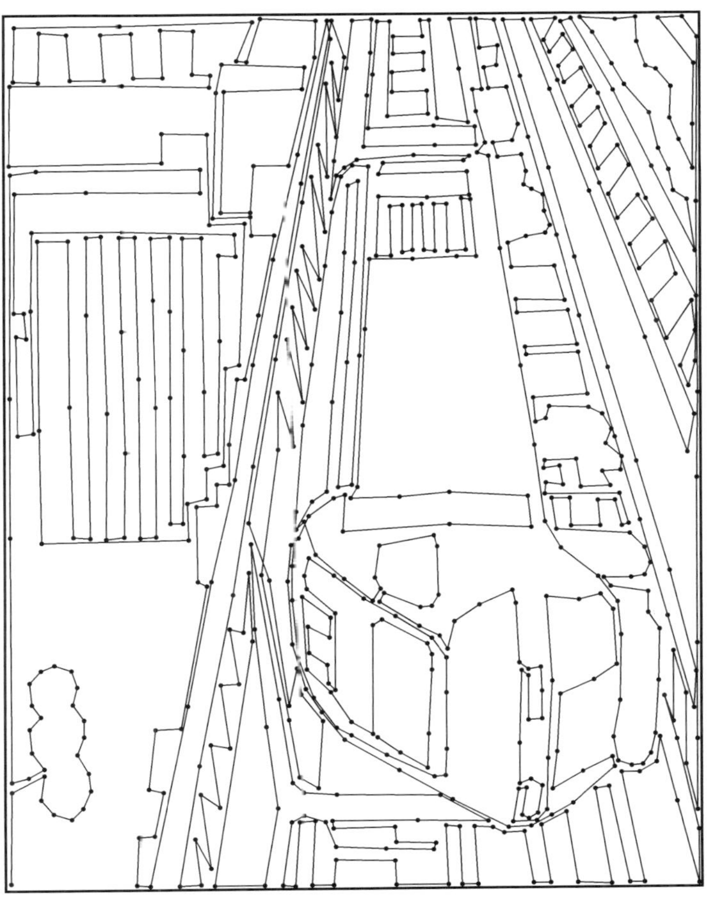

Train 27 (671 dots) -

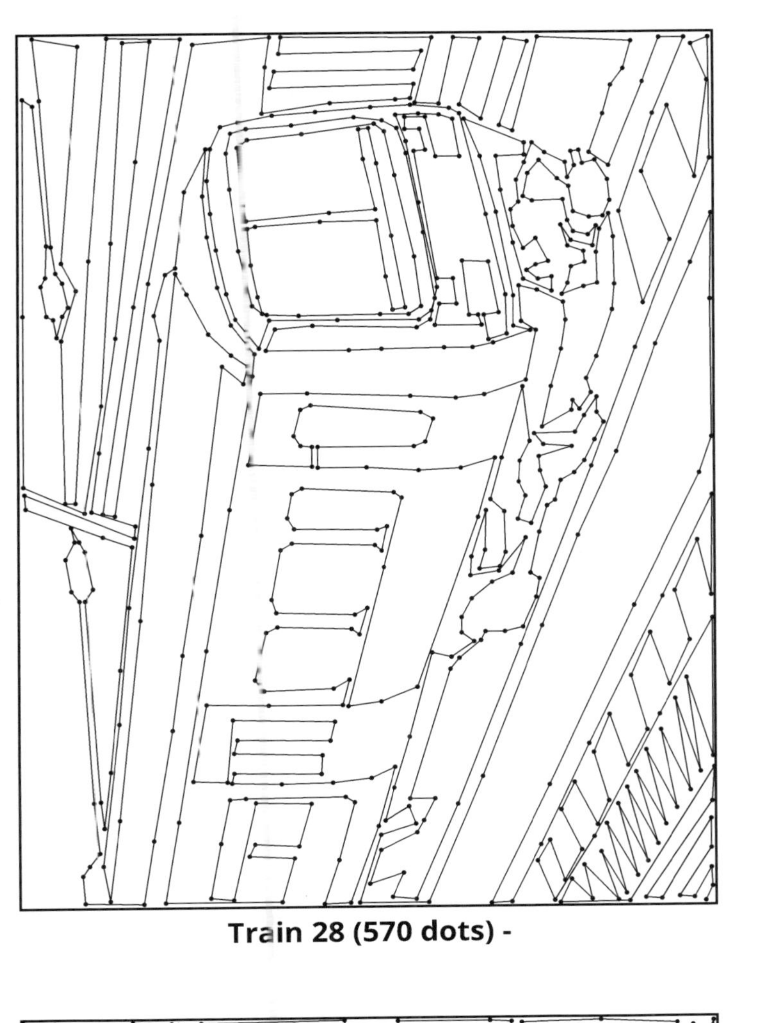

Train 28 (570 dots) -

Train 29 (515 dots) -

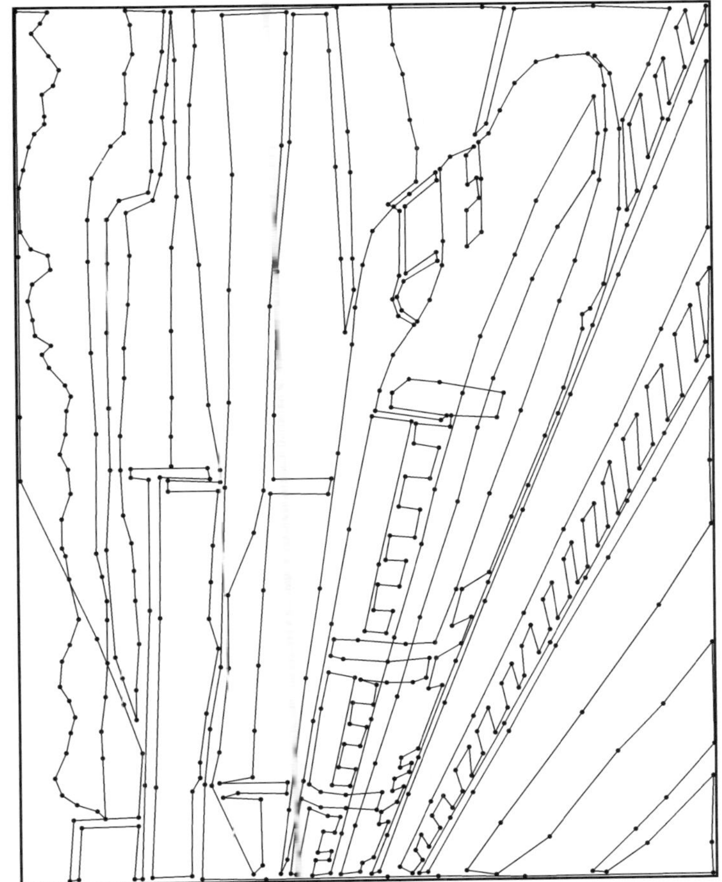

Train 3 (558 dots) -

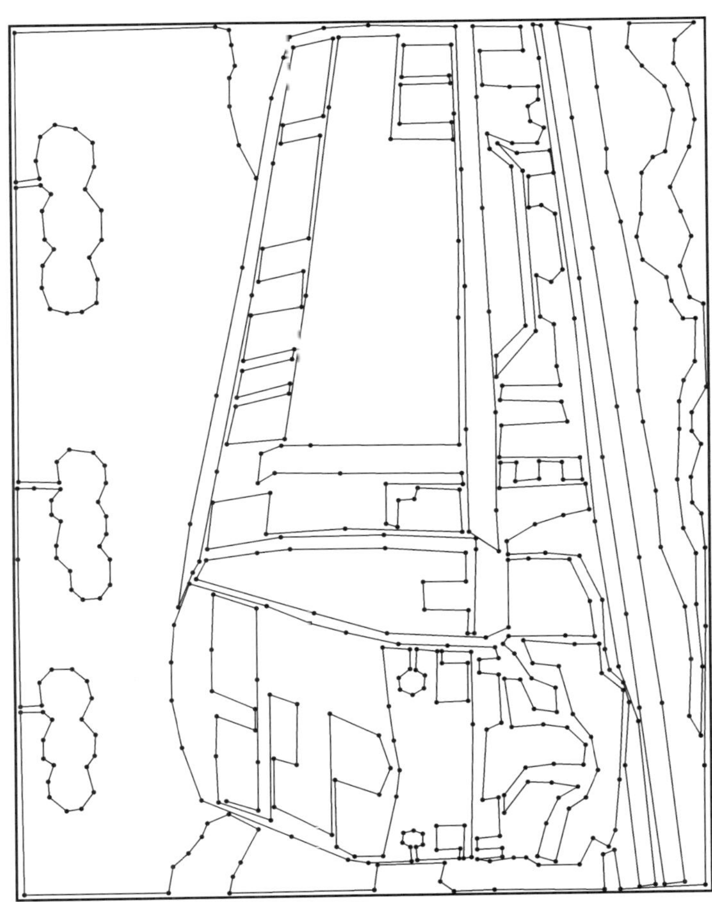

Train 30 (505 dots) -

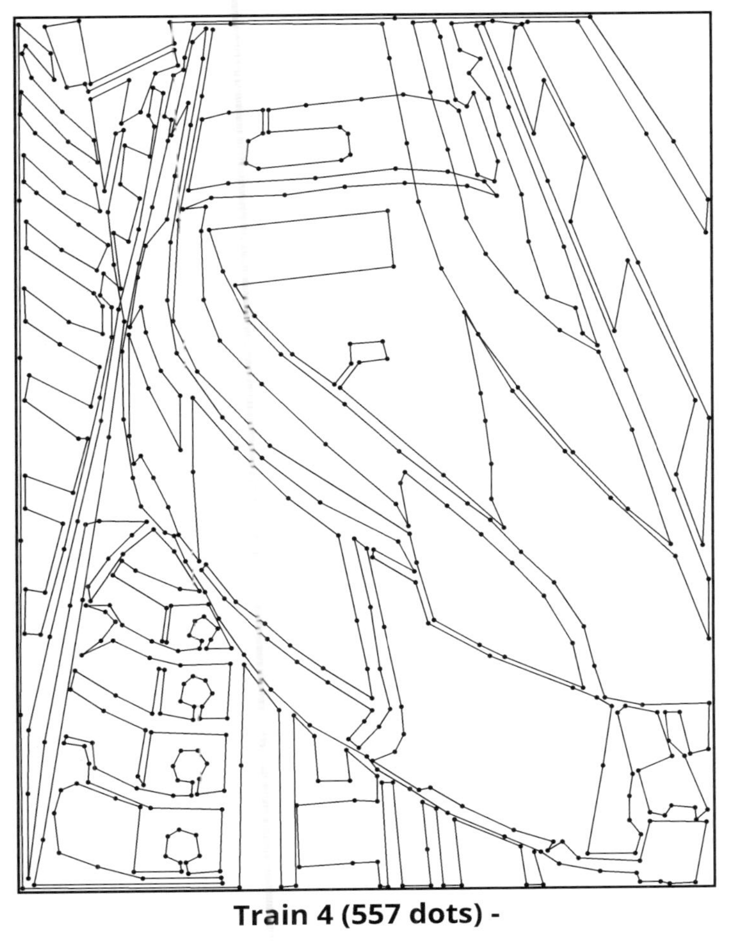

Train 4 (557 dots) -

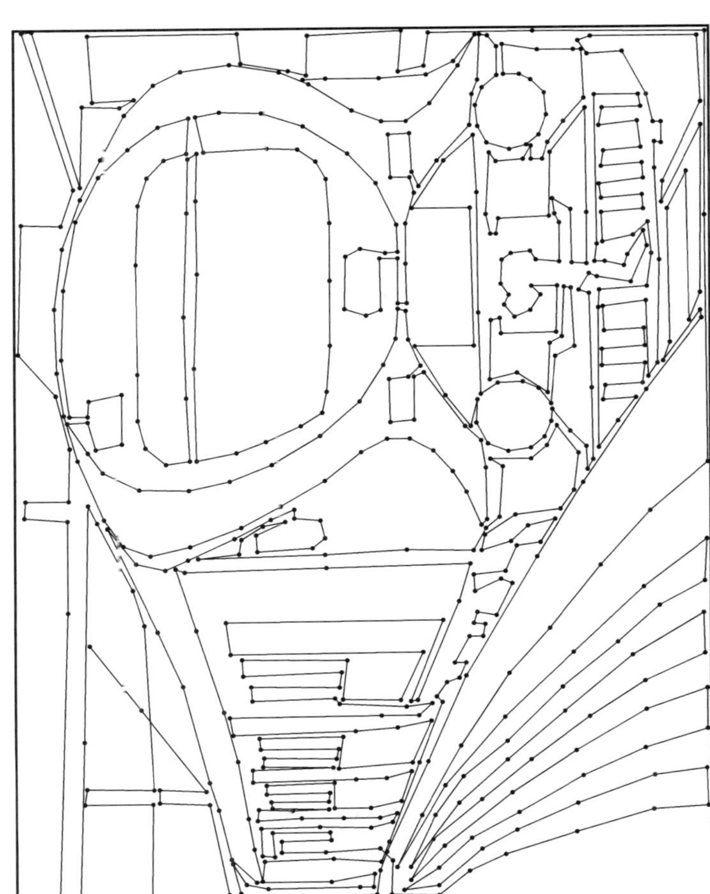

Train 5 (588 dots) -

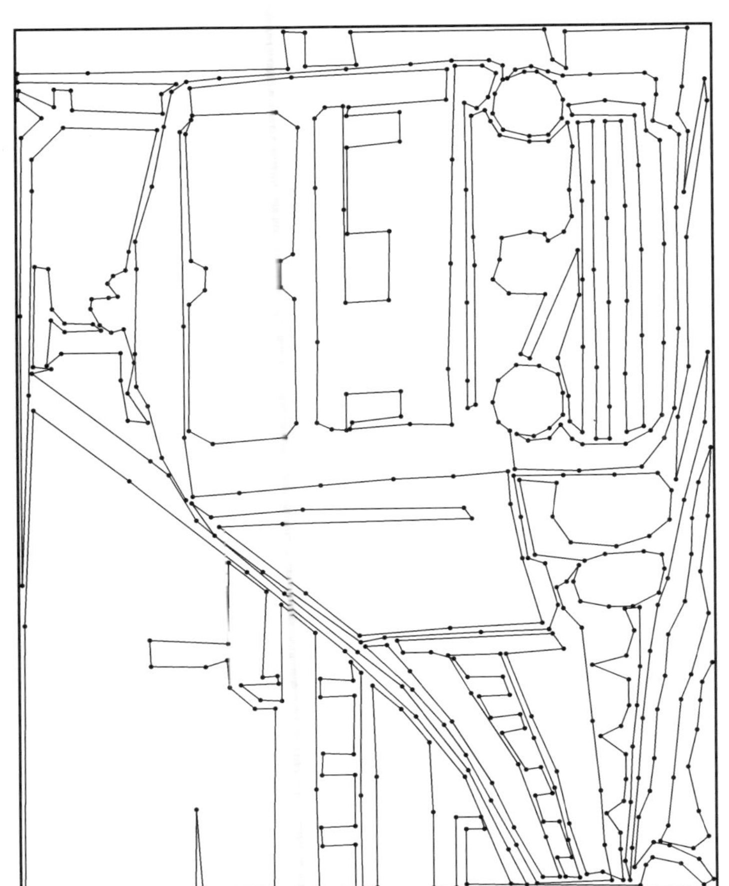

Train 6 (516 dots) -

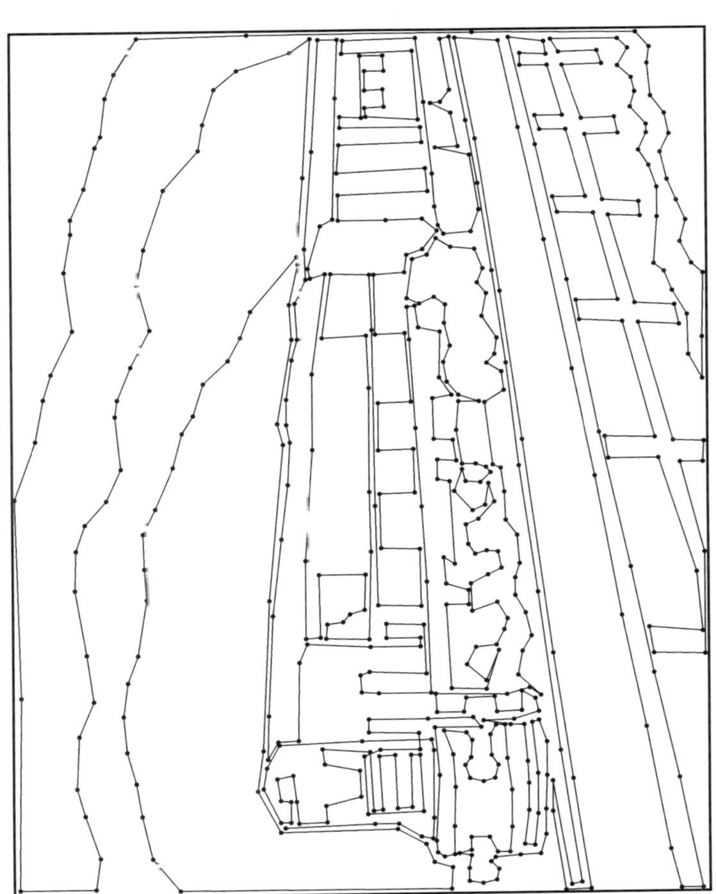

Train 7 (525 dots) -

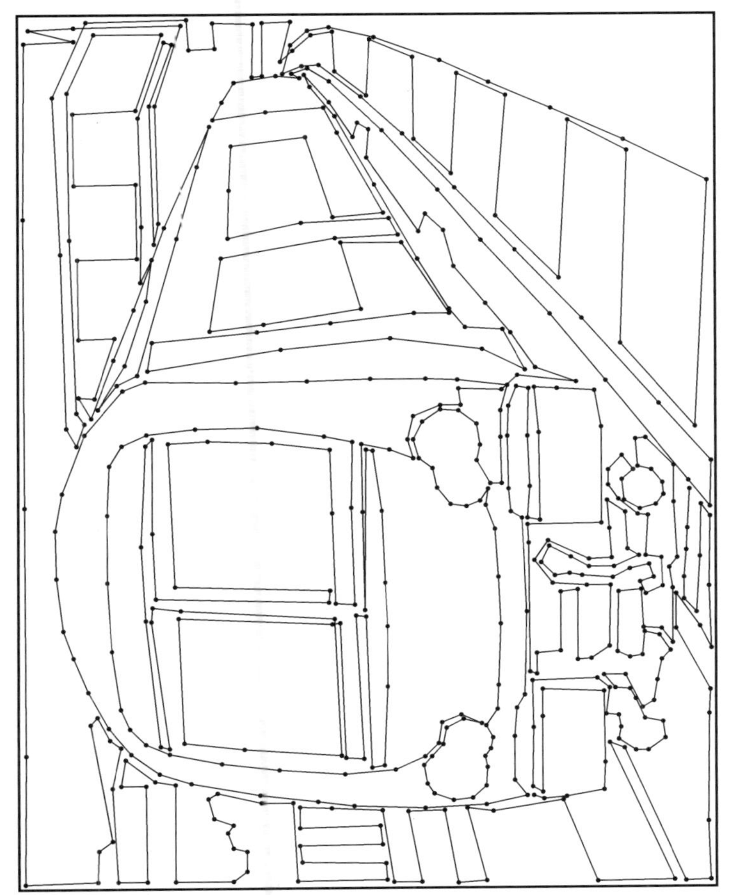
Train 8 (500 dots) -

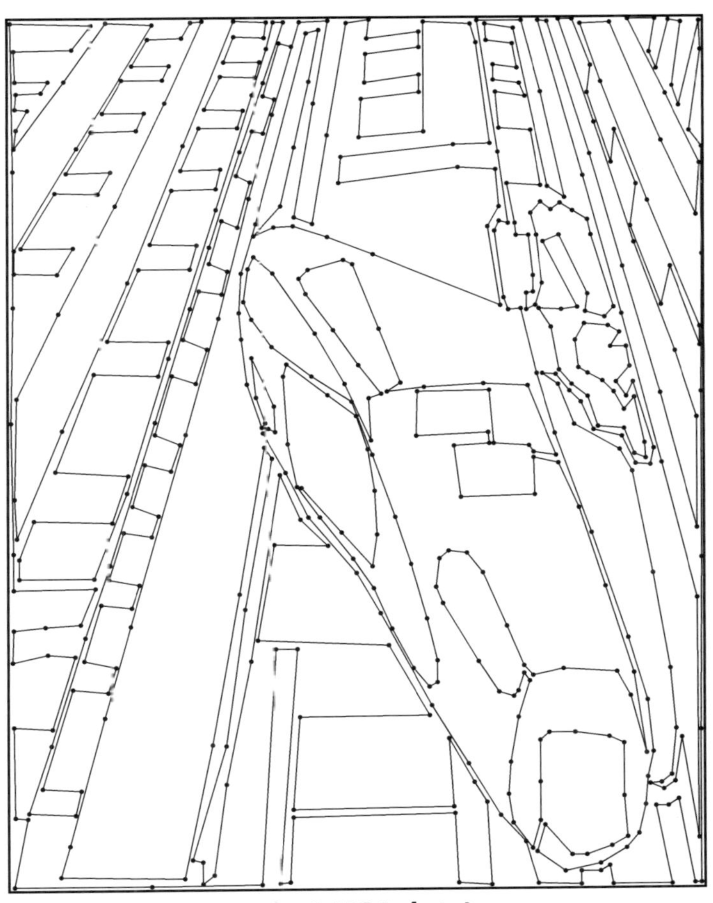
Train 9 (531 dots) -

Made in the USA
Columbia, SC
29 April 2025

57293088R00046

THIS BOOK BELONGS TO:

____

OVERWHELMED?

Being overwhelmed feels a little like being in a boat surrounded by alligators.

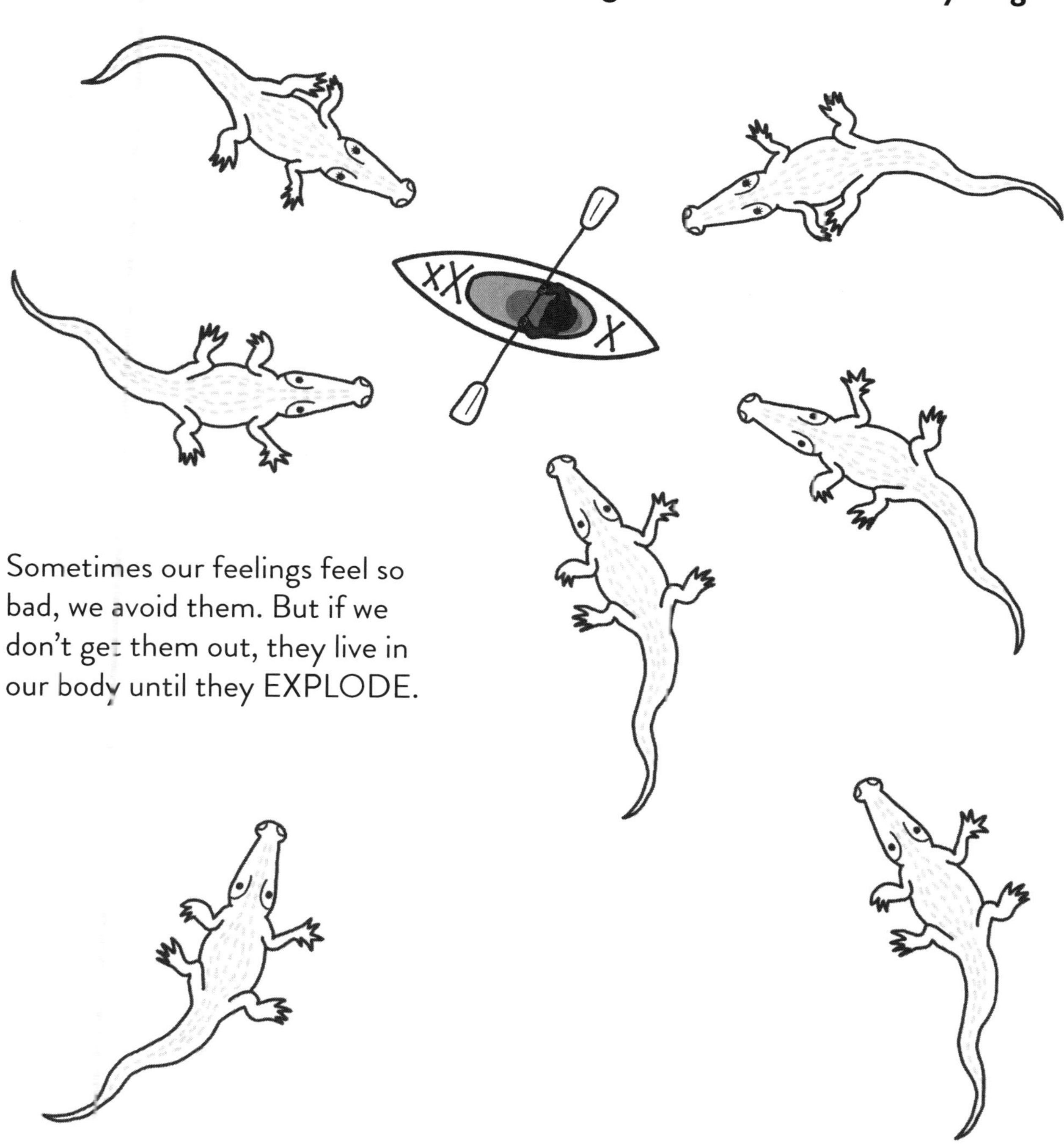

Sometimes our feelings feel so bad, we avoid them. But if we don't get them out, they live in our body until they EXPLODE.

Rate how you're feeling right now by circling a number:

1 - 2 - 3 - 4 - 5 - 6 - 7 - 8 - 9 - 10

totally calm (1) · right in the middle (5) · totally overwhelmed (10)

Brain Dump

1. In the circle, write every single thing floating around your brain, worrying you or stressing you out.

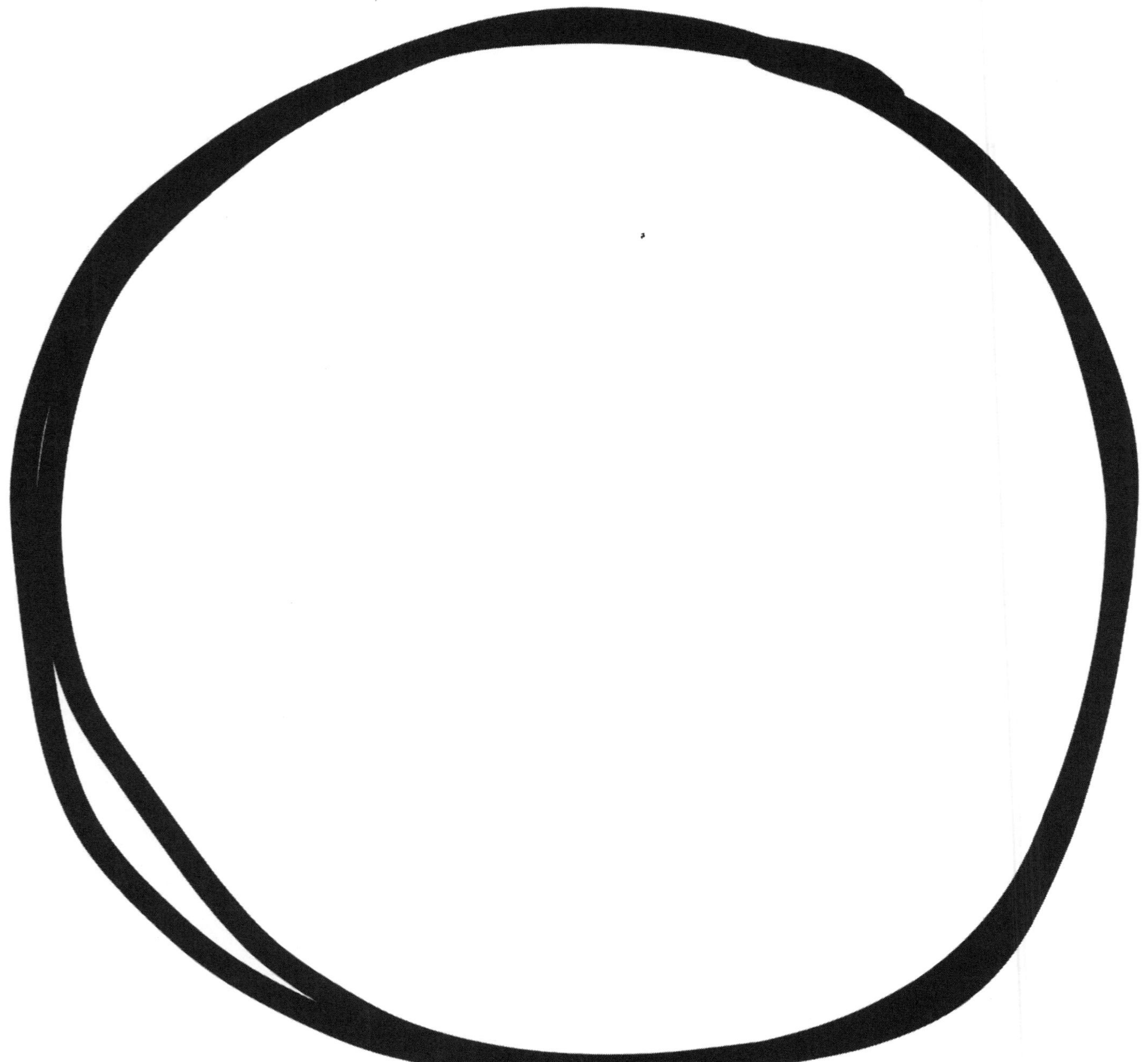

2. Circle the things that are stressing you the most.
3. Underline or highlight the things that are smaller or easier to do/solve.

List the underlined, easy things to do from the brain dump:

Rate how you're feeling right now by circling a number:

1 - 2 - 3 - 4 - 5 - 6 - 7 - 8 - 9 - 10

totally calm | right in the middle | totally overwhelmed

The circled things in your "brain dump" circle are your big and scary "alligator" worries.

Name your alligator (or multiple alligators):

Draw a crown on the alligator that feels the biggest or scariest.

That is the alligator closest to your boat.

When we are overwhelmed, it feels like we have too many problems.
The way to feel better is to deal with the alligator closest to your boat **first**.

Brainstorm some solutions for the alligator closest to your boat.

What might make this situation better? No ideas are bad ideas here. List them all in the circles below.

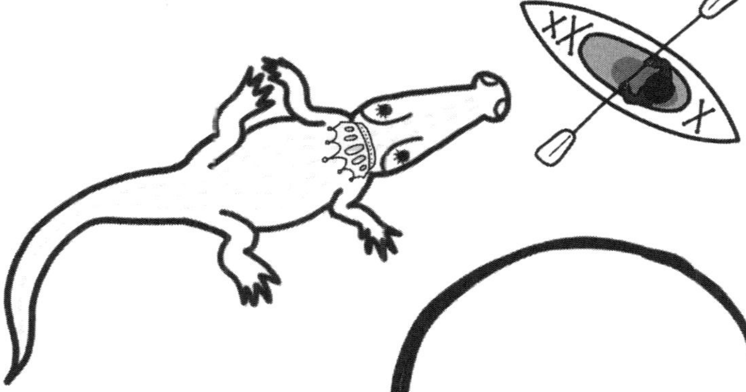

Look at each of your ideas. What might happen if you try each one? Thinking about what could happen will help you decide which solutions are better than others.

Cross out any ideas you think won't work very well.
Now decide which solution you'll try first. Put a star next to it.

There is no one "right answer." If this idea doesn't work, you will try a different one!
You got this! We can do hard things.

Rate how you're feeling right now by circling a number:

1 - 2 - 3 - 4 - 5 - 6 - 7 - 8 - 9 - 10

totally calm (1) · right in the middle (5) · totally overwhelmed (10)

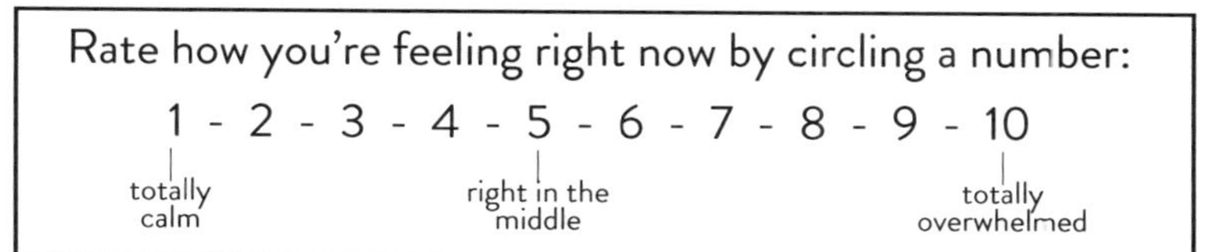

OVERWHELMED?

Being overwhelmed feels a little like being in a boat surrounded by alligators.

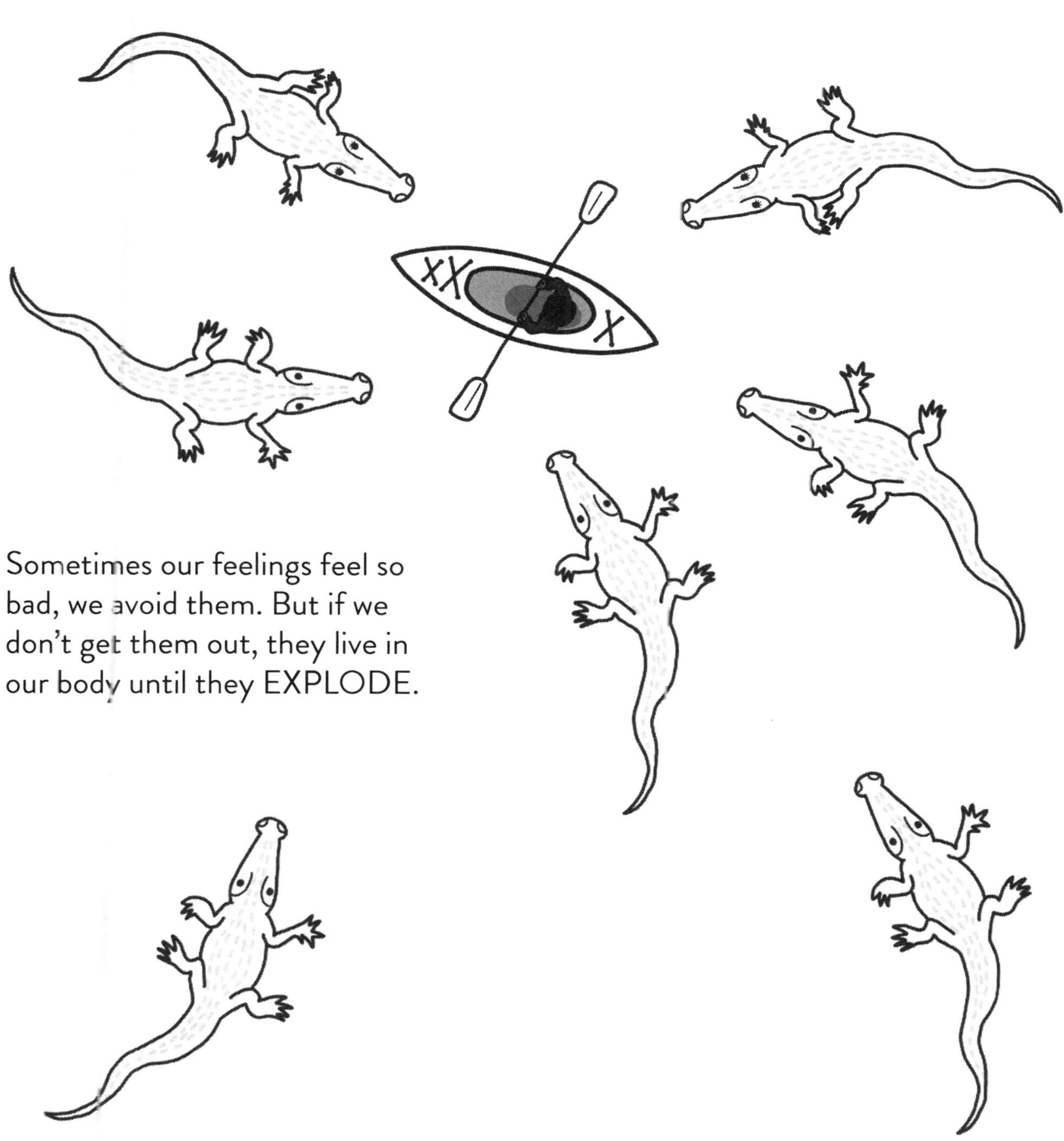

Sometimes our feelings feel so bad, we avoid them. But if we don't get them out, they live in our body until they EXPLODE.

Rate how you're feeling right now by circling a number:

1 - 2 - 3 - 4 - 5 - 6 - 7 - 8 - 9 - 10

totally calm (1) — right in the middle (5) — totally overwhelmed (10)

Brain Dump

(1) In the circle, write every single thing floating around your brain, worrying you or stressing you out.

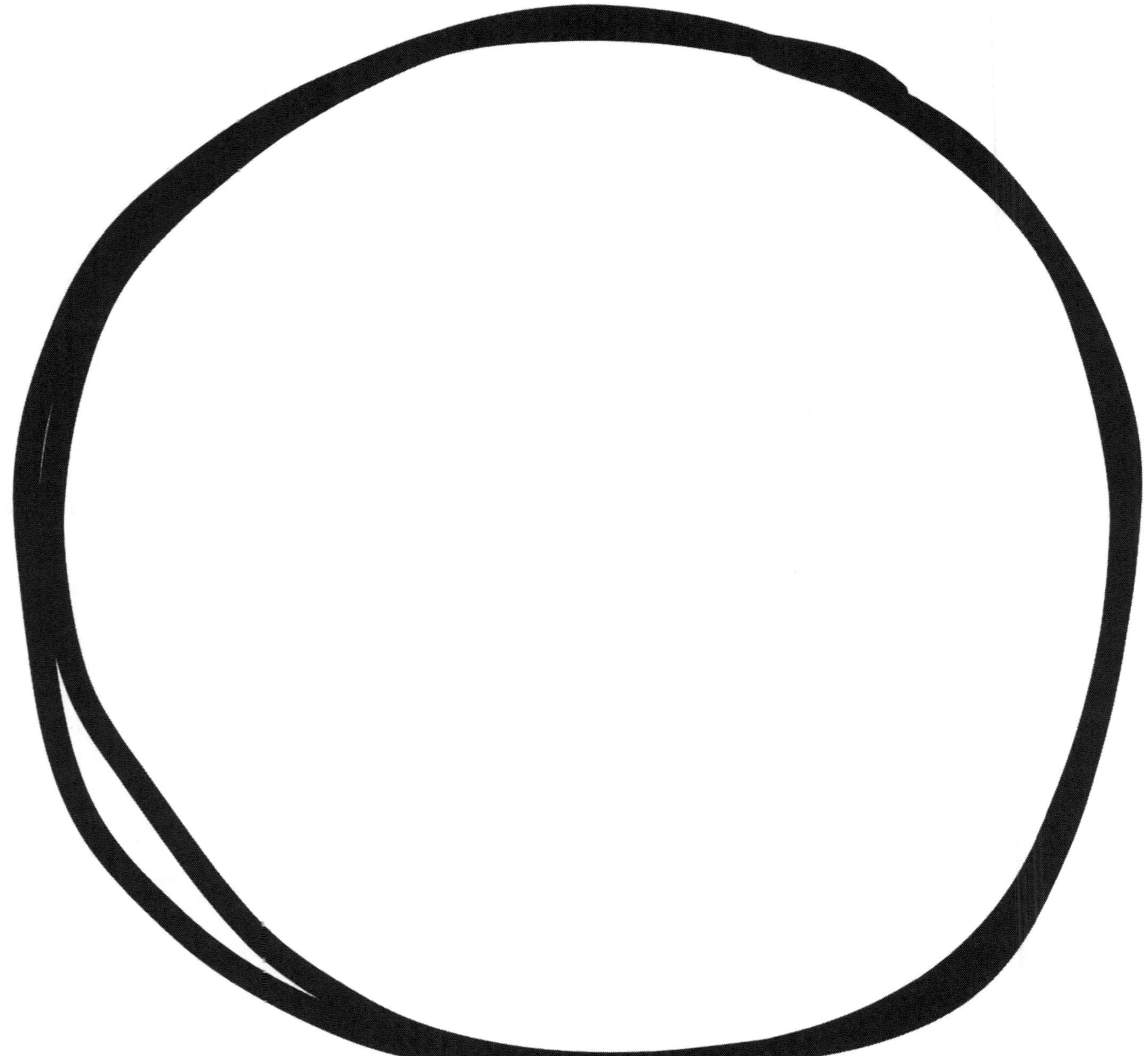

(2) Circle the things that are stressing you the most.

(3) Underline or highlight the things that are smaller or easier to do/solve.

List the underlined, easy things to do from the brain dump:

Rate how you're feeling right now by circling a number:

1 - 2 - 3 - 4 - 5 - 6 - 7 - 8 - 9 - 10

totally calm | right in the middle | totally overwhelmed

The circled things in your "brain dump" circle are your big and scary "alligator" worries.

Name your alligator (or multiple alligators):

Draw a crown on the alligator that feels the biggest or scariest.

That is the alligator closest to your boat.

When we are overwhelmed, it feels like we have too many problems.
The way to feel better is to deal with the alligator closest to your boat **first**.

Brainstorm some solutions for the alligator closest to your boat.

What might make this situation better? No ideas are bad ideas here. List them all in the circles below.

Look at each of your ideas. What might happen if you try each one? Thinking about what could happen will help you decide which solutions are better than others.

Cross out any ideas you think won't work very well.
Now decide which solution you'll try first. Put a star next to it.

There is no one "right answer." If this idea doesn't work, you will try a different one! You got this! We can do hard things.

Rate how you're feeling right now by circling a number:

1 - 2 - 3 - 4 - 5 - 6 - 7 - 8 - 9 - 10

totally calm | right in the middle | totally overwhelmed

OVERWHELMED?

Being overwhelmed feels a little like being in a boat surrounded by alligators.

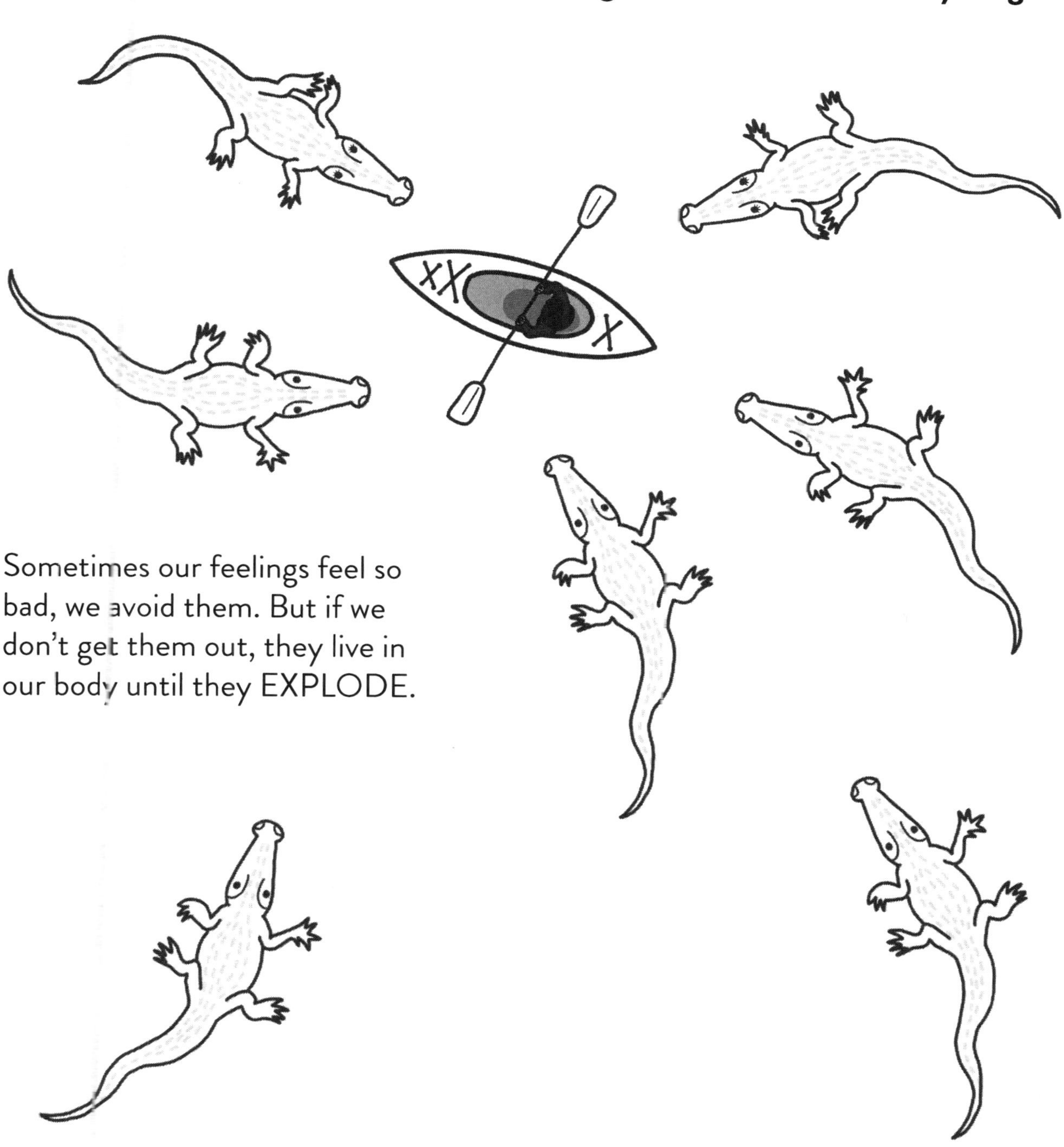

Sometimes our feelings feel so bad, we avoid them. But if we don't get them out, they live in our body until they EXPLODE.

Rate how you're feeling right now by circling a number:

1 - 2 - 3 - 4 - 5 - 6 - 7 - 8 - 9 - 10

totally calm | right in the middle | totally overwhelmed

Brain Dump

1. In the circle, write every single thing floating around your brain, worrying you or stressing you out.

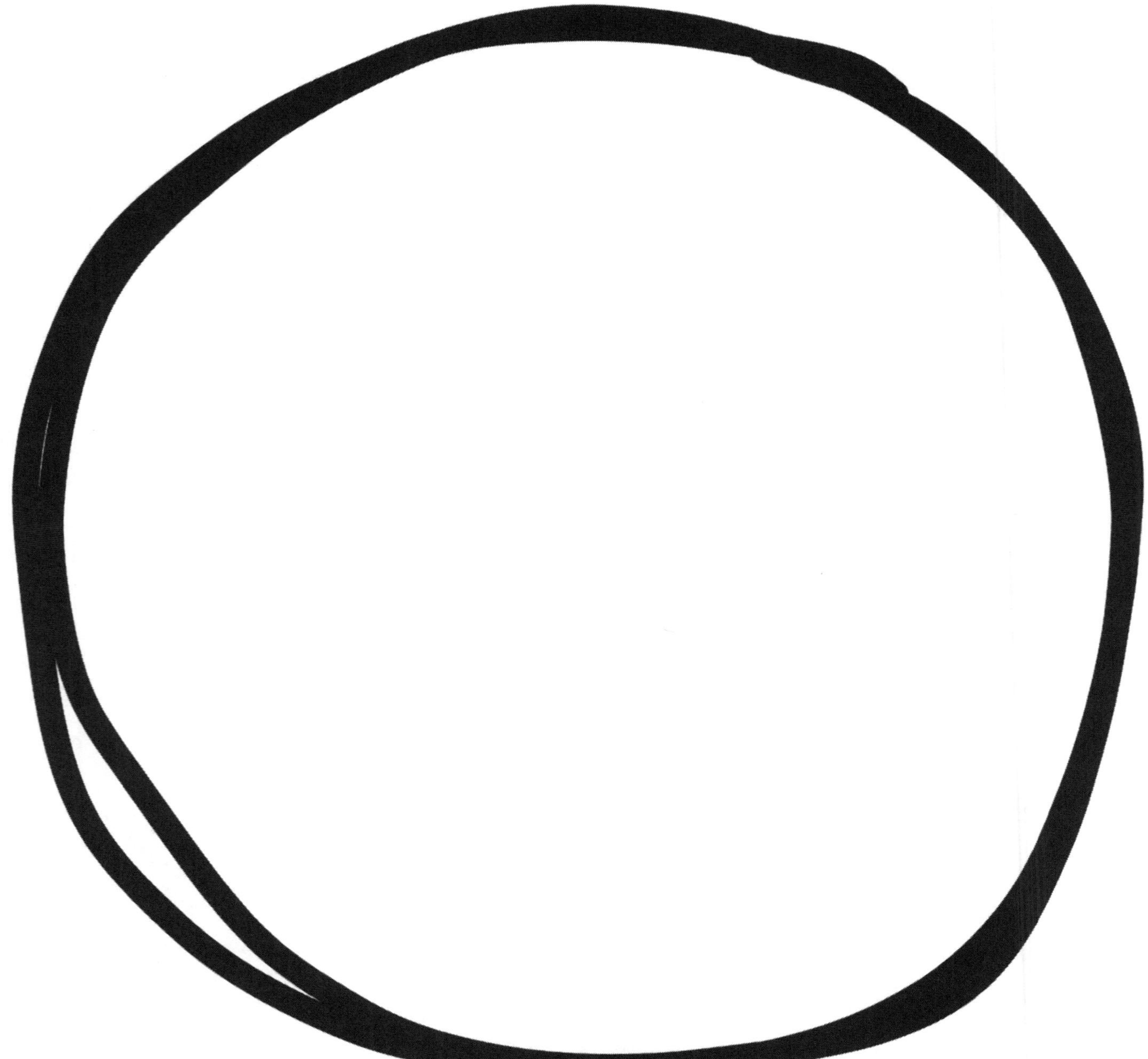

2. Circle the things that are stressing you the most.
3. Underline or highlight the things that are smaller or easier to do/solve.

List the underlined, easy things to do from the brain dump:

Rate how you're feeling right now by circling a number:

1 - 2 - 3 - 4 - 5 - 6 - 7 - 8 - 9 - 10

totally calm | right in the middle | totally overwhelmed

The circled things in your "brain dump" circle are your big and scary "alligator" worries.

Name your alligator (or multiple alligators):

Draw a crown on the alligator that feels the biggest or scariest.

That is the alligator closest to your boat.

When we are overwhelmed, it feels like we have too many problems.
The way to feel better is to deal with the alligator closest to your boat **first**.

Brainstorm some solutions for the alligator closest to your boat.

What might make this situation better? No ideas are bad ideas here. List them all in the circles below.

Look at each of your ideas. What might happen if you try each one? Thinking about what could happen will help you decide which solutions are better than others.

Cross out any ideas you think won't work very well.
Now decide which solution you'll try first. Put a star next to it.

There is no one "right answer." If this idea doesn't work, you will try a different one! You got this! We can do hard things.

Rate how you're feeling right now by circling a number:

1 - 2 - 3 - 4 - 5 - 6 - 7 - 8 - 9 - 10

totally calm | right in the middle | totally overwhelmed

OVERWHELMED?

Being overwhelmed feels a little like being in a boat surrounded by alligators.

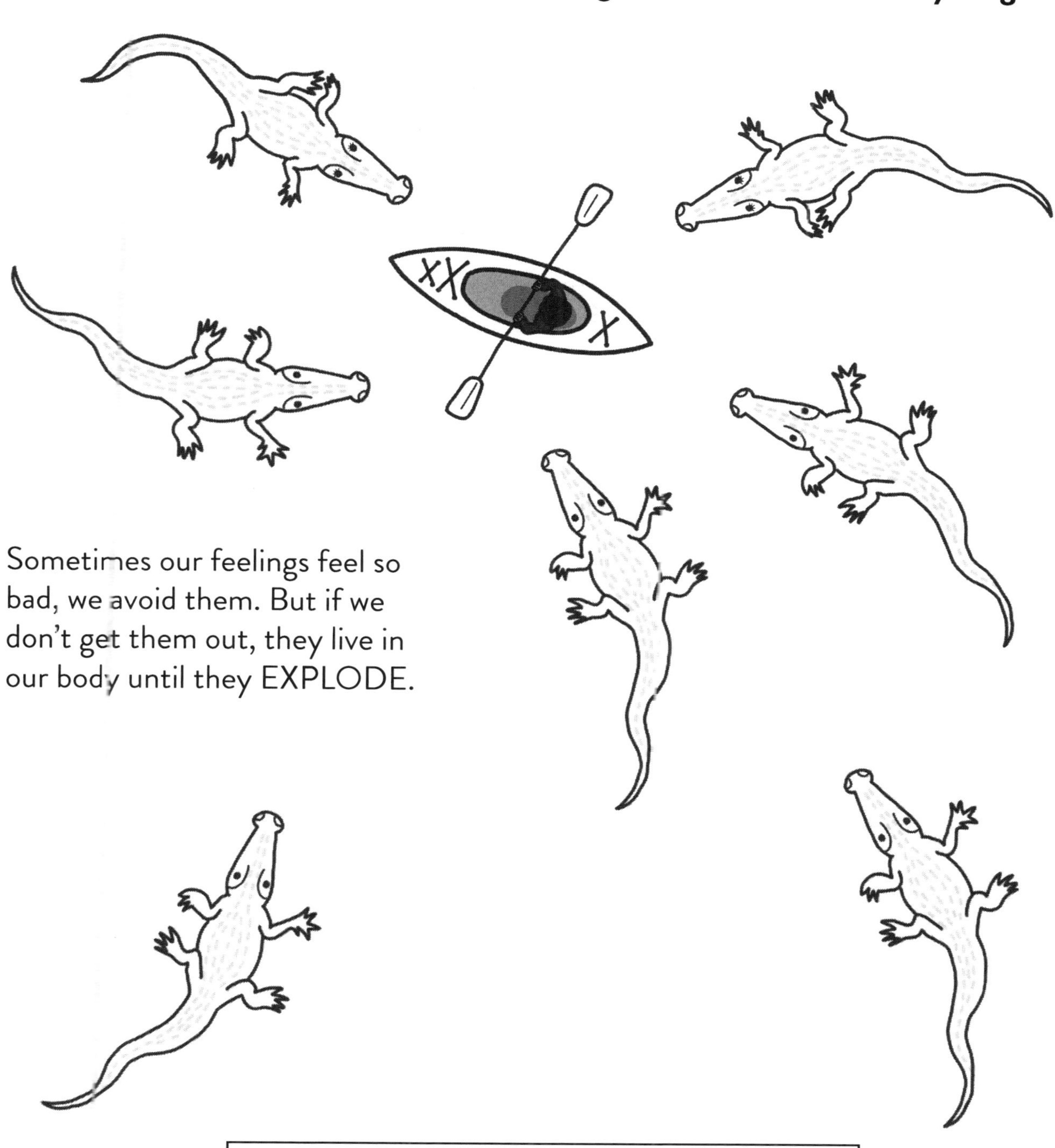

Sometimes our feelings feel so bad, we avoid them. But if we don't get them out, they live in our body until they EXPLODE.

Rate how you're feeling right now by circling a number:

1 - 2 - 3 - 4 - 5 - 6 - 7 - 8 - 9 - 10

1 = totally calm; 5 = right in the middle; 10 = totally overwhelmed

Brain Dump

1. In the circle, write every single thing floating around your brain, worrying you or stressing you out.

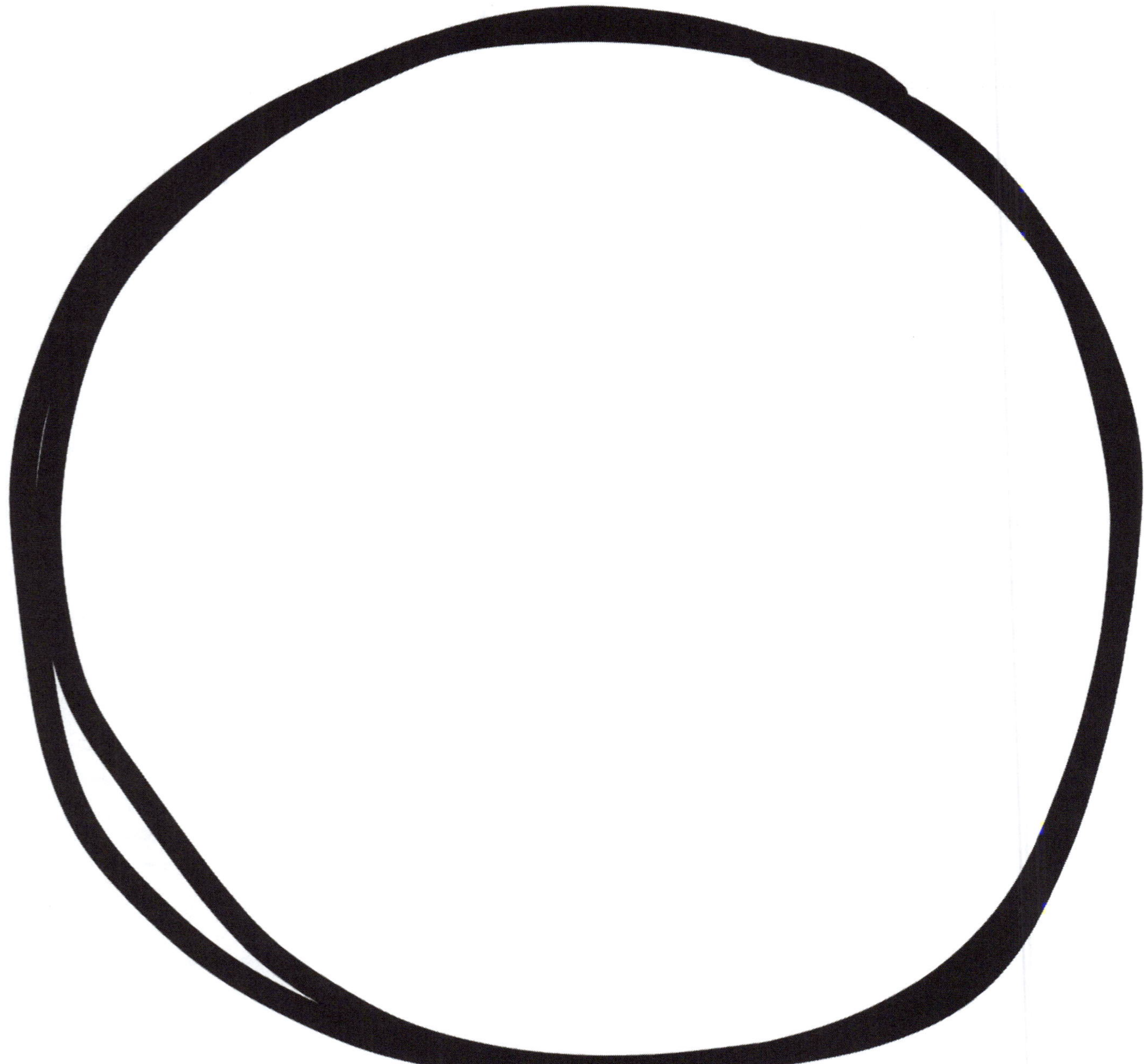

2. Circle the things that are stressing you the most.

3. Underline or highlight the things that are smaller or easier to do/solve.

List the underlined, easy things to do from the brain dump:

Rate how you're feeling right now by circling a number:

1 - 2 - 3 - 4 - 5 - 6 - 7 - 8 - 9 - 10

totally calm | right in the middle | totally overwhelmed

The circled things in your "brain dump" circle are your big and scary "alligator" worries.

Name your alligator (or multiple alligators):

Draw a crown on the alligator that feels the biggest or scariest.

That is the alligator closest to your boat.

When we are overwhelmed, it feels like we have too many problems.
The way to feel better is to deal with the alligator closest to your boat **first**.

Brainstorm some solutions for the alligator closest to your boat.

What might make this situation better? No ideas are bad ideas here. List them all in the circles below.

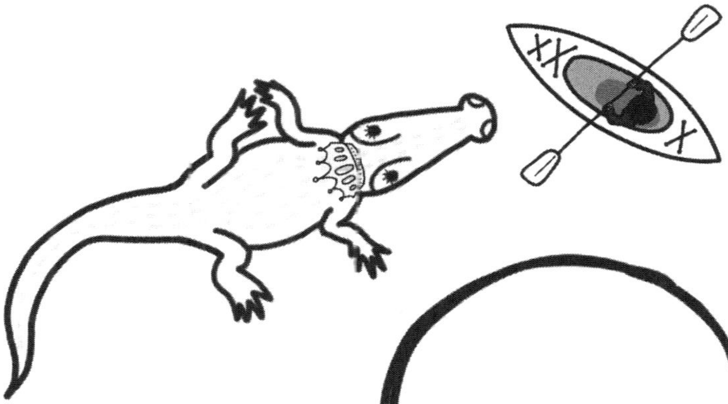

Look at each of your ideas. What might happen if you try each one? Thinking about what could happen will help you decide which solutions are better than others.

Cross out any ideas you think won't work very well.
Now decide which solution you'll try first. Put a star next to it.

There is no one "right answer." If this idea doesn't work, you will try a different one!
You got this! We can do hard things.

Rate how you're feeling right now by circling a number:

1 - 2 - 3 - 4 - 5 - 6 - 7 - 8 - 9 - 10

1 = totally calm; 5 = right in the middle; 10 = totally overwhelmed

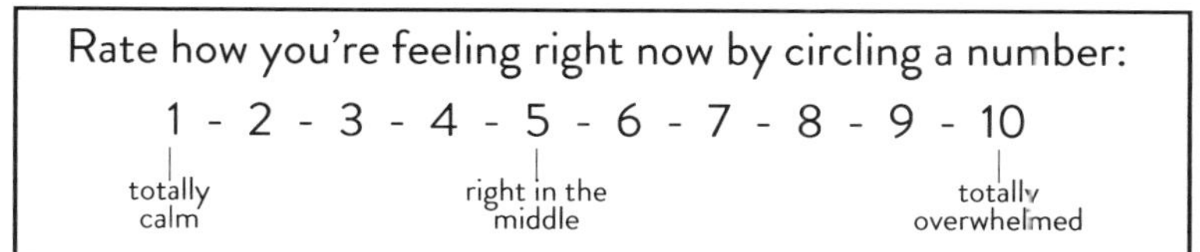

OVERWHELMED?

Being overwhelmed feels a little like being in a boat surrounded by alligators.

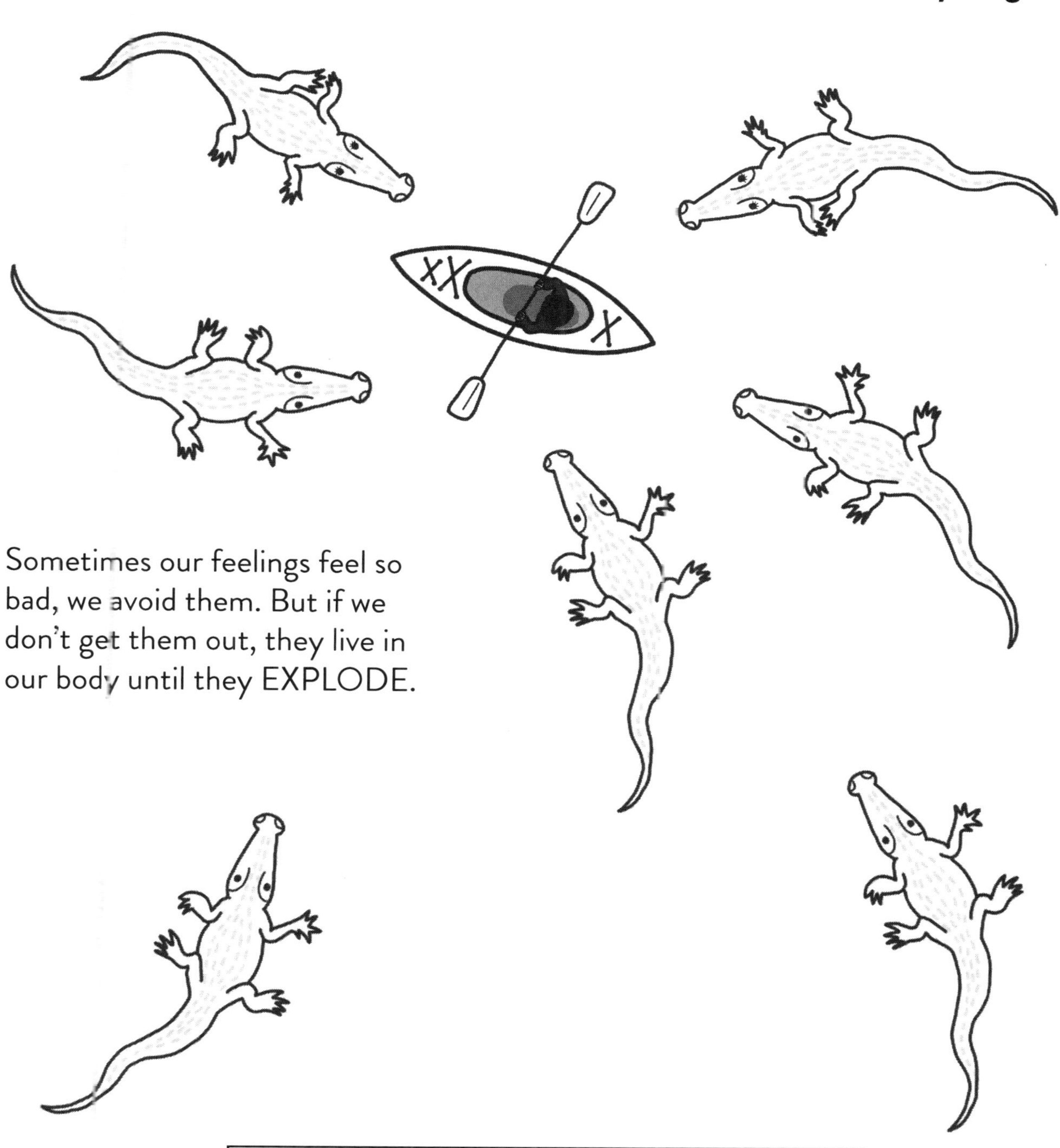

Sometimes our feelings feel so bad, we avoid them. But if we don't get them out, they live in our body until they EXPLODE.

Rate how you're feeling right now by circling a number:

1 - 2 - 3 - 4 - 5 - 6 - 7 - 8 - 9 - 10

totally calm (1) | right in the middle (5) | totally overwhelmed (10)

Brain Dump

1. In the circle, write every single thing floating around your brain, worrying you or stressing you out.

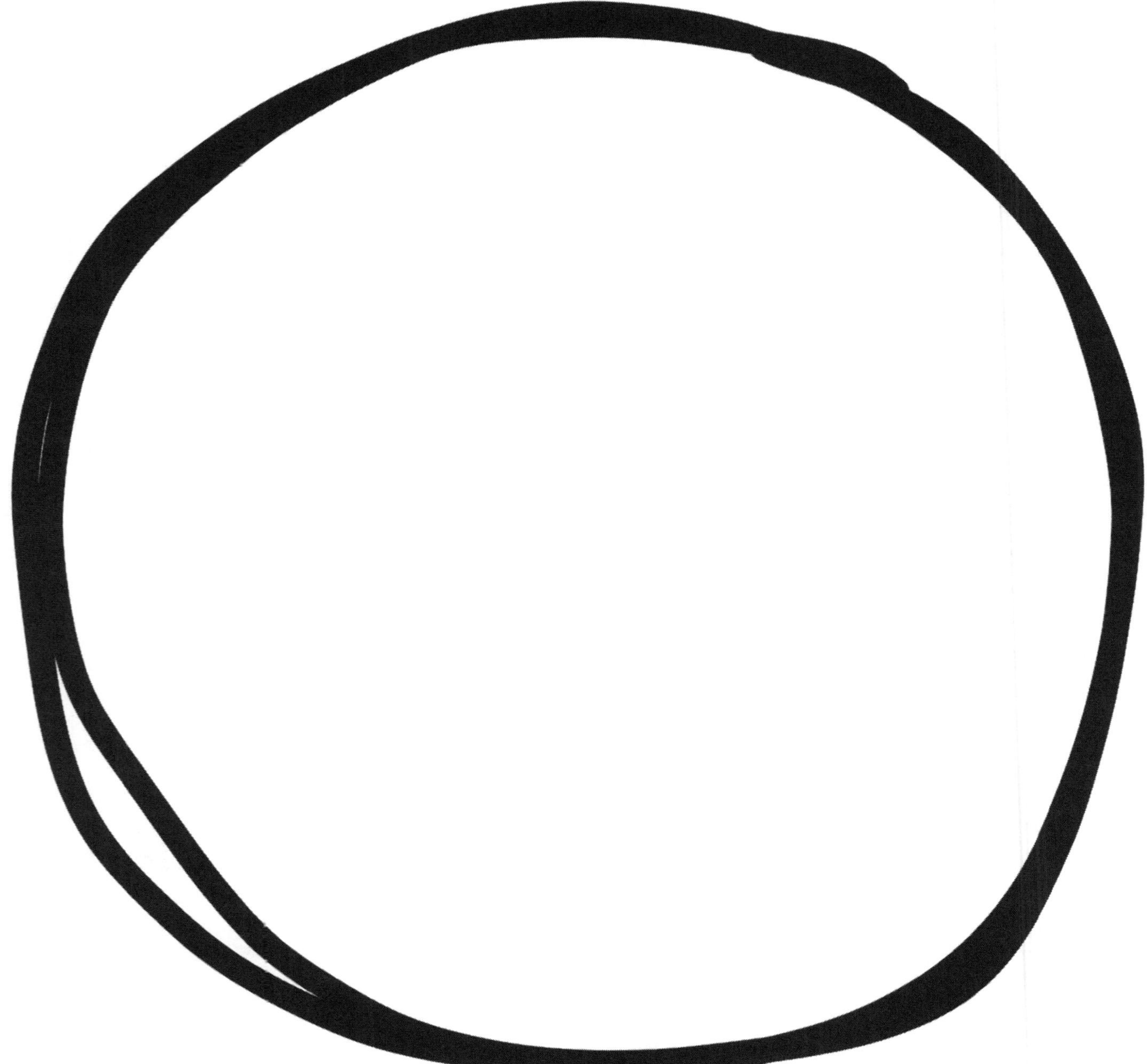

2. Circle the things that are stressing you the most.

3. Underline or highlight the things that are smaller or easier to do/solve.

List the underlined, easy things to do from the brain dump:

Rate how you're feeling right now by circling a number:

1 - 2 - 3 - 4 - 5 - 6 - 7 - 8 - 9 - 10

totally calm | right in the middle | totally overwhelmed

The circled things in your "brain dump" circle are your big and scary "alligator" worries.

Name your alligator (or multiple alligators):

Draw a crown on the alligator that feels the biggest or scariest.

That is the alligator closest to your boat.

When we are overwhelmed, it feels like we have too many problems.
The way to feel better is to deal with the alligator closest to your boat **first**.

Brainstorm some solutions for the alligator closest to your boat.

What might make this situation better? No ideas are bad ideas here. List them all in the circles below.

Look at each of your ideas. What might happen if you try each one? Thinking about what could happen will help you decide which solutions are better than others.

Cross out any ideas you think won't work very well.
Now decide which solution you'll try first. Put a star next to it.

There is no one "right answer." If this idea doesn't work, you will try a different one!
You got this! We can do hard things.

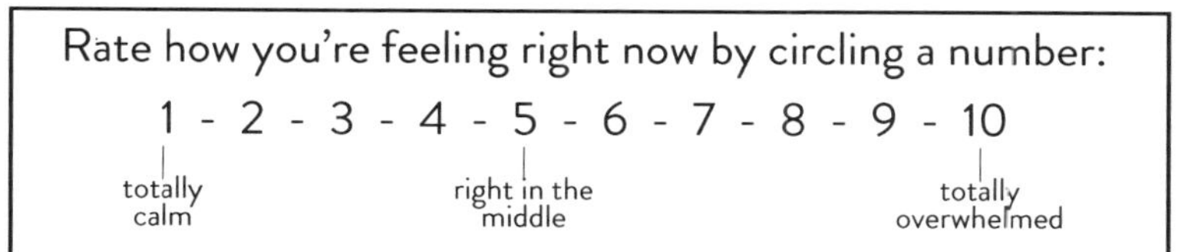
Rate how you're feeling right now by circling a number:

1 - 2 - 3 - 4 - 5 - 6 - 7 - 8 - 9 - 10

totally calm — right in the middle — totally overwhelmed

OVERWHELMED?

Being overwhelmed feels a little like being in a boat surrounded by alligators.

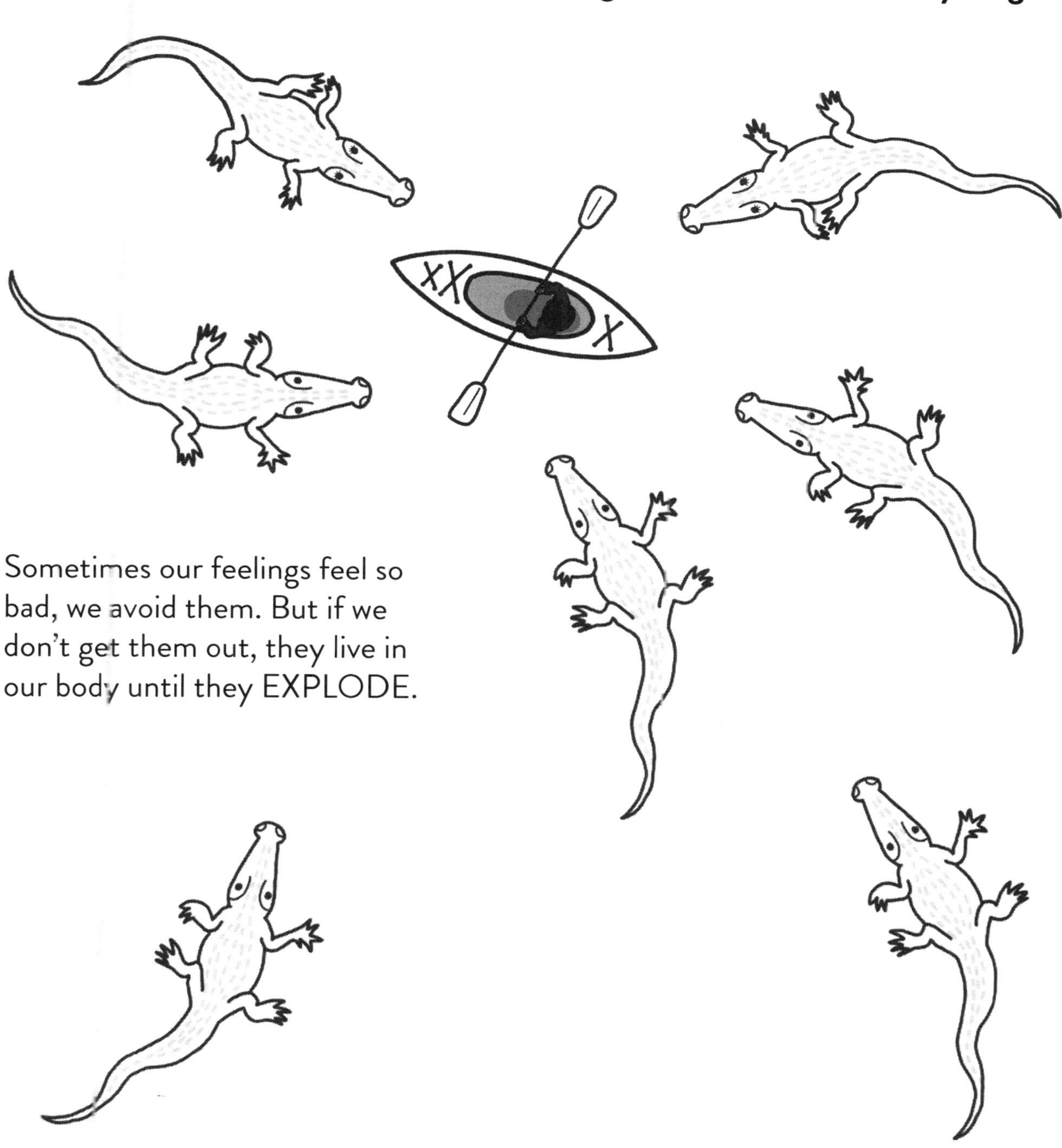

Sometimes our feelings feel so bad, we avoid them. But if we don't get them out, they live in our body until they EXPLODE.

Rate how you're feeling right now by circling a number:

1 - 2 - 3 - 4 - 5 - 6 - 7 - 8 - 9 - 10

totally calm | right in the middle | totally overwhelmed

Brain Dump

1. In the circle, write every single thing floating around your brain, worrying you or stressing you out.

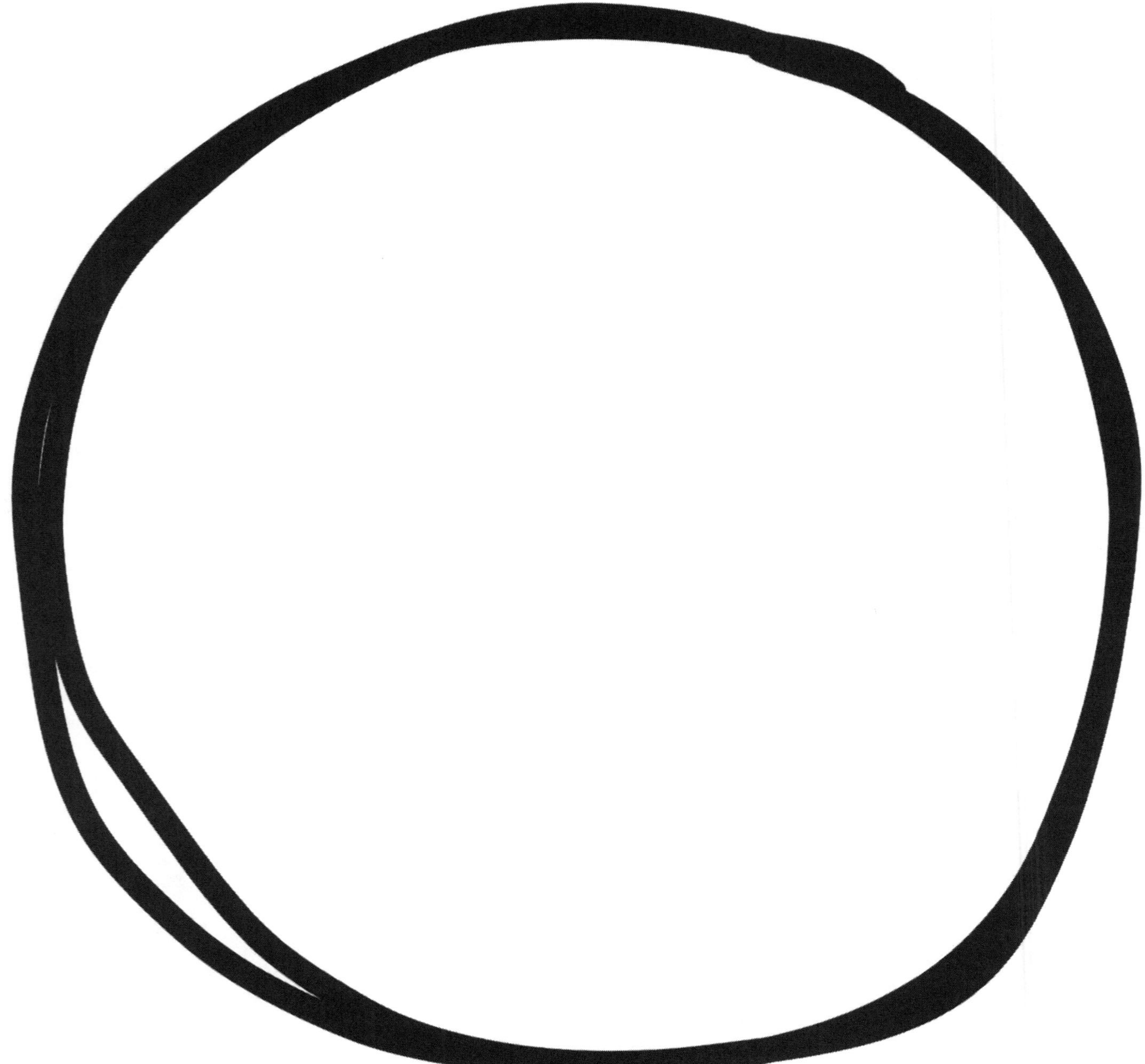

2. Circle the things that are stressing you the most.

3. Underline or highlight the things that are smaller or easier to do/solve.

List the underlined, easy things to do from the brain dump:

Rate how you're feeling right now by circling a number:

1 - 2 - 3 - 4 - 5 - 6 - 7 - 8 - 9 - 10

totally calm | right in the middle | totally overwhelmed

The circled things in your "brain dump" circle are your big and scary "alligator" worries.

Name your alligator (or multiple alligators):

Draw a crown on the alligator that feels the biggest or scariest.

That is the alligator closest to your boat.

When we are overwhelmed, it feels like we have too many problems.
The way to feel better is to deal with the alligator closest to your boat **first**.

Brainstorm some solutions for the alligator closest to your boat.

What might make this situation better? No ideas are bad ideas here. List them all in the circles below.

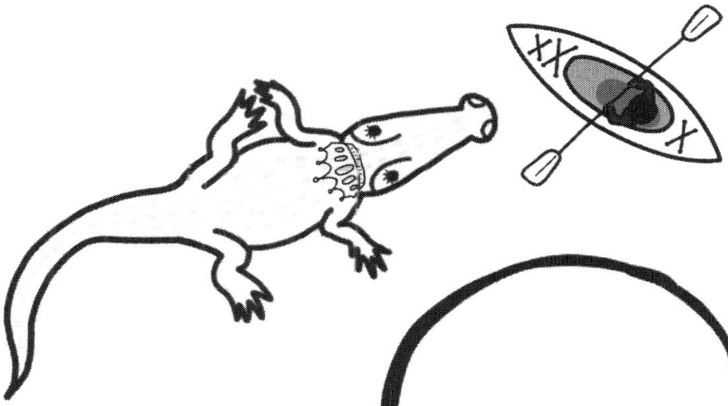

Look at each of your ideas. What might happen if you try each one? Thinking about what could happen will help you decide which solutions are better than others.

Cross out any ideas you think won't work very well.
Now decide which solution you'll try first. Put a star next to it.

There is no one "right answer." If this idea doesn't work, you will try a different one!
You got this! We can do hard things.

Rate how you're feeling right now by circling a number:

1 - 2 - 3 - 4 - 5 - 6 - 7 - 8 - 9 - 10

totally calm (1) | right in the middle (5) | totally overwhelmed (10)

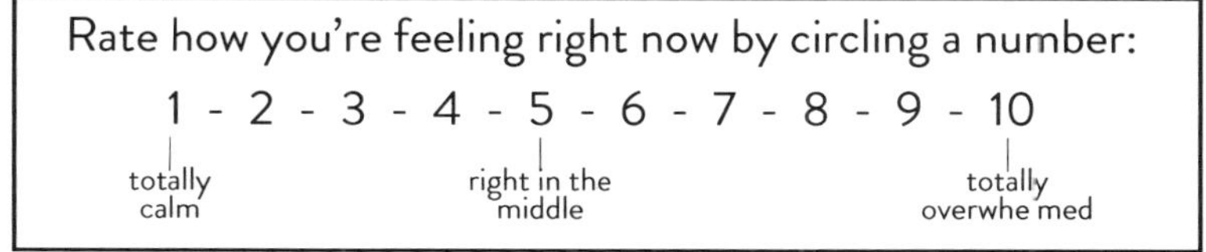

OVERWHELMED?

Being overwhelmed feels a little like being in a boat surrounded by alligators.

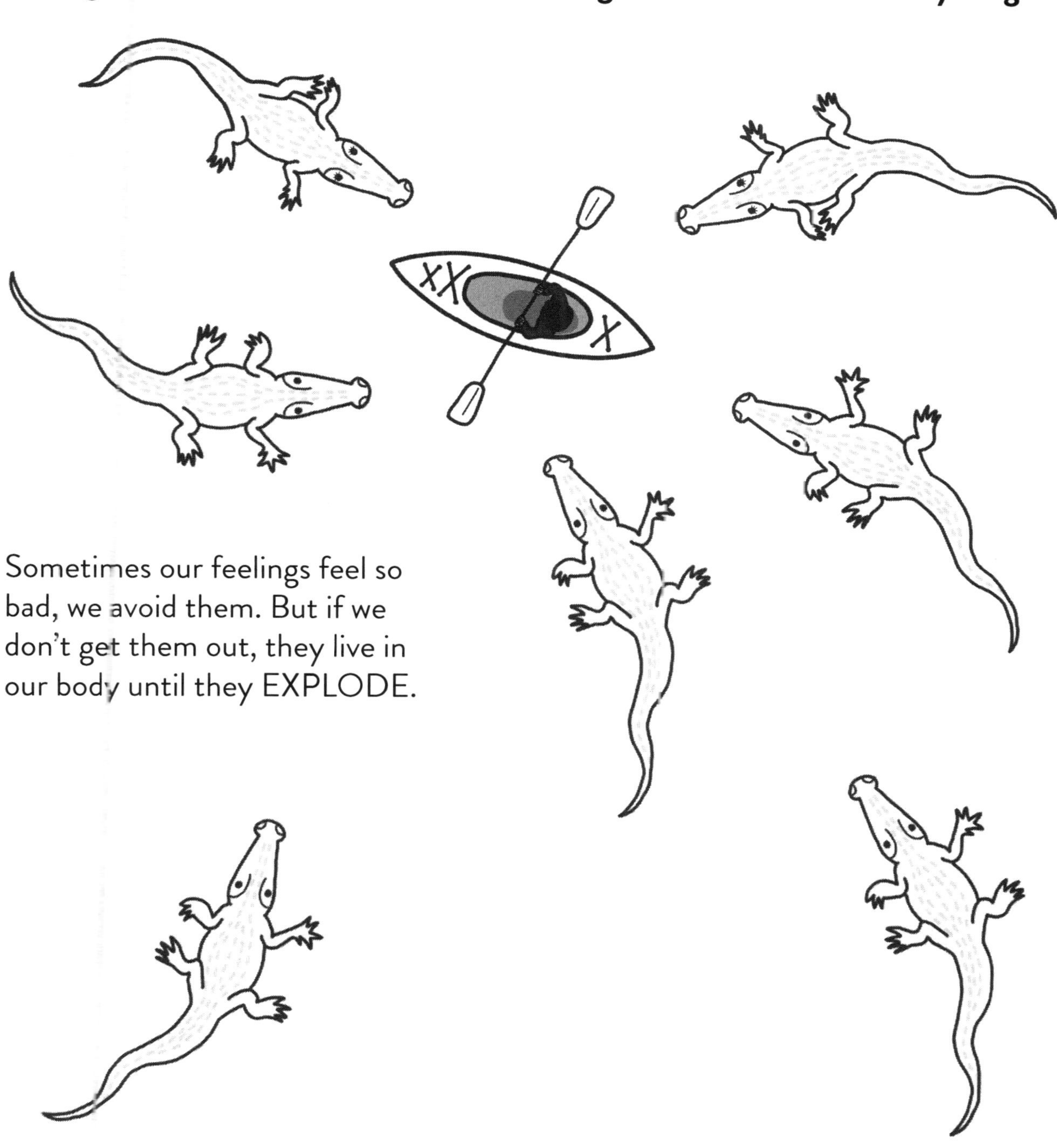

Sometimes our feelings feel so bad, we avoid them. But if we don't get them out, they live in our body until they EXPLODE.

Rate how you're feeling right now by circling a number:

1 - 2 - 3 - 4 - 5 - 6 - 7 - 8 - 9 - 10

1: totally calm
5: right in the middle
10: totally overwhelmed

Brain Dump

1. In the circle, write every single thing floating around your brain, worrying you or stressing you out.

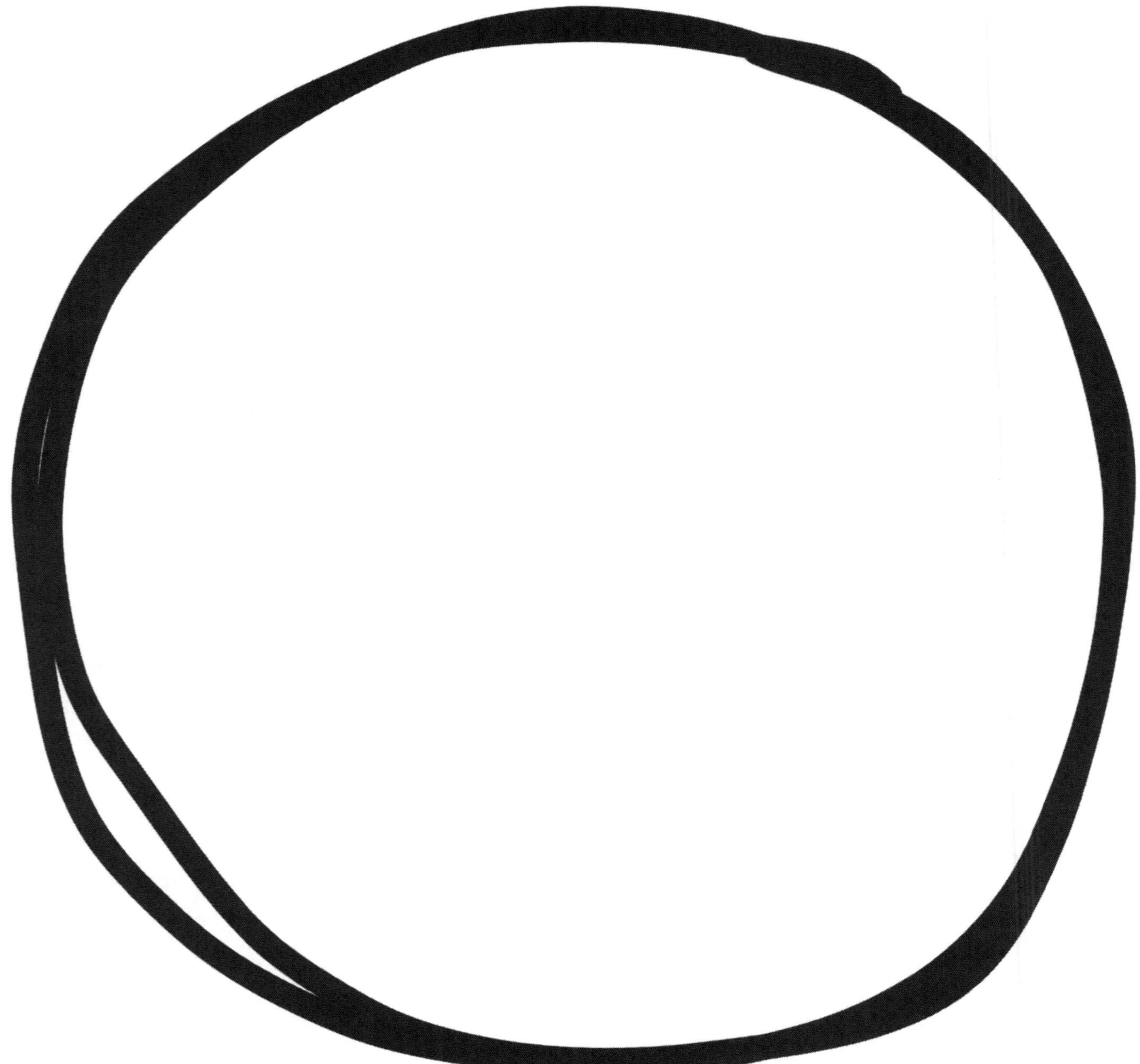

2. Circle the things that are stressing you the most.

3. Underline or highlight the things that are smaller or easier to do/solve.

List the underlined, easy things to do from the brain dump:

Rate how you're feeling right now by circling a number:

1 - 2 - 3 - 4 - 5 - 6 - 7 - 8 - 9 - 10

totally calm — right in the middle — totally overwhelmed

The circled things in your "brain dump" circle are your big and scary "alligator" worries.

Name your alligator (or multiple alligators):

Draw a crown on the alligator that feels the biggest or scariest.

That is the alligator closest to your boat.

When we are overwhelmed, it feels like we have too many problems.
The way to feel better is to deal with the alligator closest to your boat **first**.

Brainstorm some solutions for the alligator closest to your boat.

What might make this situation better? No ideas are bad ideas here. List them all in the circles below.

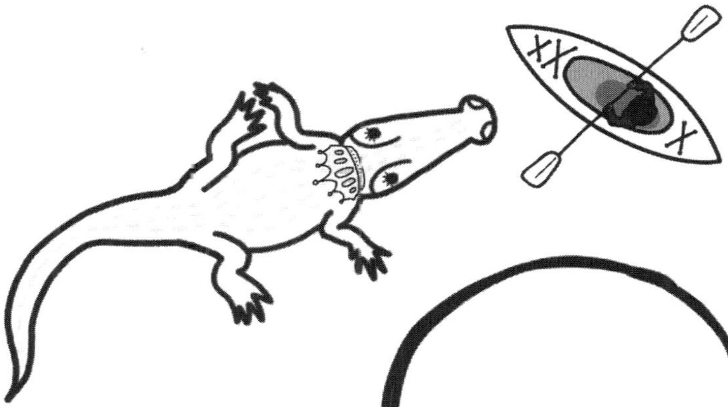

Look at each of your ideas. What might happen if you try each one? Thinking about what could happen will help you decide which solutions are better than others.

Cross out any ideas you think won't work very well.
Now decide which solution you'll try first. Put a star next to it.

There is no one "right answer." If this idea doesn't work, you will try a different one! You got this! We can do hard things.

Rate how you're feeling right now by circling a number:

1 - 2 - 3 - 4 - 5 - 6 - 7 - 8 - 9 - 10

1: totally calm; 5: right in the middle; 10: totally overwhelmed

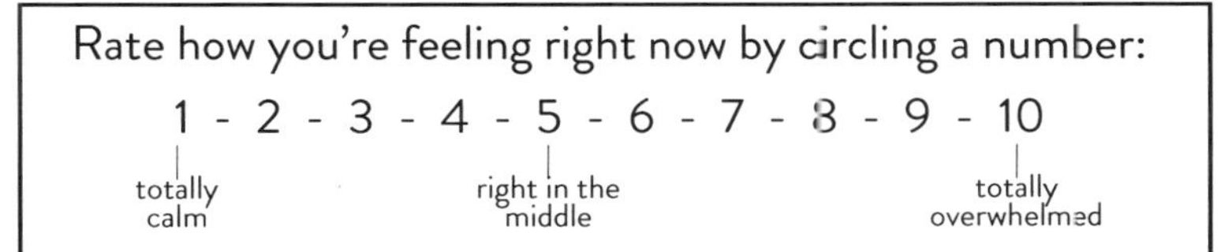

OVERWHELMED?

Being overwhelmed feels a little like being in a boat surrounded by alligators.

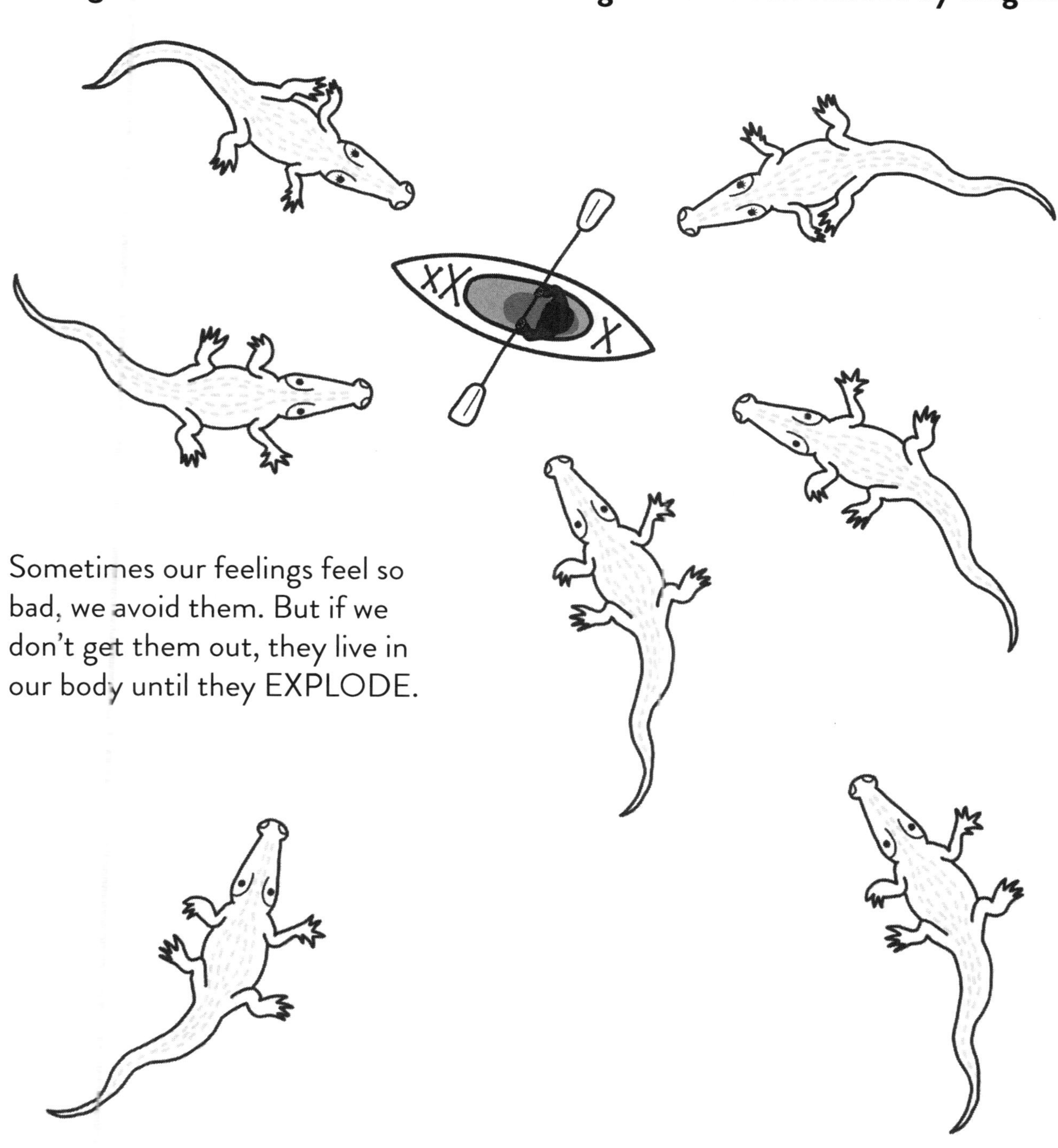

Sometimes our feelings feel so bad, we avoid them. But if we don't get them out, they live in our body until they EXPLODE.

Rate how you're feeling right now by circling a number:

1 - 2 - 3 - 4 - 5 - 6 - 7 - 8 - 9 - 10

totally calm (1) · right in the middle (5) · totally overwhelmed (10)

Brain Dump

1. In the circle, write every single thing floating around your brain, worrying you or stressing you out.

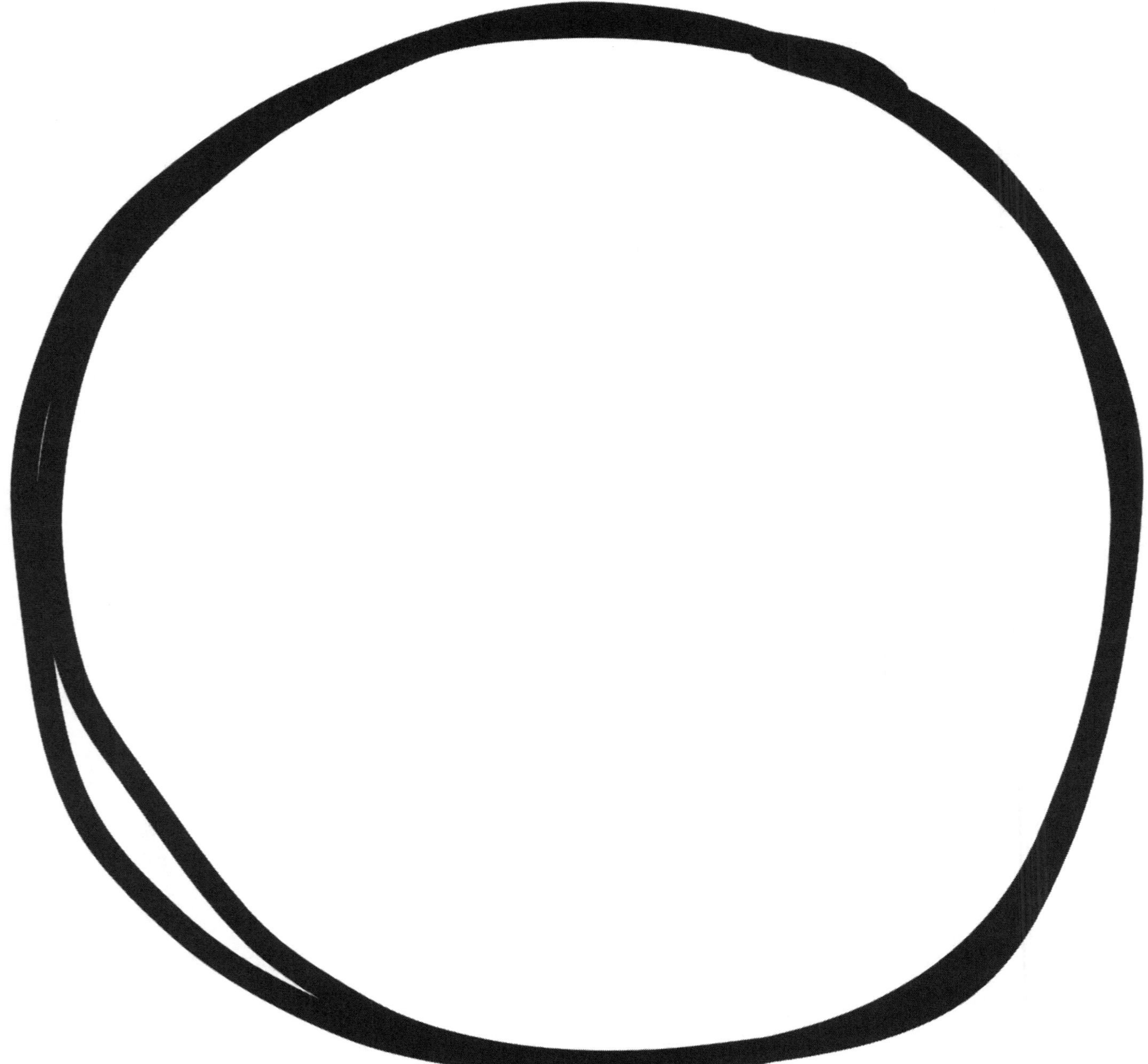

2. Circle the things that are stressing you the most.

3. Underline or highlight the things that are smaller or easier to do/solve.

List the underlined, easy things to do from the brain dump:

Rate how you're feeling right now by circling a number:

1 - 2 - 3 - 4 - 5 - 6 - 7 - 8 - 9 - 10

totally calm | right in the middle | totally overwhelmed

The circled things in your "brain dump" circle are your big and scary "alligator" worries.

Name your alligator (or multiple alligators):

Draw a crown on the alligator that feels the biggest or scariest.

That is the alligator closest to your boat.

When we are overwhelmed, it feels like we have too many problems.
The way to feel better is to deal with the alligator closest to your boat **first**.

Brainstorm some solutions for the alligator closest to your boat.

What might make this situation better? No ideas are bad ideas here. List them all in the circles below.

Look at each of your ideas. What might happen if you try each one? Thinking about what could happen will help you decide which solutions are better than others.

Cross out any ideas you think won't work very well.
Now decide which solution you'll try first. Put a star next to it.

There is no one "right answer." If this idea doesn't work, you will try a different one! You got this! We can do hard things.

Rate how you're feeling right now by circling a number:

1 - 2 - 3 - 4 - 5 - 6 - 7 - 8 - 9 - 10

totally calm | right in the middle | totally overwhelmed

OVERWHELMED?

Being overwhelmed feels a little like being in a boat surrounded by alligators.

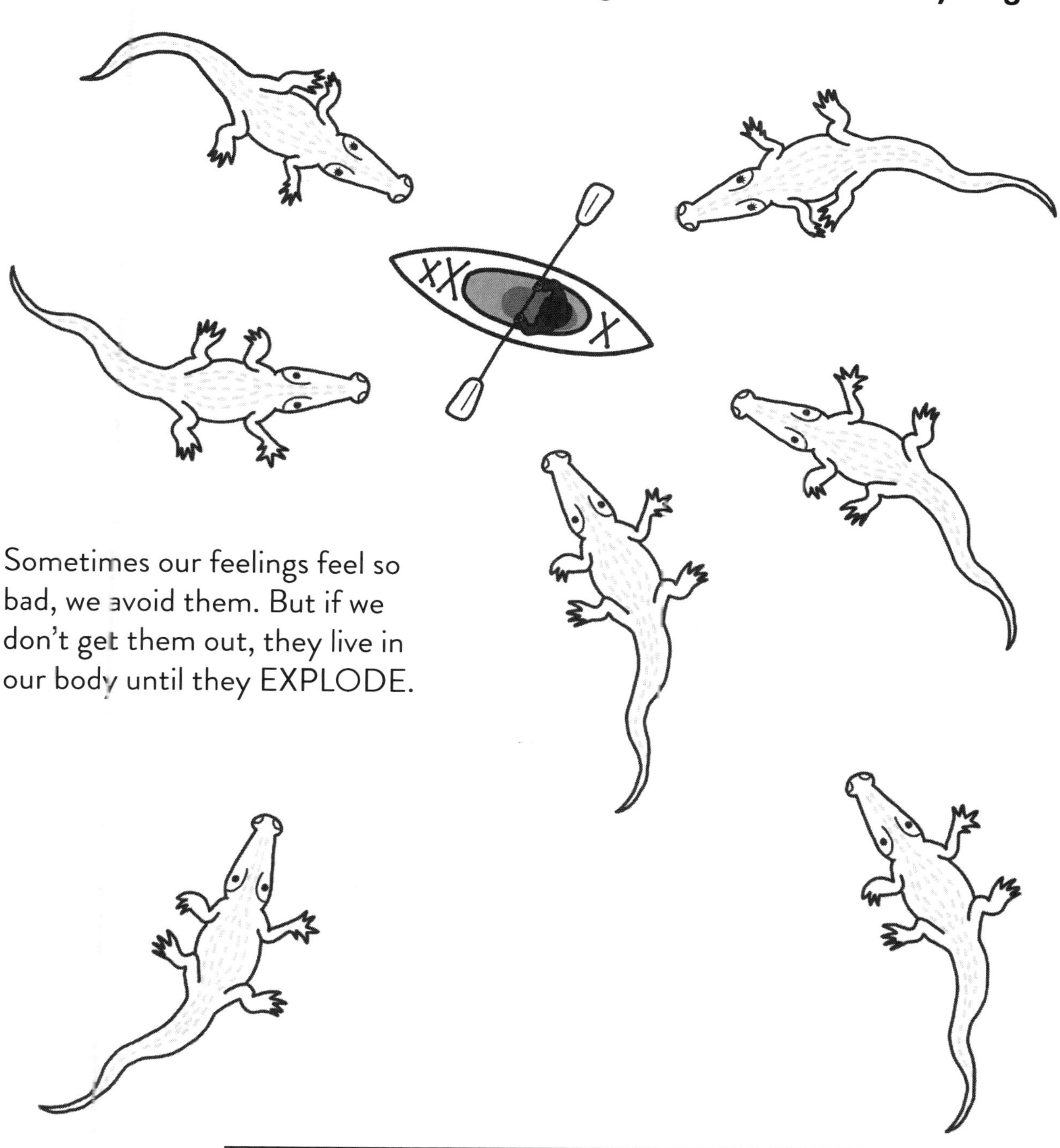

Sometimes our feelings feel so bad, we avoid them. But if we don't get them out, they live in our body until they EXPLODE.

Rate how you're feeling right now by circling a number:

1 - 2 - 3 - 4 - 5 - 6 - 7 - 8 - 9 - 10

totally calm | right in the middle | totally overwhelmed

Brain Dump

① In the circle, write every single thing floating around your brain, worrying you or stressing you out.

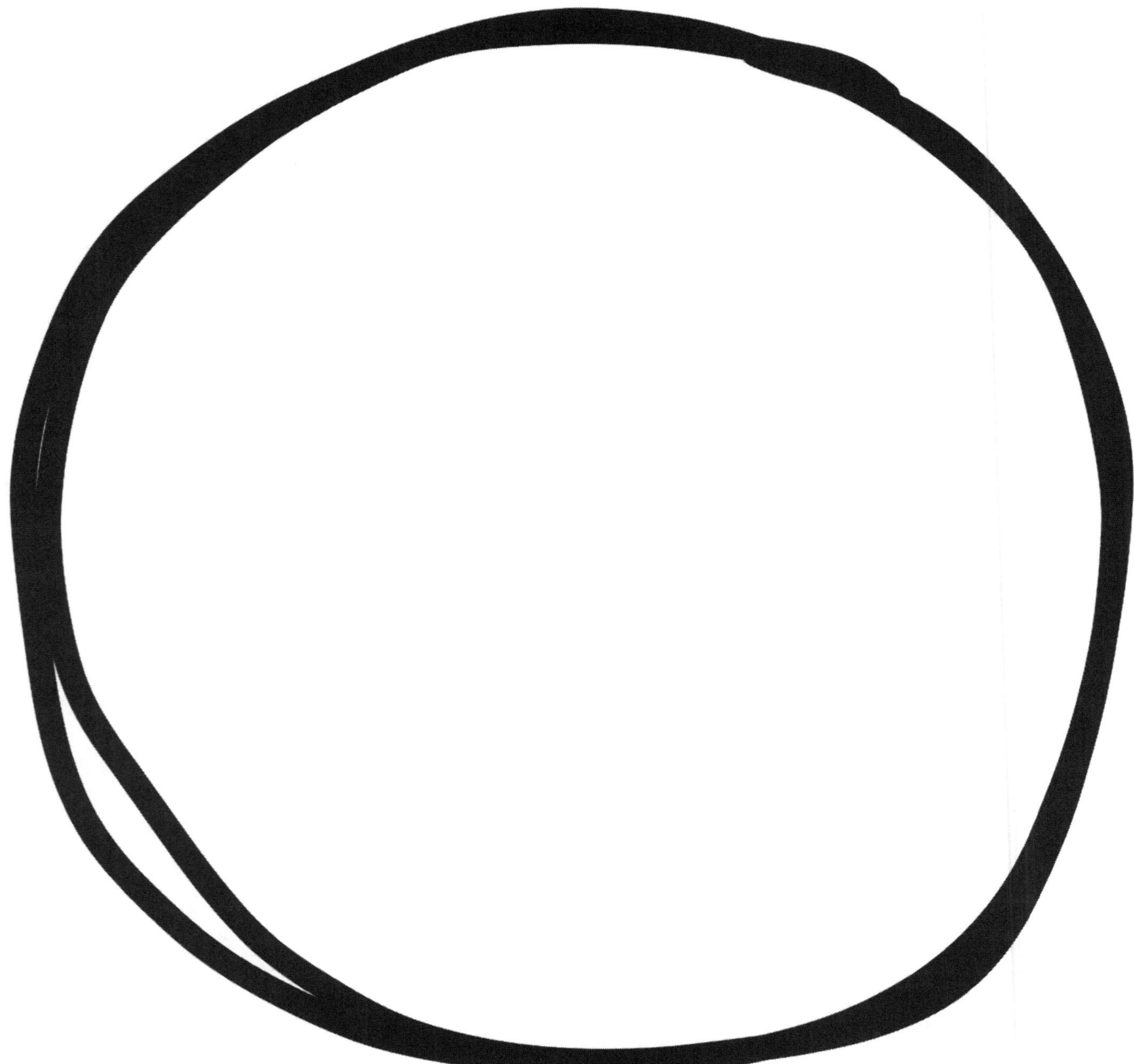

② Circle the things that are stressing you the most.

③ Underline or highlight the things that are smaller or easier to do/solve.

List the underlined, easy things to do from the brain dump:

Rate how you're feeling right now by circling a number:

1 - 2 - 3 - 4 - 5 - 6 - 7 - 8 - 9 - 10

totally calm | right in the middle | totally overwhelmed

The circled things in your "brain dump" circle are your big and scary "alligator" worries.

Name your alligator (or multiple alligators):

Draw a crown on the alligator that feels the biggest or scariest.

That is the alligator closest to your boat.

When we are overwhelmed, it feels like we have too many problems.
The way to feel better is to deal with the alligator closest to your boat **first**.

Brainstorm some solutions for the alligator closest to your boat.

What might make this situation better? No ideas are bad ideas here. List them all in the circles below.

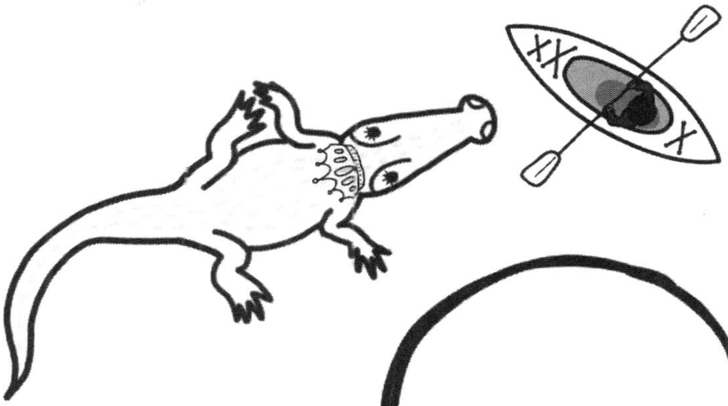

Look at each of your ideas. What might happen if you try each one? Thinking about what could happen will help you decide which solutions are better than others.

Cross out any ideas you think won't work very well.
Now decide which solution you'll try first. Put a star next to it.

There is no one "right answer." If this idea doesn't work, you will try a different one! You got this! We can do hard things.

Rate how you're feeling right now by circling a number:

1 - 2 - 3 - 4 - 5 - 6 - 7 - 8 - 9 - 10

totally calm (1) | right in the middle (5) | totally overwhelmed (10)

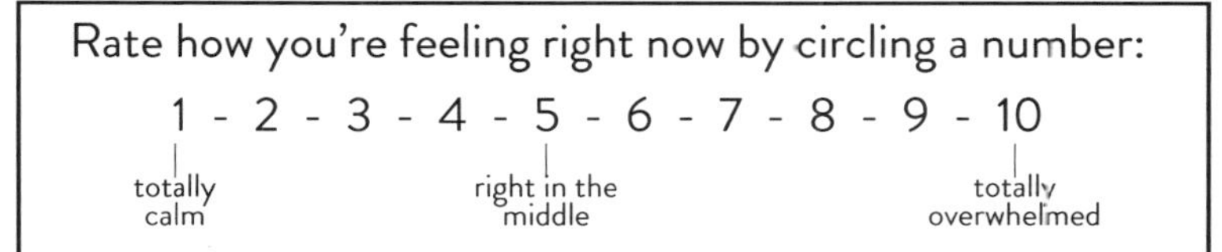

OVERWHELMED?

Being overwhelmed feels a little like being in a boat surrounded by alligators.

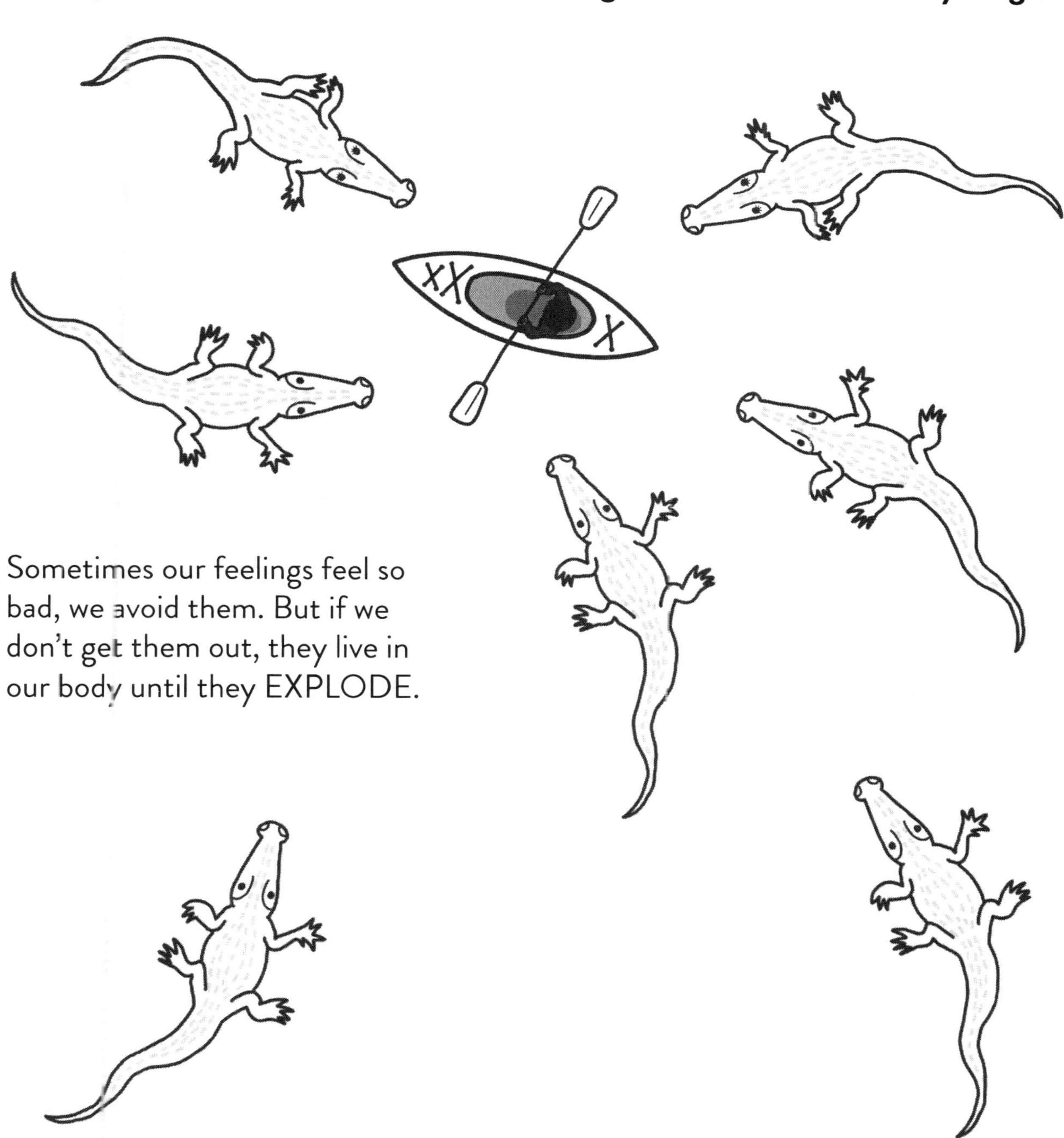

Sometimes our feelings feel so bad, we avoid them. But if we don't get them out, they live in our body until they EXPLODE.

Rate how you're feeling right now by circling a number:

1 - 2 - 3 - 4 - 5 - 6 - 7 - 8 - 9 - 10

1: totally calm
5: right in the middle
10: totally overwhelmed

Brain Dump

1. In the circle, write every single thing floating around your brain, worrying you or stressing you out.

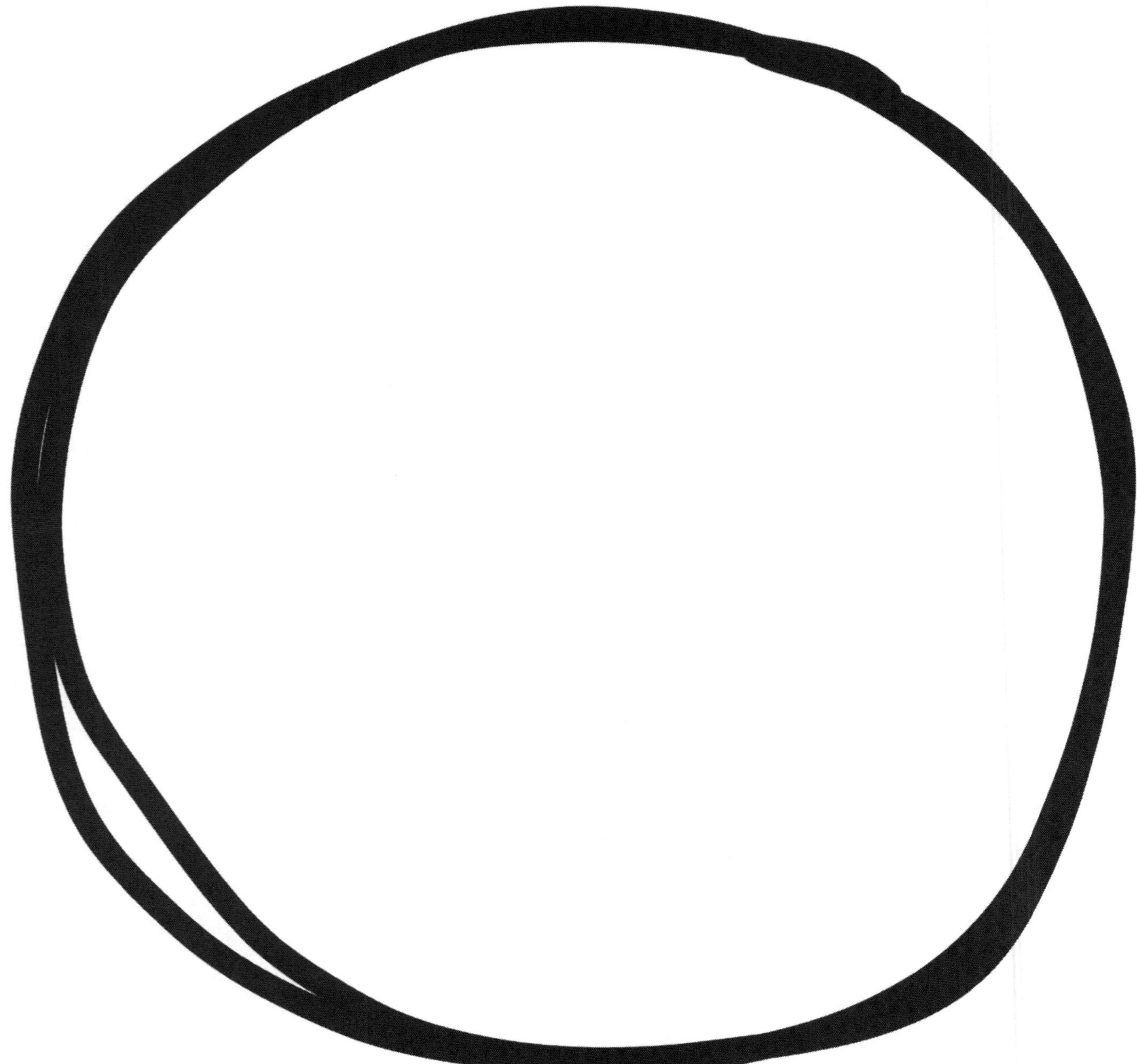

2. Circle the things that are stressing you the most.

3. Underline or highlight the things that are smaller or easier to do/solve.

List the underlined, easy things to do from the brain dump:

Rate how you're feeling right now by circling a number:

1 - 2 - 3 - 4 - 5 - 6 - 7 - 8 - 9 - 10

totally calm — right in the middle — totally overwhelmed

The circled things in your "brain dump" circle are your big and scary "alligator" worries.

Name your alligator (or multiple alligators):

Draw a crown on the alligator that feels the biggest or scariest.

That is the alligator closest to your boat.

When we are overwhelmed, it feels like we have too many problems.
The way to feel better is to deal with the alligator closest to your boat **first**.

Brainstorm some solutions for the alligator closest to your boat.

What might make this situation better? No ideas are bad ideas here. List them all in the circles below.

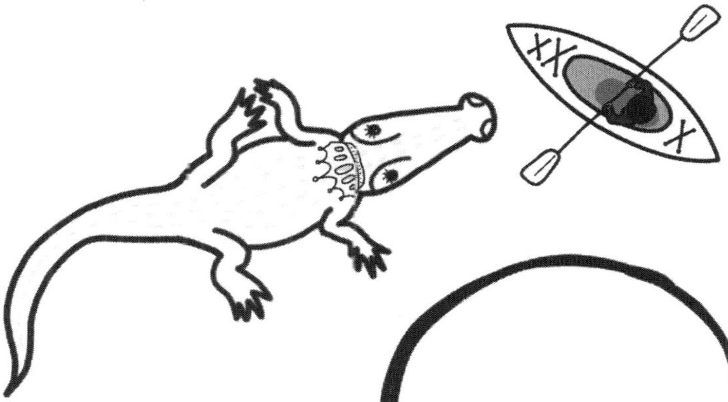

Look at each of your ideas. What might happen if you try each one? Thinking about what could happen will help you decide which solutions are better than others.

Cross out any ideas you think won't work very well.
Now decide which solution you'll try first. Put a star next to it.

There is no one "right answer." If this idea doesn't work, you will try a different one! You got this! We can do hard things.

Rate how you're feeling right now by circling a number:

1 - 2 - 3 - 4 - 5 - 6 - 7 - 8 - 9 - 10

totally calm (1) · right in the middle (5) · totally overwhelmed (10)

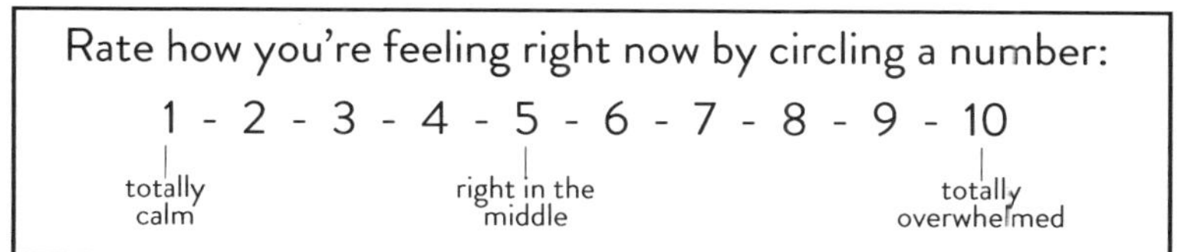

OVERWHELMED?

Being overwhelmed feels a little like being in a boat surrounded by alligators.

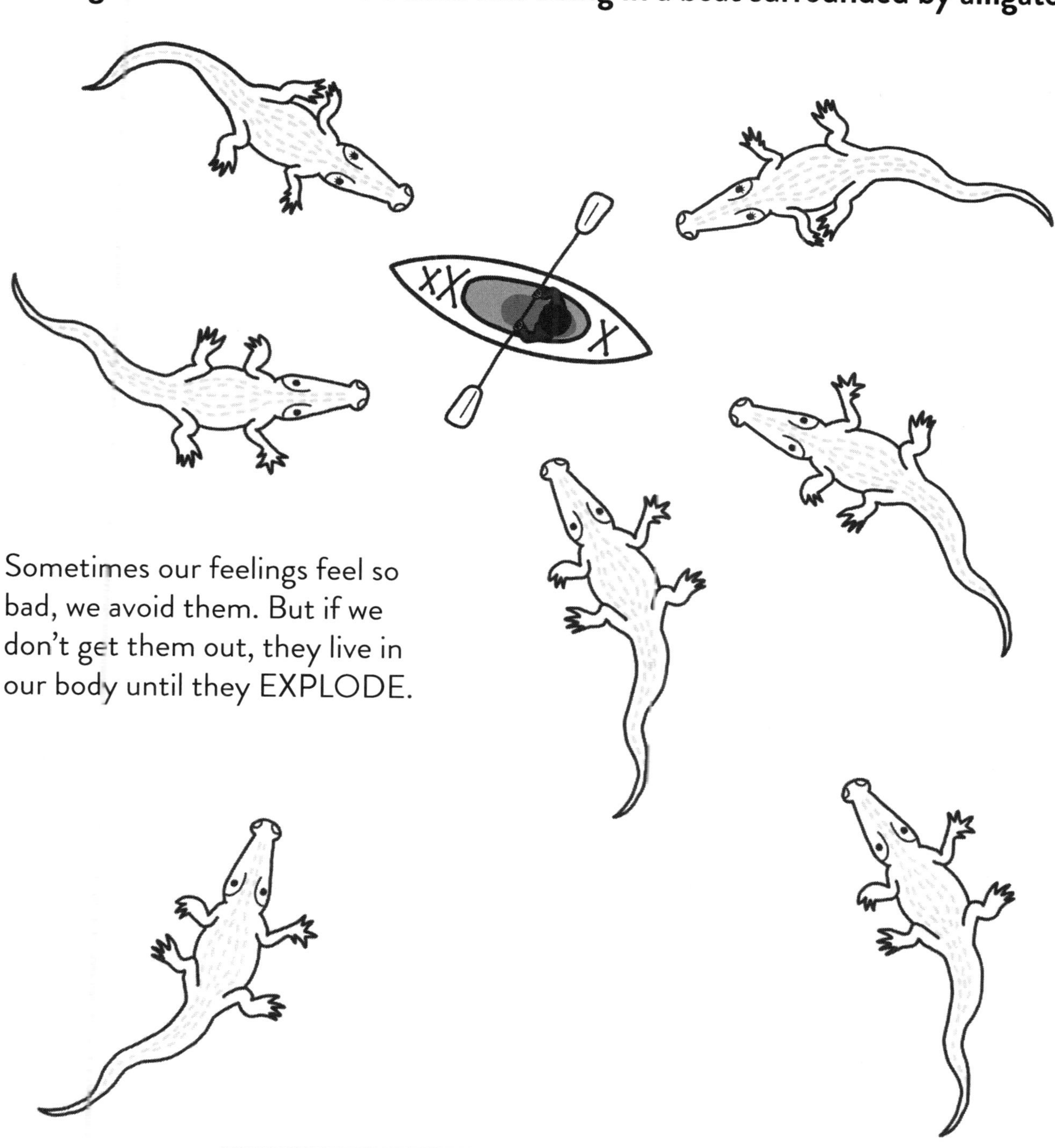

Sometimes our feelings feel so bad, we avoid them. But if we don't get them out, they live in our body until they EXPLODE.

Rate how you're feeling right now by circling a number:

1 - 2 - 3 - 4 - 5 - 6 - 7 - 8 - 9 - 10

1: totally calm
5: right in the middle
10: totally overwhelmed

Brain Dump

1. In the circle, write every single thing floating around your brain, worrying you or stressing you out.

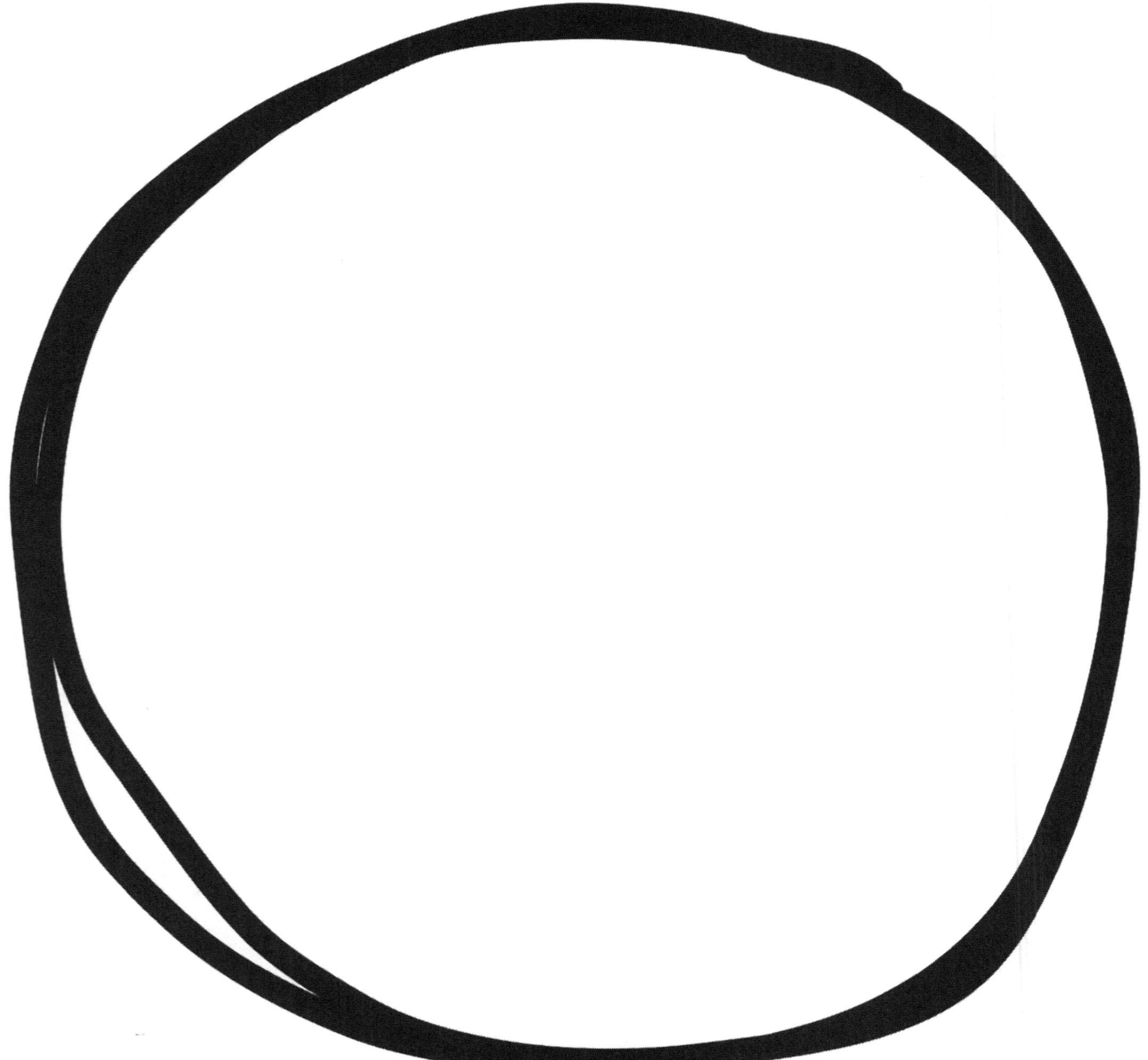

2. Circle the things that are stressing you the most.

3. Underline or highlight the things that are smaller or easier to do/solve.

List the underlined, easy things to do from the brain dump:

Rate how you're feeling right now by circling a number:

1 - 2 - 3 - 4 - 5 - 6 - 7 - 8 - 9 - 10

totally calm | right in the middle | totally overwhelmed

The circled things in your "brain dump" circle are your big and scary "alligator" worries.

Name your alligator (or multiple alligators):

Draw a crown on the alligator that feels the biggest or scariest.

That is the alligator closest to your boat.

When we are overwhelmed, it feels like we have too many problems.
The way to feel better is to deal with the alligator closest to your boat **first**.

Brainstorm some solutions for the alligator closest to your boat.

What might make this situation better? No ideas are bad ideas here. List them all in the circles below.

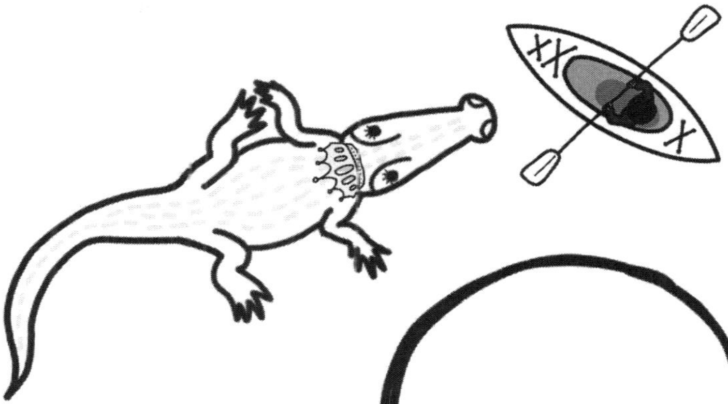

Look at each of your ideas. What might happen if you try each one? Thinking about what could happen will help you decide which solutions are better than others.

Cross out any ideas you think won't work very well.
Now decide which solution you'll try first. Put a star next to it.

There is no one "right answer." If this idea doesn't work, you will try a different one!
You got this! We can do hard things.

Rate how you're feeling right now by circling a number:

1 - 2 - 3 - 4 - 5 - 6 - 7 - 8 - 9 - 10

1: totally calm; 5: right in the middle; 10: totally overwhelmed

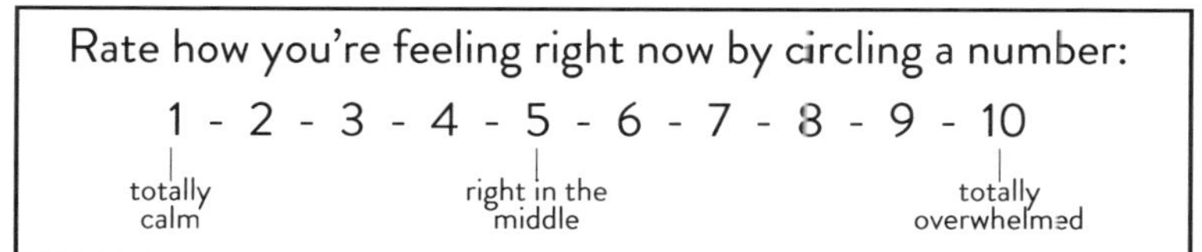

OVERWHELMED?

Being overwhelmed feels a little like being in a boat surrounded by alligators.

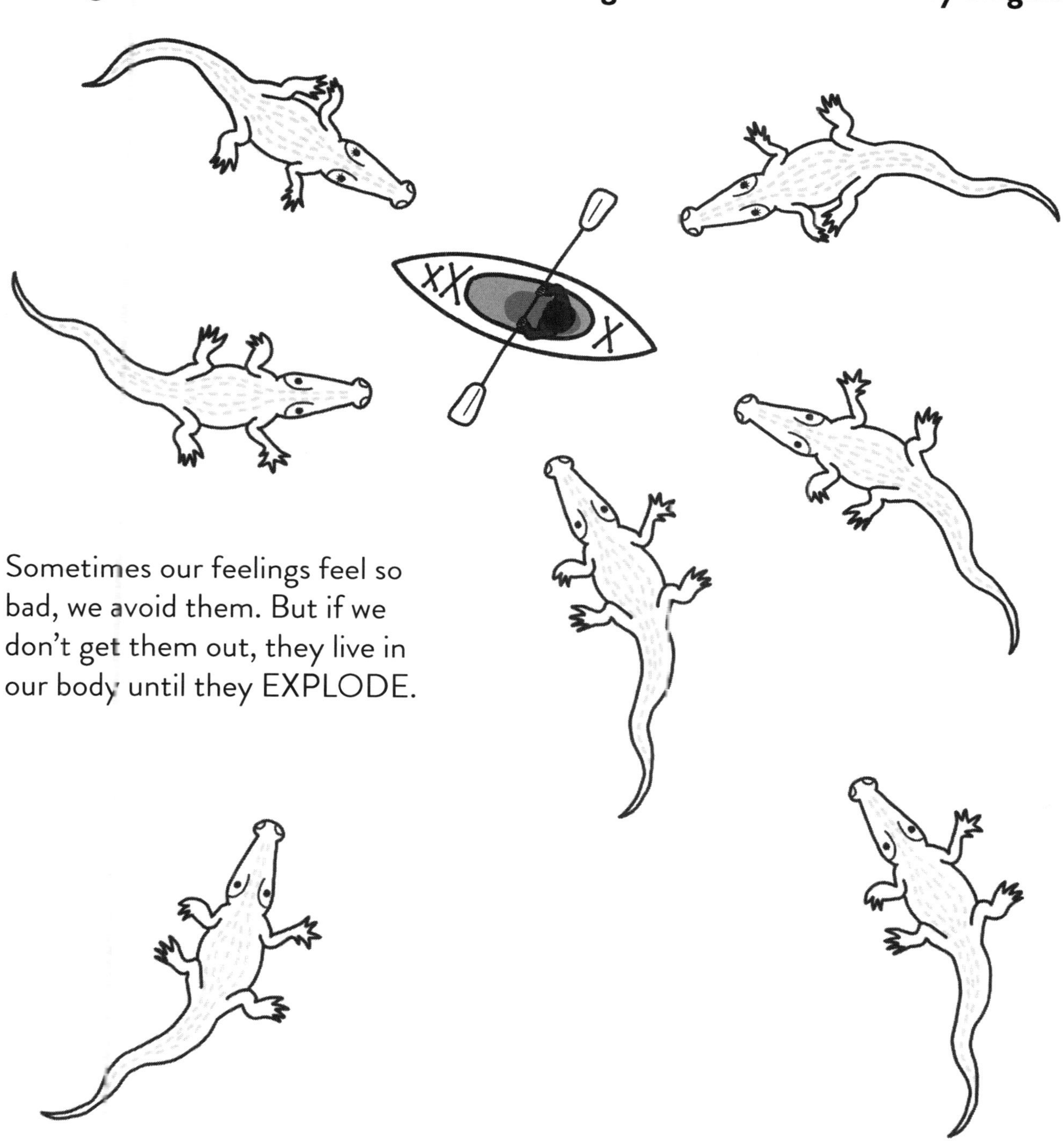

Sometimes our feelings feel so bad, we avoid them. But if we don't get them out, they live in our body until they EXPLODE.

Rate how you're feeling right now by circling a number:

1 - 2 - 3 - 4 - 5 - 6 - 7 - 8 - 9 - 10

totally calm (1) · right in the middle (5) · totally overwhelmed (10)

Brain Dump

1. In the circle, write every single thing floating around your brain, worrying you or stressing you out.

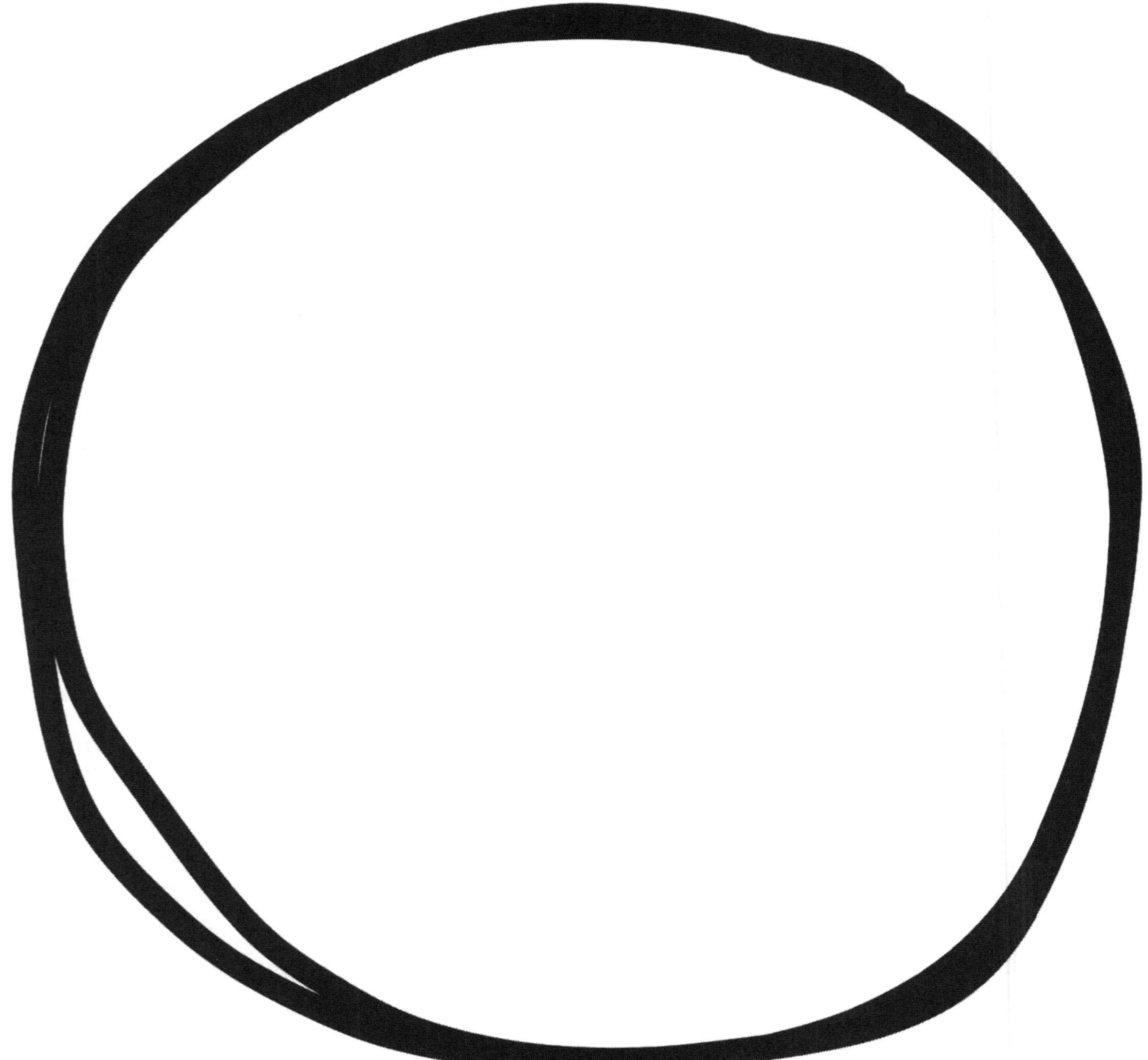

2. Circle the things that are stressing you the most.

3. Underline or highlight the things that are smaller or easier to do/solve.

List the underlined, easy things to do from the brain dump:

Rate how you're feeling right now by circling a number:

1 - 2 - 3 - 4 - 5 - 6 - 7 - 8 - 9 - 10

totally calm — right in the middle — totally overwhelmed

The circled things in your "brain dump" circle are your big and scary "alligator" worries.

Name your alligator (or multiple alligators):

Draw a crown on the alligator that feels the biggest or scariest.

That is the alligator closest to your boat.

When we are overwhelmed, it feels like we have too many problems.
The way to feel better is to deal with the alligator closest to your boat **first**.

Brainstorm some solutions for the alligator closest to your boat.

What might make this situation better? No ideas are bad ideas here. List them all in the circles below.

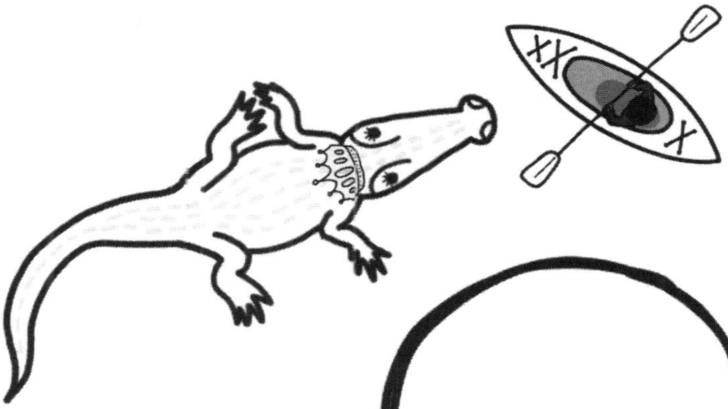

Look at each of your ideas. What might happen if you try each one? Thinking about what could happen will help you decide which solutions are better than others.

Cross out any ideas you think won't work very well.
Now decide which solution you'll try first. Put a star next to it.

There is no one "right answer." If this idea doesn't work, you will try a different one!
You got this! We can do hard things.

Rate how you're feeling right now by circling a number:

1 - 2 - 3 - 4 - 5 - 6 - 7 - 8 - 9 - 10

totally calm (1) · right in the middle (5) · totally overwhelmed (10)

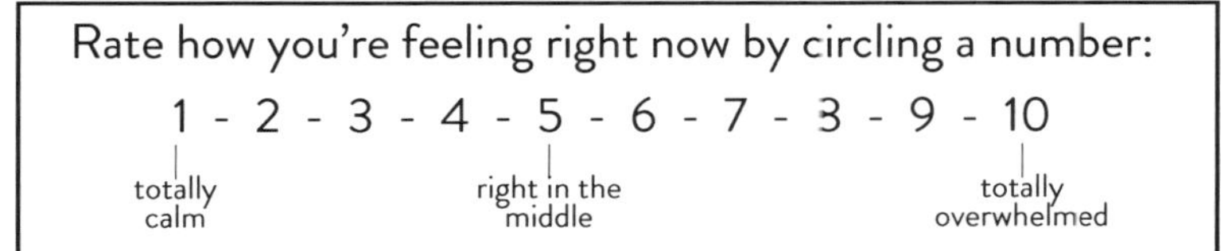

OVERWHELMED?

Being overwhelmed feels a little like being in a boat surrounded by alligators.

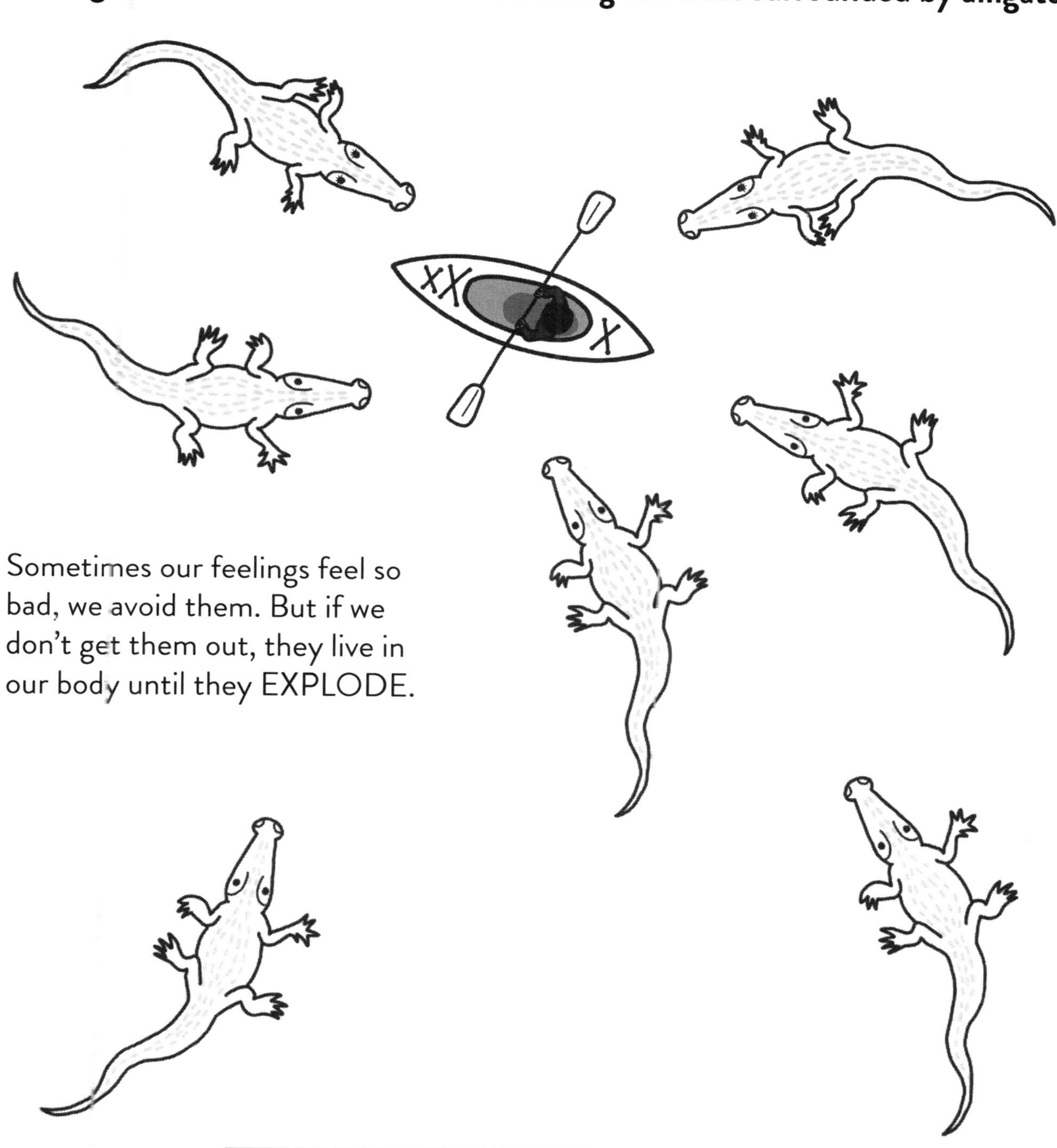

Sometimes our feelings feel so bad, we avoid them. But if we don't get them out, they live in our body until they EXPLODE.

Rate how you're feeling right now by circling a number:

1 - 2 - 3 - 4 - 5 - 6 - 7 - 8 - 9 - 10

1 = totally calm; 5 = right in the middle; 10 = totally overwhelmed

Brain Dump

1. In the circle, write every single thing floating around your brain, worrying you or stressing you out.

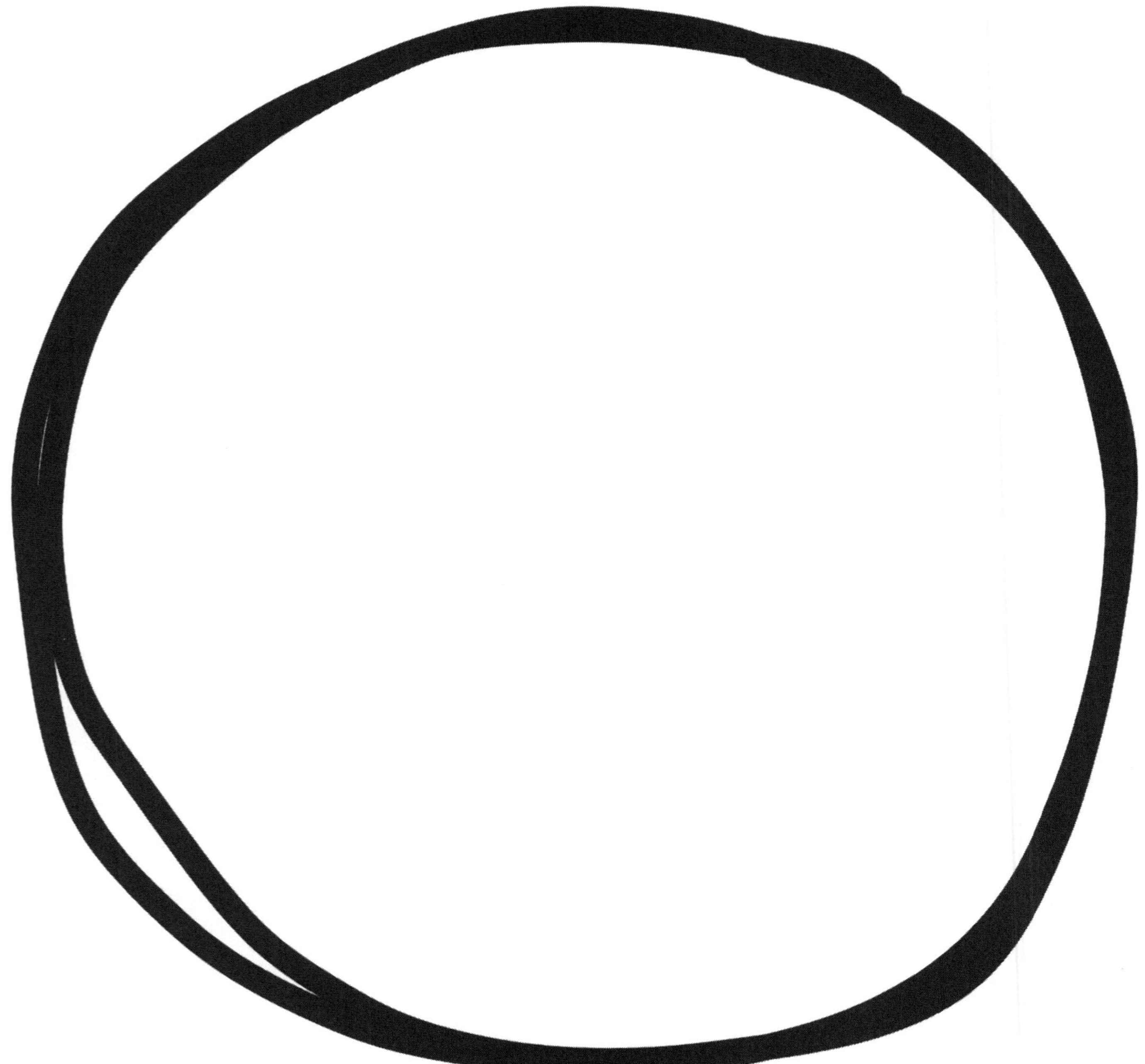

2. Circle the things that are stressing you the most.

3. Underline or highlight the things that are smaller or easier to do/solve.

List the underlined, easy things to do from the brain dump:

Rate how you're feeling right now by circling a number:

1 - 2 - 3 - 4 - 5 - 6 - 7 - 8 - 9 - 10

totally calm | right in the middle | totally overwhelmed

The circled things in your "brain dump" circle are your big and scary "alligator" worries.

Name your alligator (or multiple alligators):

Draw a crown on the alligator that feels the biggest or scariest.

That is the alligator closest to your boat.

When we are overwhelmed, it feels like we have too many problems.
The way to feel better is to deal with the alligator closest to your boat **first**.

Brainstorm some solutions for the alligator closest to your boat.

What might make this situation better? No ideas are bad ideas here. List them all in the circles below.

Look at each of your ideas. What might happen if you try each one? Thinking about what could happen will help you decide which solutions are better than others.

Cross out any ideas you think won't work very well.
Now decide which solution you'll try first. Put a star next to it.

There is no one "right answer." If this idea doesn't work, you will try a different one! You got this! We can do hard things.

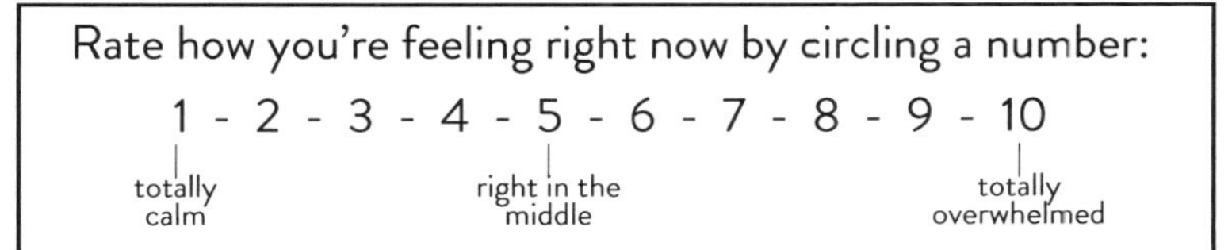
Rate how you're feeling right now by circling a number:

1 - 2 - 3 - 4 - 5 - 6 - 7 - 8 - 9 - 10

totally calm | right in the middle | totally overwhelmed

OVERWHELMED?

Being overwhelmed feels a little like being in a boat surrounded by alligators.

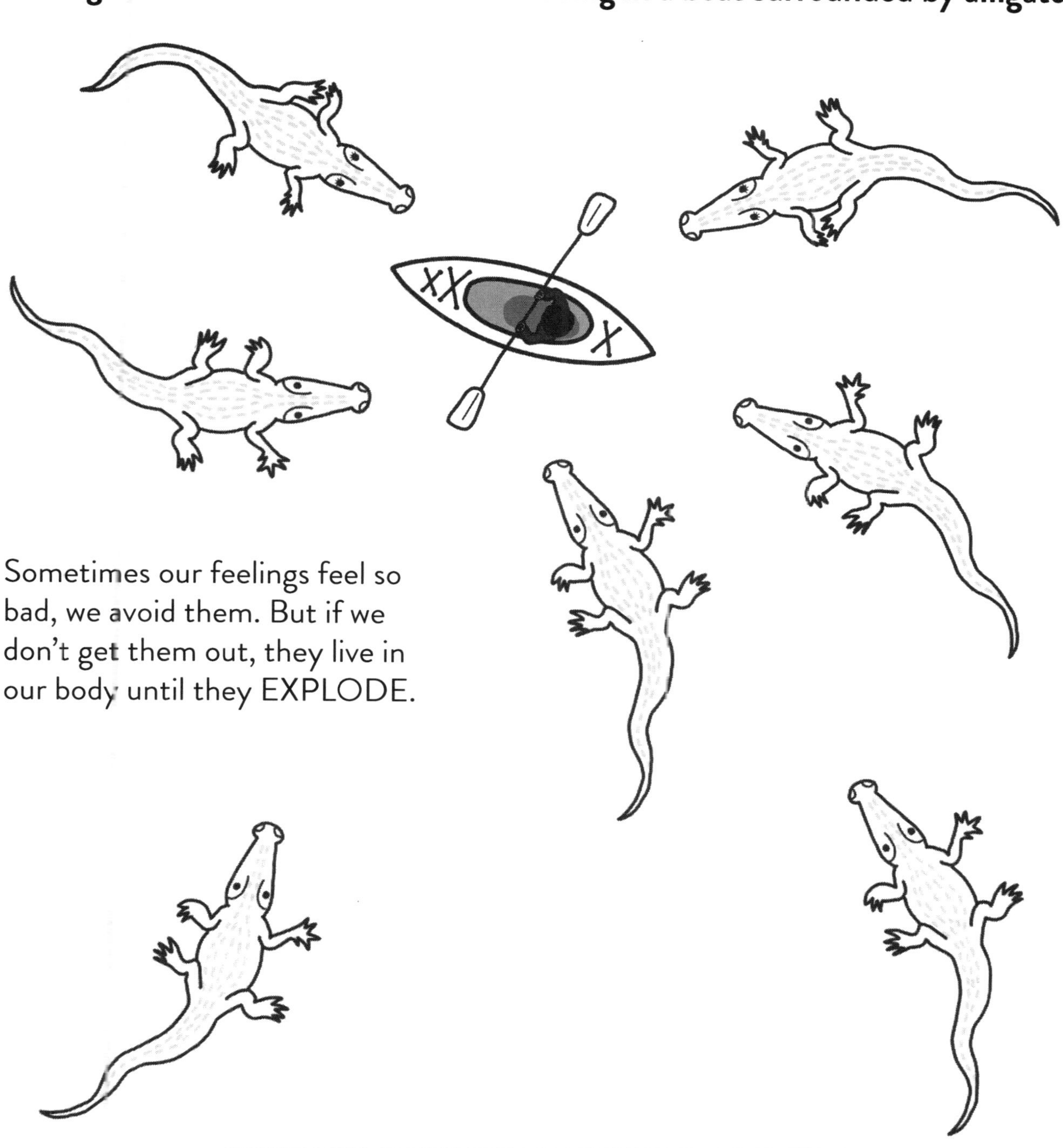

Sometimes our feelings feel so bad, we avoid them. But if we don't get them out, they live in our body until they EXPLODE.

Rate how you're feeling right now by circling a number:

1 - 2 - 3 - 4 - 5 - 6 - 7 - 8 - 9 - 10

1 = totally calm; 5 = right in the middle; 10 = totally overwhelmed

Brain Dump

1. In the circle, write every single thing floating around your brain, worrying you or stressing you out.

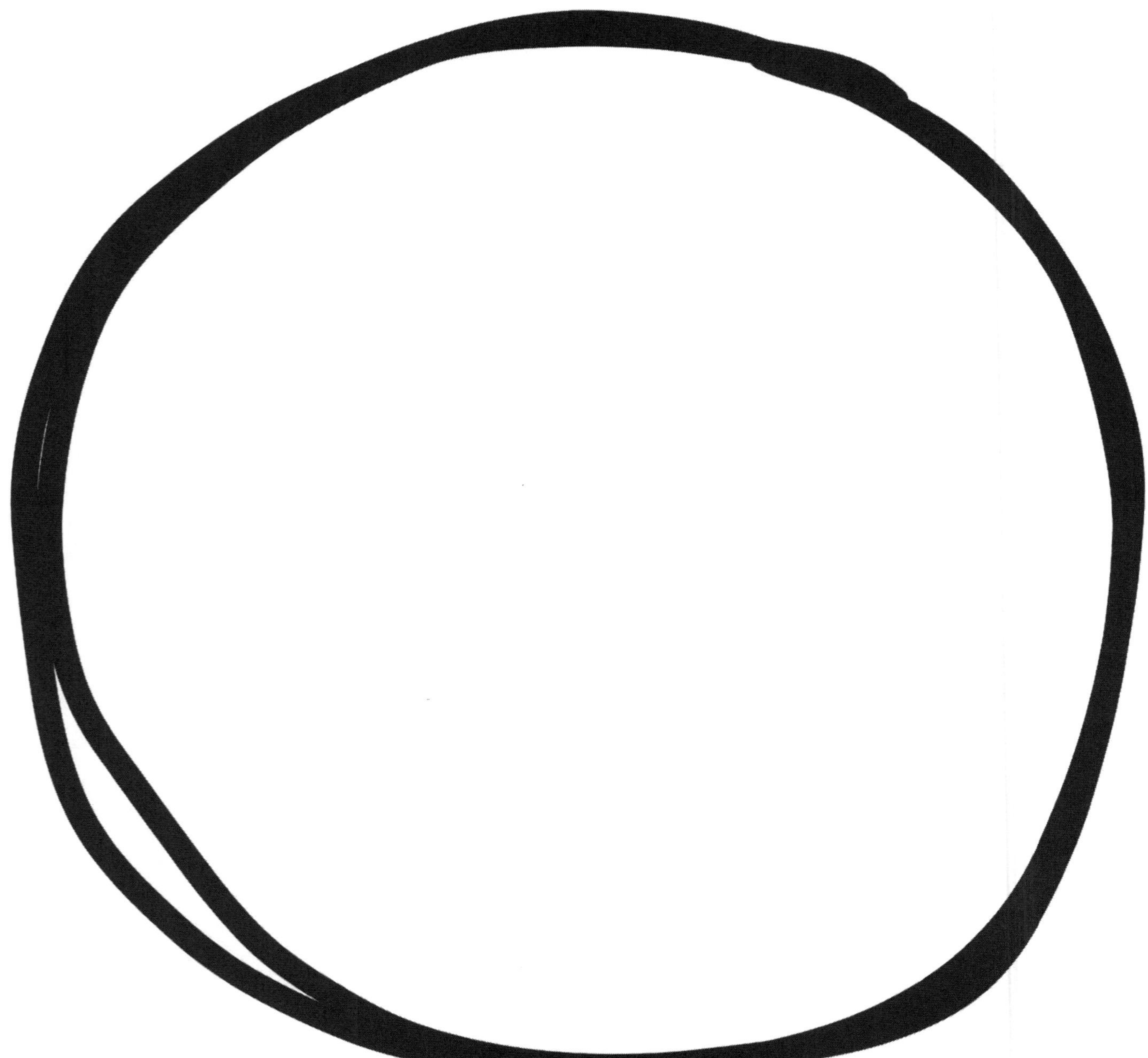

2. Circle the things that are stressing you the most.

3. Underline or highlight the things that are smaller or easier to do/solve.

List the underlined, easy things to do from the brain dump:

Rate how you're feeling right now by circling a number:

1 - 2 - 3 - 4 - 5 - 6 - 7 - 8 - 9 - 10

totally calm — right in the middle — totally overwhelmed

The circled things in your "brain dump" circle are your big and scary "alligator" worries.

Name your alligator (or multiple alligators):

Draw a crown on the alligator that feels the biggest or scariest.

That is the alligator closest to your boat.

When we are overwhelmed, it feels like we have too many problems.
The way to feel better is to deal with the alligator closest to your boat **first**.

Brainstorm some solutions for the alligator closest to your boat.

What might make this situation better? No ideas are bad ideas here. List them all in the circles below.

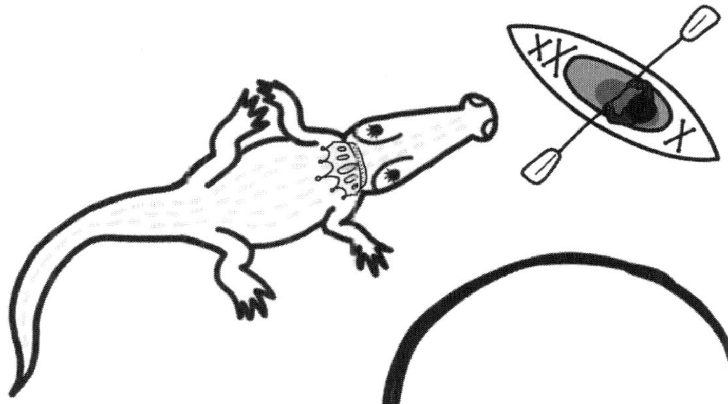

Look at each of your ideas. What might happen if you try each one? Thinking about what could happen will help you decide which solutions are better than others.

Cross out any ideas you think won't work very well.
Now decide which solution you'll try first. Put a star next to it.

There is no one "right answer." If this idea doesn't work, you will try a different one! You got this! We can do hard things.

Rate how you're feeling right now by circling a number:

1 - 2 - 3 - 4 - 5 - 6 - 7 - 8 - 9 - 10

totally calm | right in the middle | totally overwhelmed

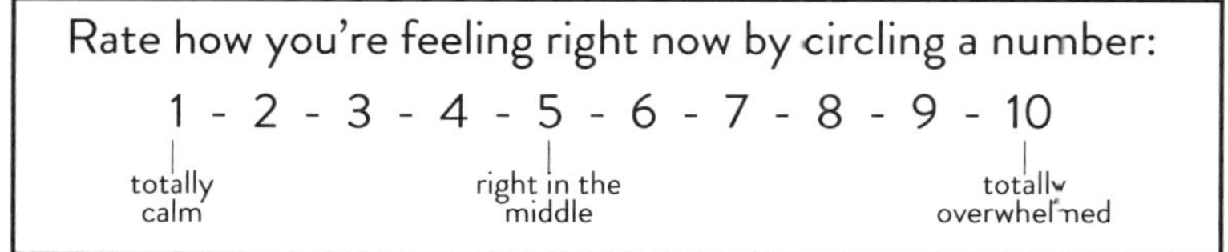

OVERWHELMED?

Being overwhelmed feels a little like being in a boat surrounded by alligators.

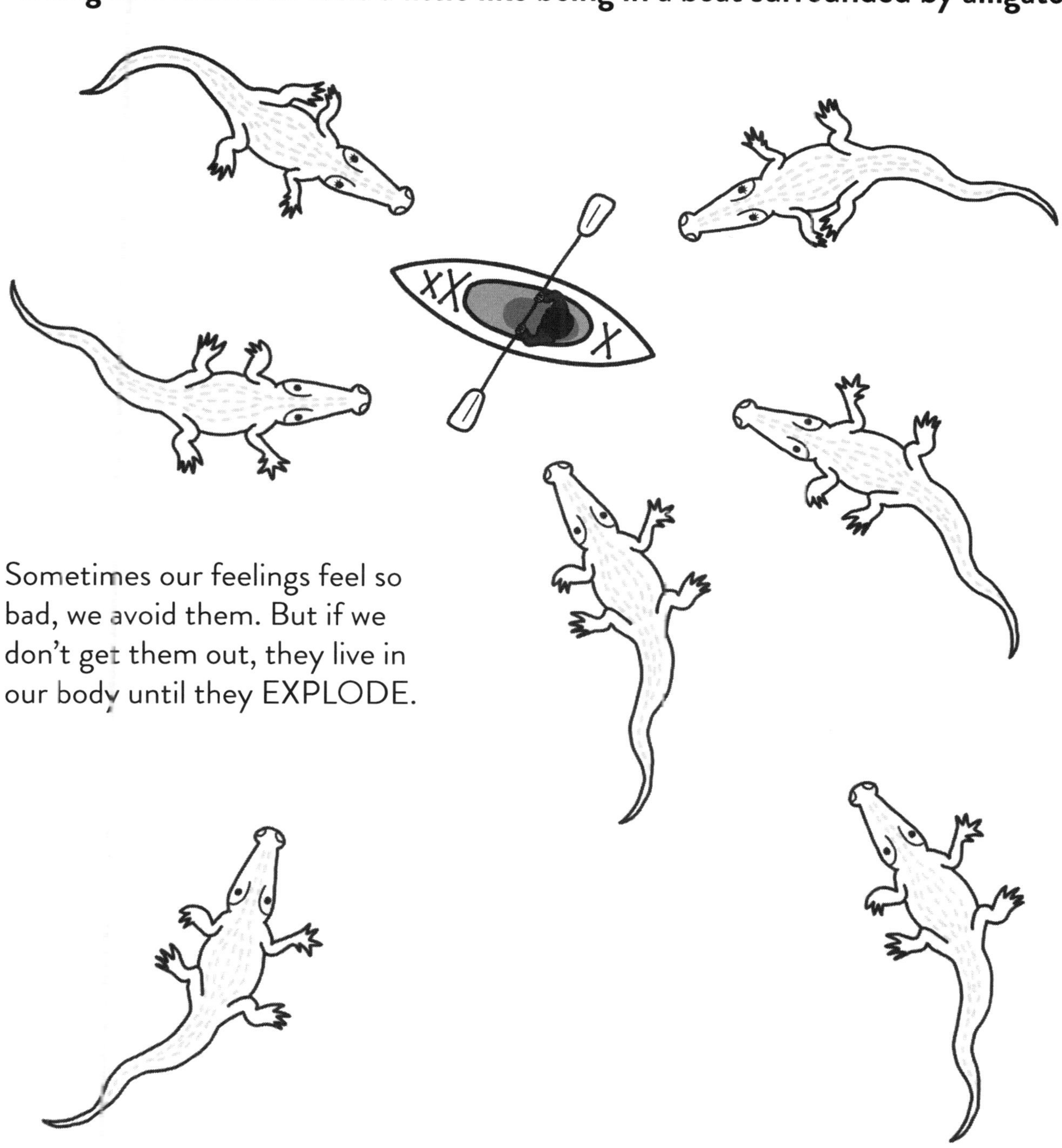

Sometimes our feelings feel so bad, we avoid them. But if we don't get them out, they live in our body until they EXPLODE.

Rate how you're feeling right now by circling a number:

1 - 2 - 3 - 4 - 5 - 6 - 7 - 8 - 9 - 10

totally calm (1) — right in the middle (5) — totally overwhelmed (10)

Brain Dump

1. In the circle, write every single thing floating around your brain, worrying you or stressing you out.

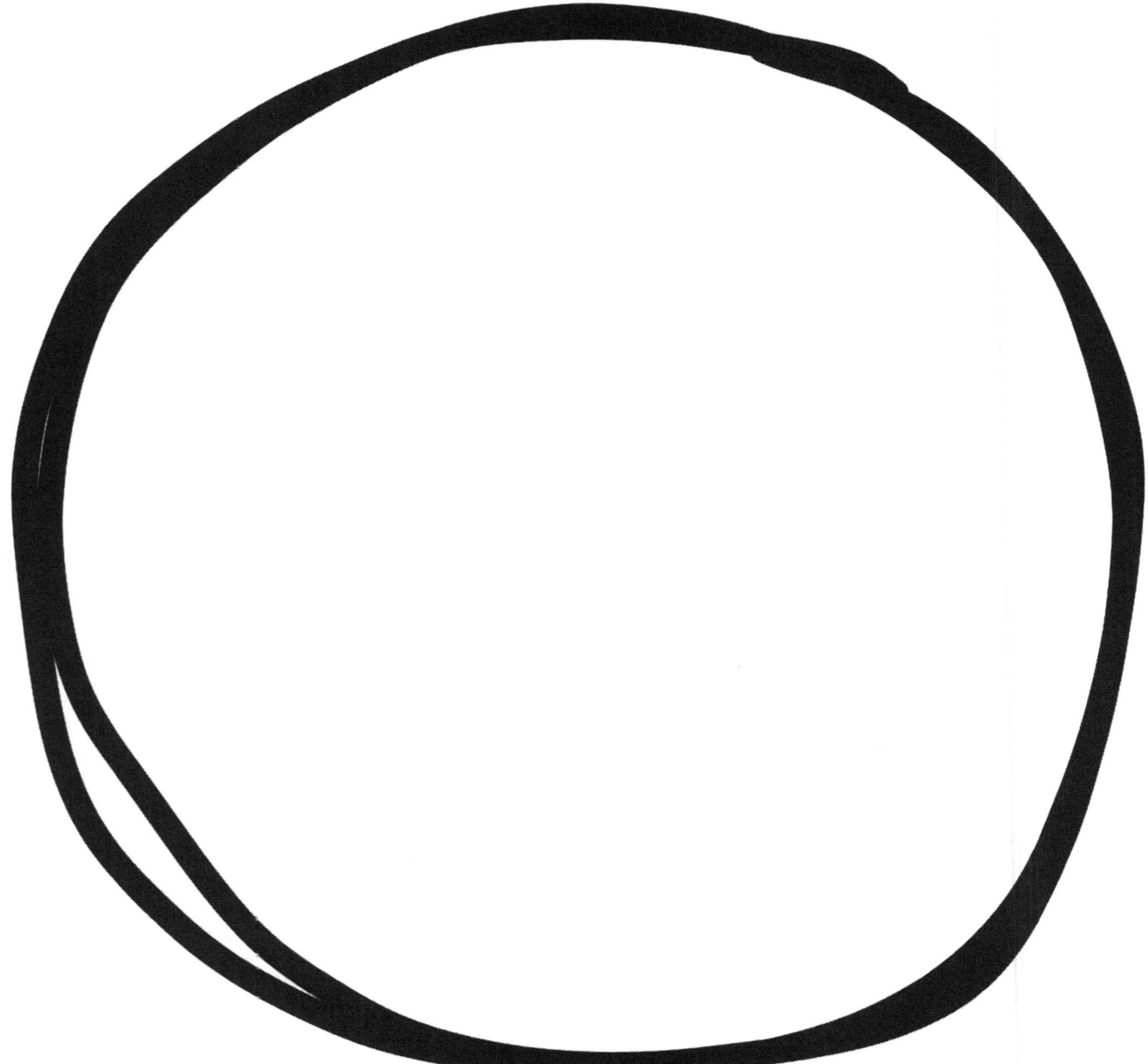

2. Circle the things that are stressing you the most.

3. Underline or highlight the things that are smaller or easier to do/solve.

List the underlined, easy things to do from the brain dump:

Rate how you're feeling right now by circling a number:

1 - 2 - 3 - 4 - 5 - 6 - 7 - 8 - 9 - 10

totally calm — right in the middle — totally overwhelmed

The circled things in your "brain dump" circle are your big and scary "alligator" worries.

Name your alligator (or multiple alligators):

Draw a crown on the alligator that feels the biggest or scariest.

That is the alligator closest to your boat.

When we are overwhelmed, it feels like we have too many problems. The way to feel better is to deal with the alligator closest to your boat **first**.

Brainstorm some solutions for the alligator closest to your boat.

What might make this situation better? No ideas are bad ideas here. List them all in the circles below.

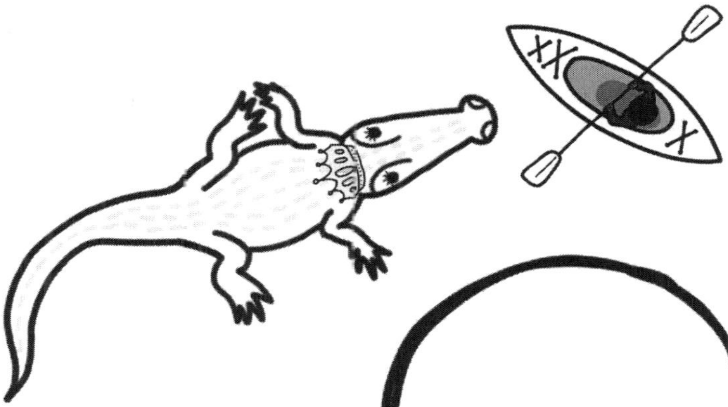

Look at each of your ideas. What might happen if you try each one? Thinking about what could happen will help you decide which solutions are better than others.

Cross out any ideas you think won't work very well.
Now decide which solution you'll try first. Put a star next to it.

There is no one "right answer." If this idea doesn't work, you will try a different one!
You got this! We can do hard things.

Rate how you're feeling right now by circling a number:

1 - 2 - 3 - 4 - 5 - 6 - 7 - 8 - 9 - 10

1 = totally calm; 5 = right in the middle; 10 = totally overwhelmed

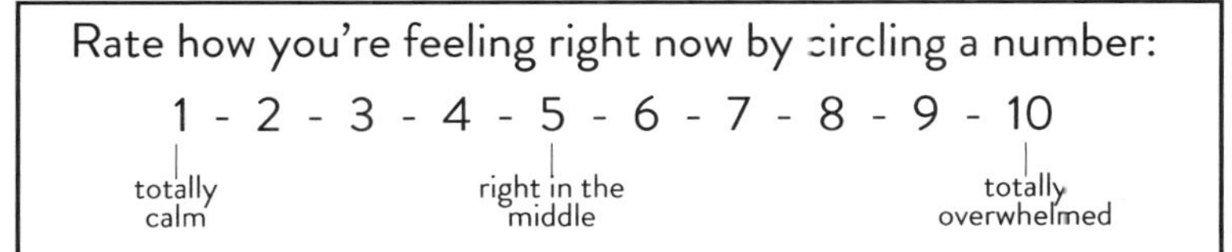

OVERWHELMED?

Being overwhelmed feels a little like being in a boat surrounded by alligators.

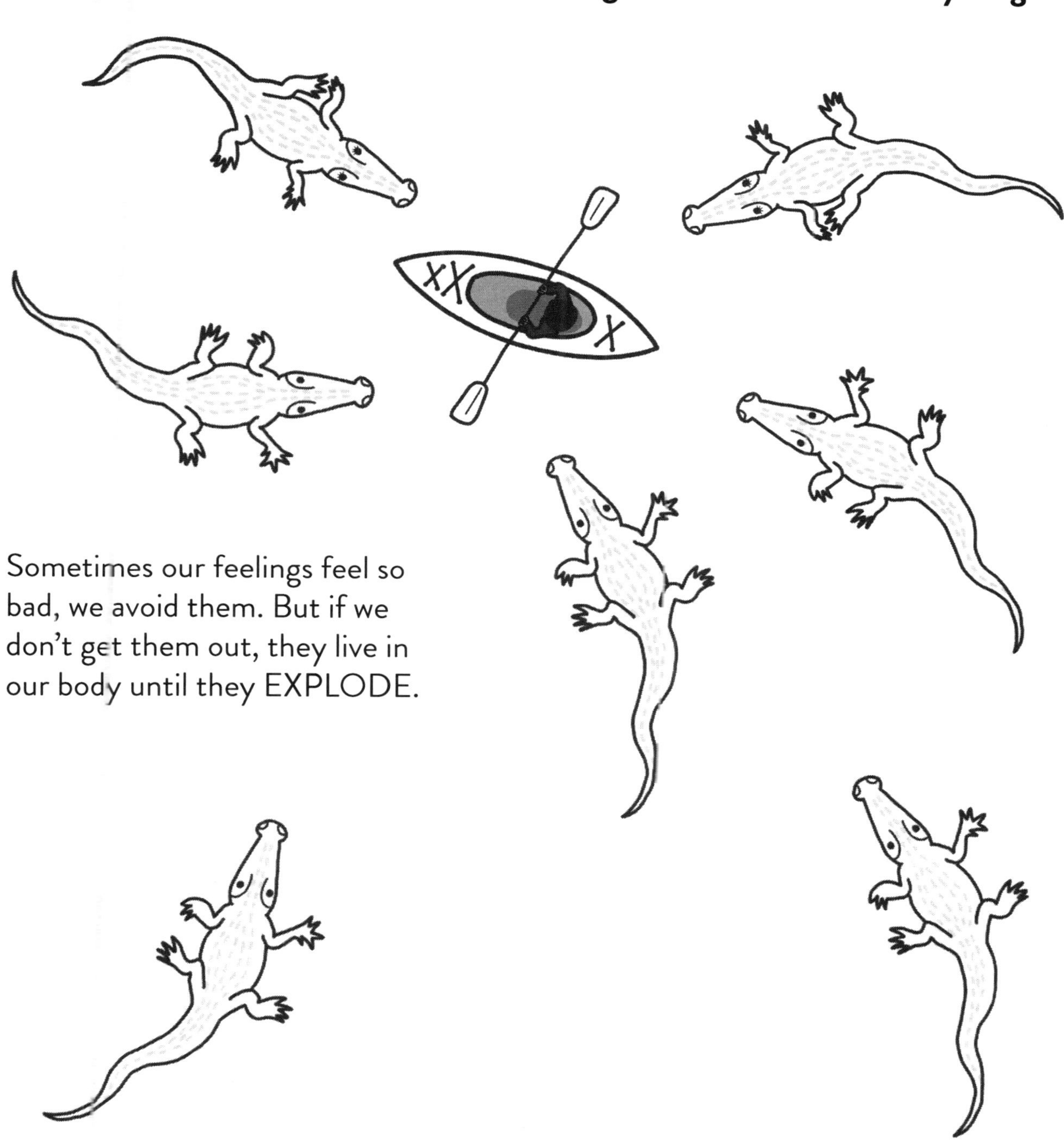

Sometimes our feelings feel so bad, we avoid them. But if we don't get them out, they live in our body until they EXPLODE.

Rate how you're feeling right now by circling a number:

1 - 2 - 3 - 4 - 5 - 6 - 7 - 8 - 9 - 10

1: totally calm — 5: right in the middle — 10: totally overwhelmed

Brain Dump

① In the circle, write every single thing floating around your brain, worrying you or stressing you out.

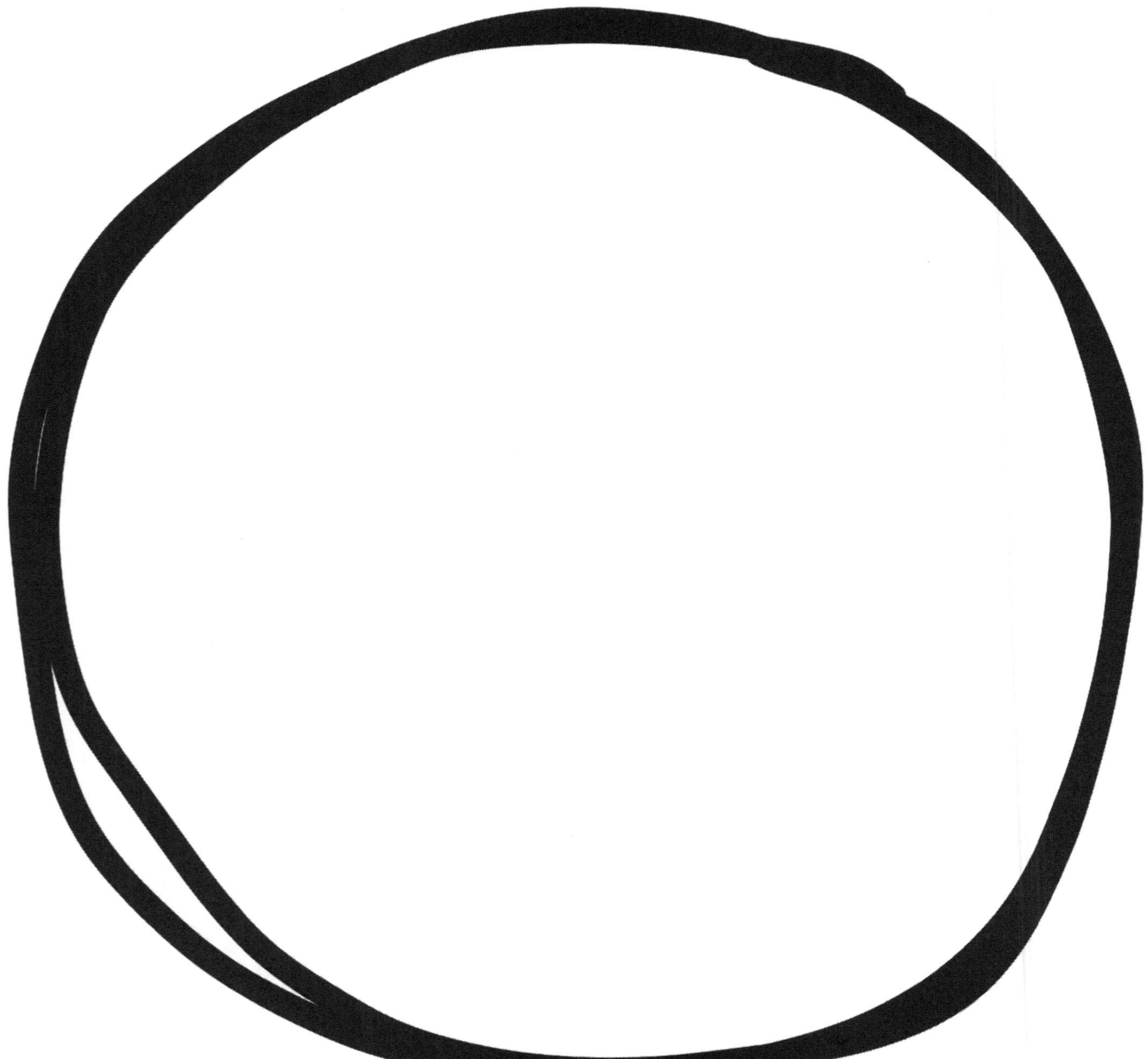

② Circle the things that are stressing you the most.

③ Underline or highlight the things that are smaller or easier to do/solve.

List the underlined, easy things to do from the brain dump:

Rate how you're feeling right now by circling a number:

1 - 2 - 3 - 4 - 5 - 6 - 7 - 8 - 9 - 10

totally calm | right in the middle | totally overwhelmed

The circled things in your "brain dump" circle are your big and scary "alligator" worries.

Name your alligator (or multiple alligators):

Draw a crown on the alligator that feels the biggest or scariest.

That is the alligator closest to your boat.

When we are overwhelmed, it feels like we have too many problems.
The way to feel better is to deal with the alligator closest to your boat **first**.

Brainstorm some solutions for the alligator closest to your boat.

What might make this situation better? No ideas are bad ideas here. List them all in the circles below.

Look at each of your ideas. What might happen if you try each one? Thinking about what could happen will help you decide which solutions are better than others.

Cross out any ideas you think won't work very well.
Now decide which solution you'll try first. Put a star next to it.

There is no one "right answer." If this idea doesn't work, you will try a different one!
You got this! We can do hard things.

Rate how you're feeling right now by circling a number:

1 - 2 - 3 - 4 - 5 - 6 - 7 - 8 - 9 - 10

totally calm | right in the middle | totally overwhelmed

OVERWHELMED?

Being overwhelmed feels a little like being in a boat surrounded by alligators.

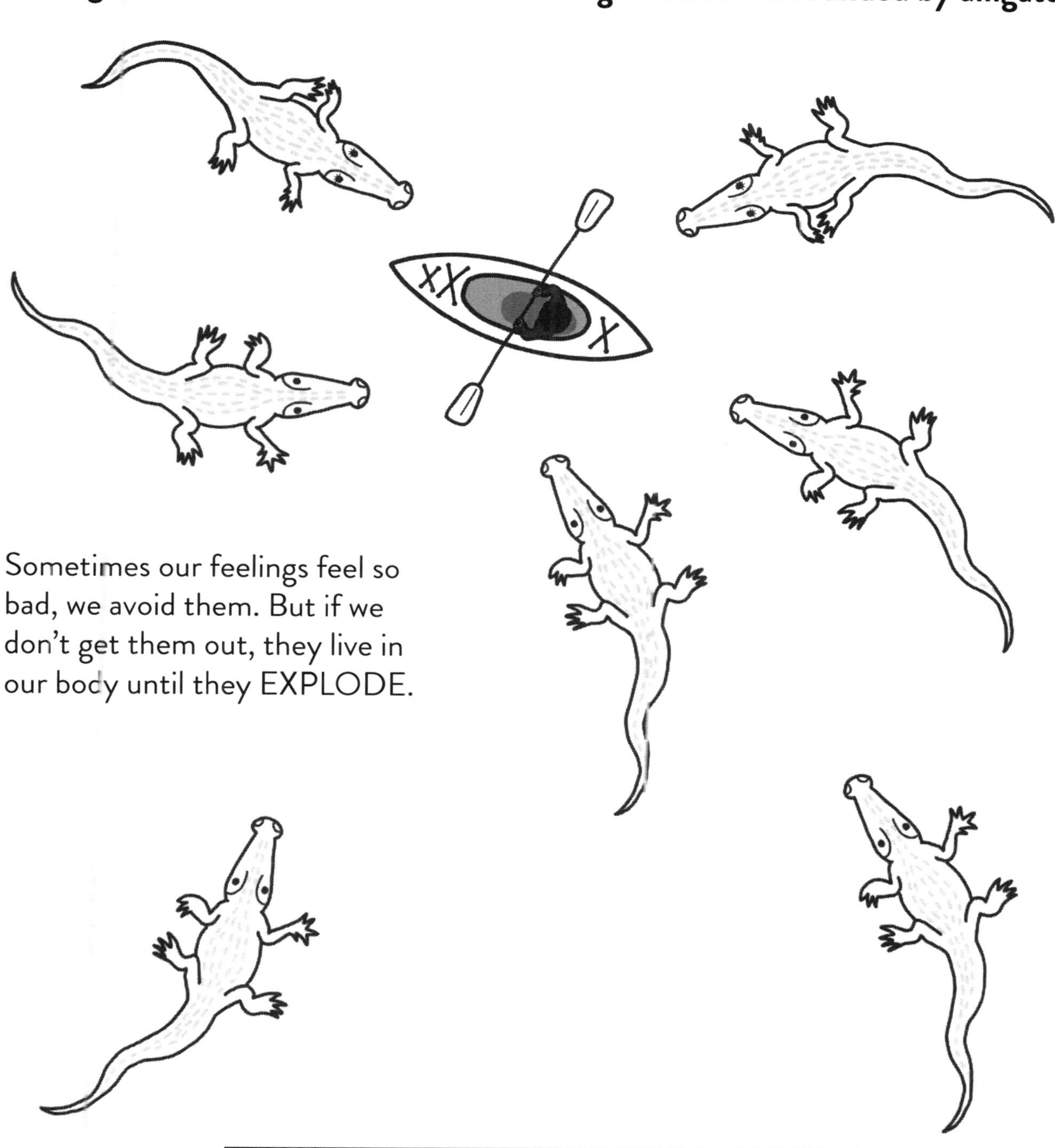

Sometimes our feelings feel so bad, we avoid them. But if we don't get them out, they live in our body until they EXPLODE.

Rate how you're feeling right now by circling a number:

1 - 2 - 3 - 4 - 5 - 6 - 7 - 8 - 9 - 10

totally calm | right in the middle | totally overwhelmed

Brain Dump

1. In the circle, write every single thing floating around your brain, worrying you or stressing you out.

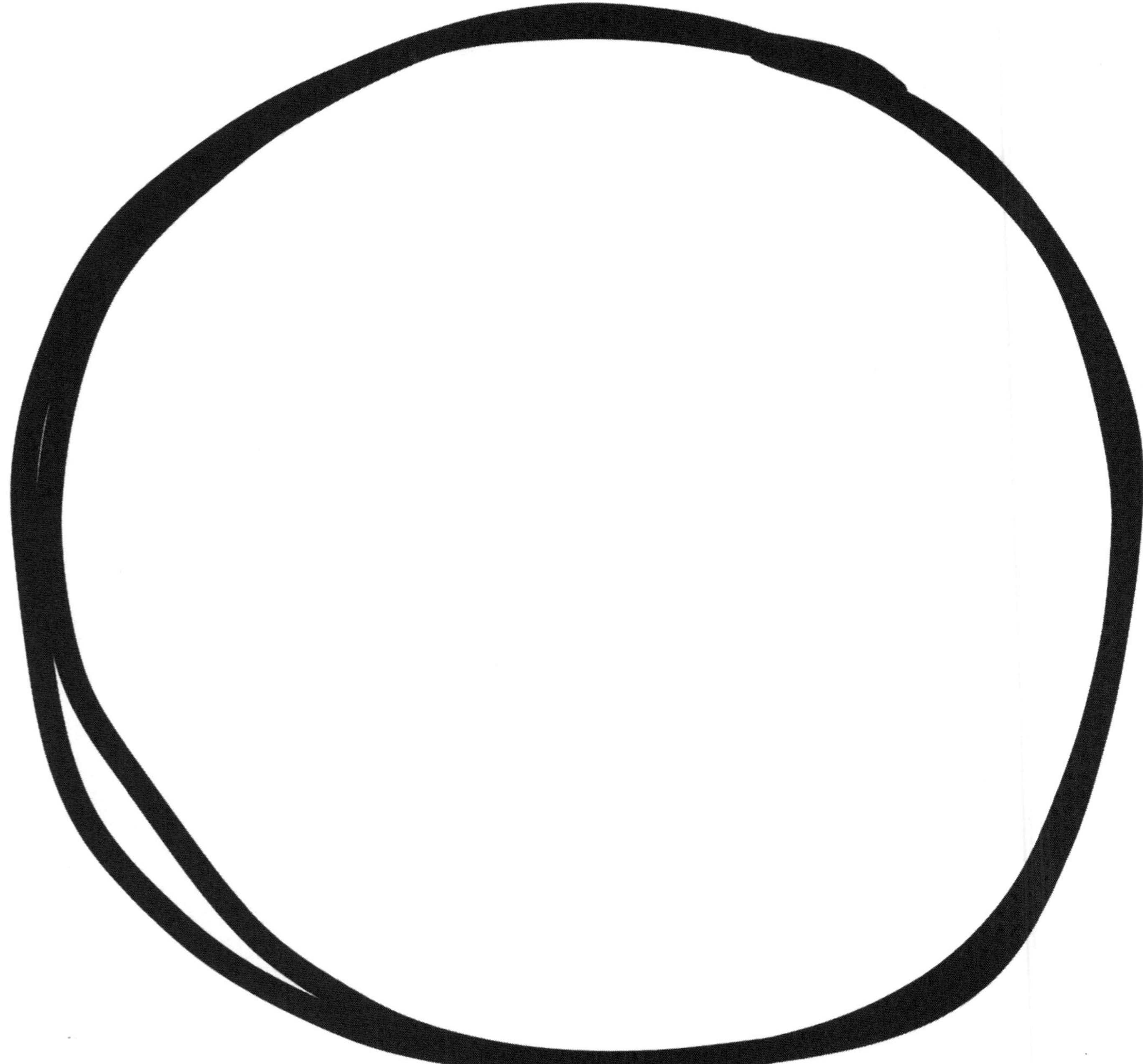

2. Circle the things that are stressing you the most.

3. Underline or highlight the things that are smaller or easier to do/solve.

List the underlined, easy things to do from the brain dump:

Rate how you're feeling right now by circling a number:

1 - 2 - 3 - 4 - 5 - 6 - 7 - 8 - 9 - 10

totally calm | right in the middle | totally overwhelmed

The circled things in your "brain dump" circle are your big and scary "alligator" worries.

Name your alligator (or multiple alligators):

Draw a crown on the alligator that feels the biggest or scariest.

That is the alligator closest to your boat.

When we are overwhelmed, it feels like we have too many problems.
The way to feel better is to deal with the alligator closest to your boat **first**.

Brainstorm some solutions for the alligator closest to your boat.

What might make this situation better? No ideas are bad ideas here. List them all in the circles below.

Look at each of your ideas. What might happen if you try each one? Thinking about what could happen will help you decide which solutions are better than others.

Cross out any ideas you think won't work very well.
Now decide which solution you'll try first. Put a star next to it.

There is no one "right answer." If this idea doesn't work, you will try a different one! You got this! We can do hard things.

Rate how you're feeling right now by circling a number:

1 - 2 - 3 - 4 - 5 - 6 - 7 - 8 - 9 - 10

totally calm (1) · right in the middle (5) · totally overwhelmed (10)

OVERWHELMED?

Being overwhelmed feels a little like being in a boat surrounded by alligators.

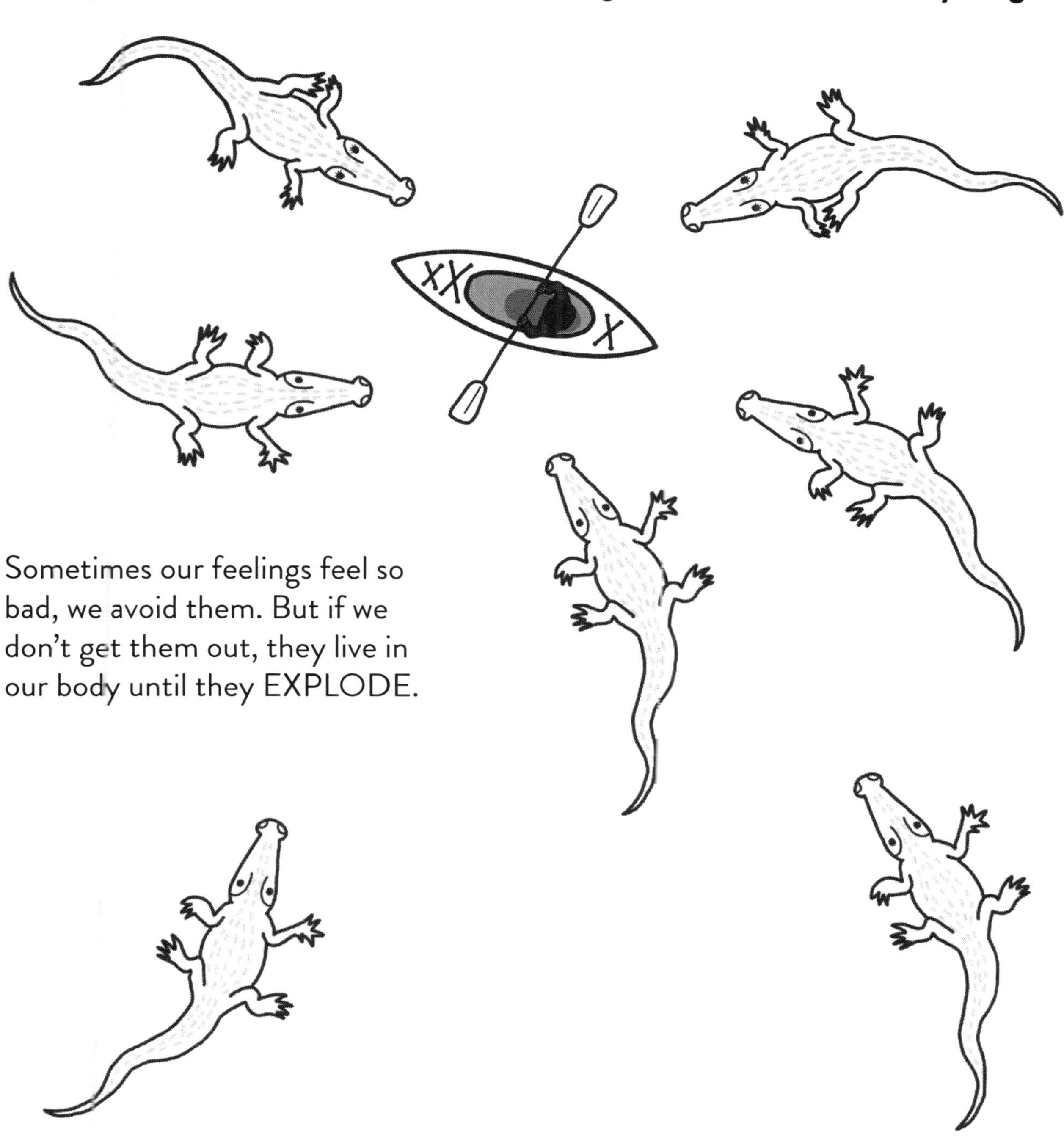

Sometimes our feelings feel so bad, we avoid them. But if we don't get them out, they live in our body until they EXPLODE.

Rate how you're feeling right now by circling a number:

1 - 2 - 3 - 4 - 5 - 6 - 7 - 8 - 9 - 10

totally calm (1) · right in the middle (5) · totally overwhelmed (10)

Brain Dump

1. In the circle, write every single thing floating around your brain, worrying you or stressing you out.

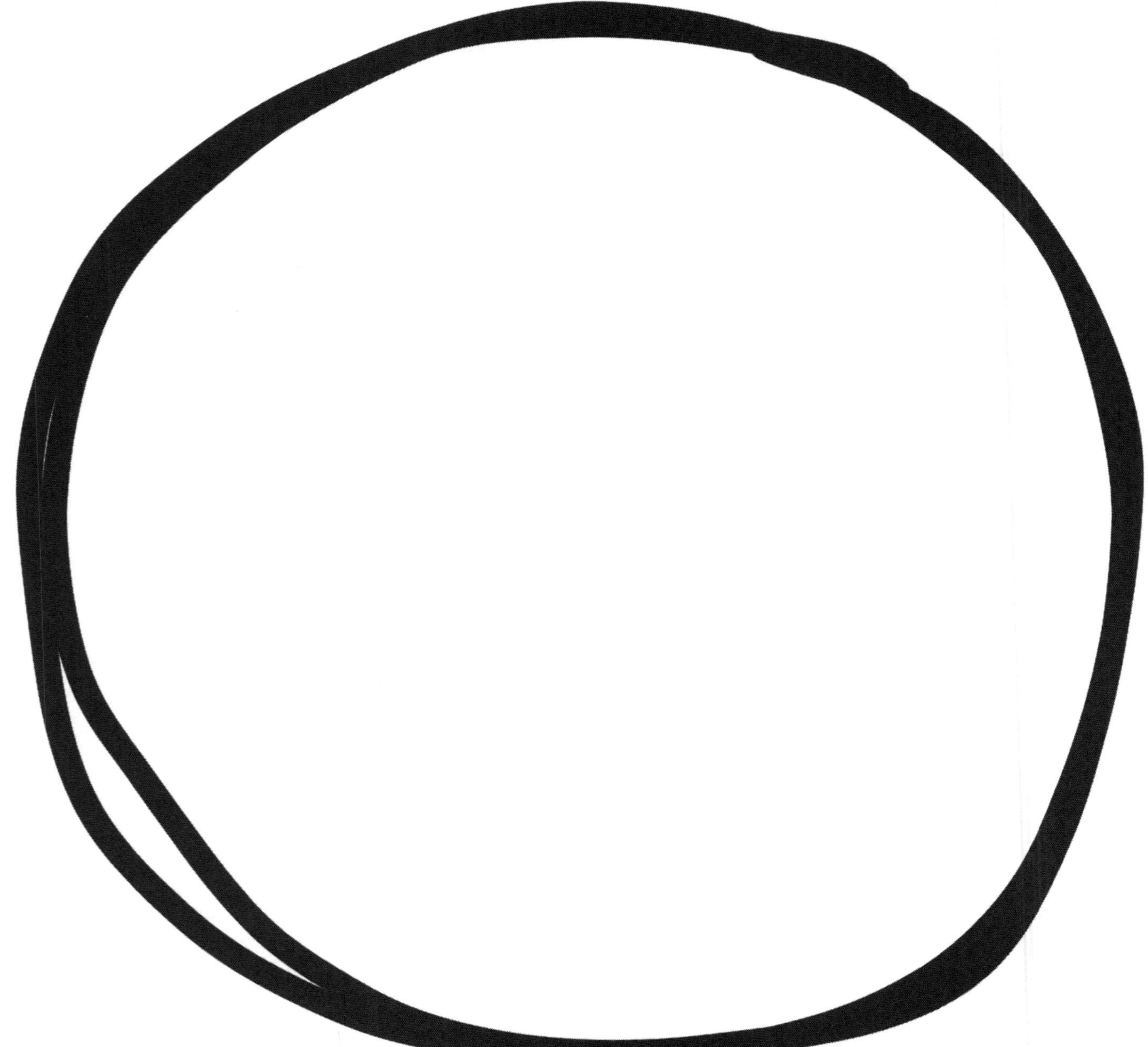

2. Circle the things that are stressing you the most.

3. Underline or highlight the things that are smaller or easier to do/solve.

List the underlined, easy things to do from the brain dump:

Rate how you're feeling right now by circling a number:

1 - 2 - 3 - 4 - 5 - 6 - 7 - 8 - 9 - 10

totally calm | right in the middle | totally overwhelmed

The circled things in your "brain dump" circle are your big and scary "alligator" worries.

Name your alligator (or multiple alligators):

Draw a crown on the alligator that feels the biggest or scariest.

That is the alligator closest to your boat.

When we are overwhelmed, it feels like we have too many problems.
The way to feel better is to deal with the alligator closest to your boat **first**.

Brainstorm some solutions for the alligator closest to your boat.

What might make this situation better? No ideas are bad ideas here. List them all in the circles below.

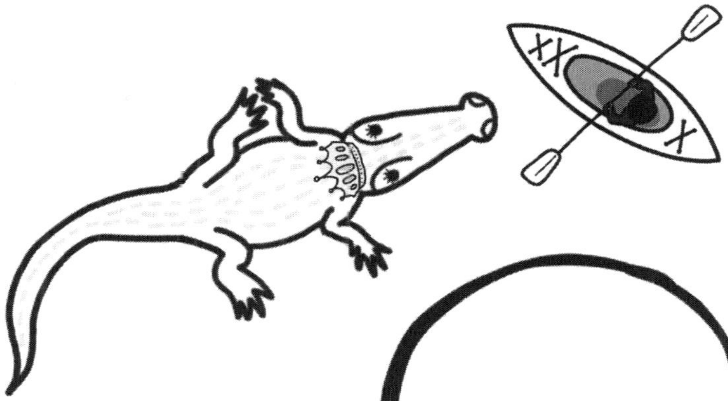

Look at each of your ideas. What might happen if you try each one? Thinking about what could happen will help you decide which solutions are better than others.

Cross out any ideas you think won't work very well.
Now decide which solution you'll try first. Put a star next to it.

There is no one "right answer." If this idea doesn't work, you will try a different one!
You got this! We can do hard things.

Rate how you're feeling right now by circling a number:

1 - 2 - 3 - 4 - 5 - 6 - 7 - 8 - 9 - 10

totally calm (1) · right in the middle (5) · totally overwhelmed (10)

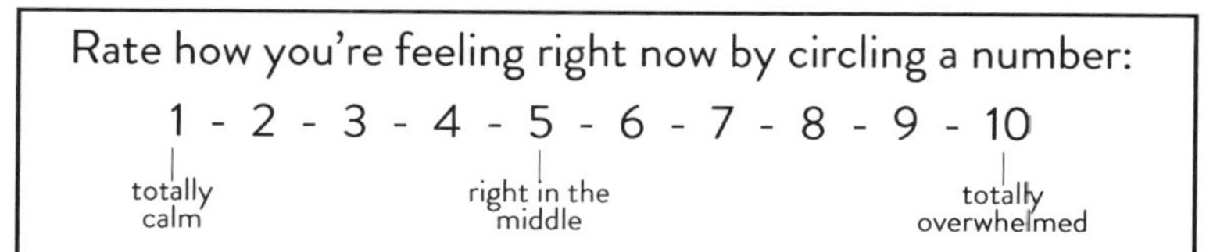

OVERWHELMED?

Being overwhelmed feels a little like being in a boat surrounded by alligators.

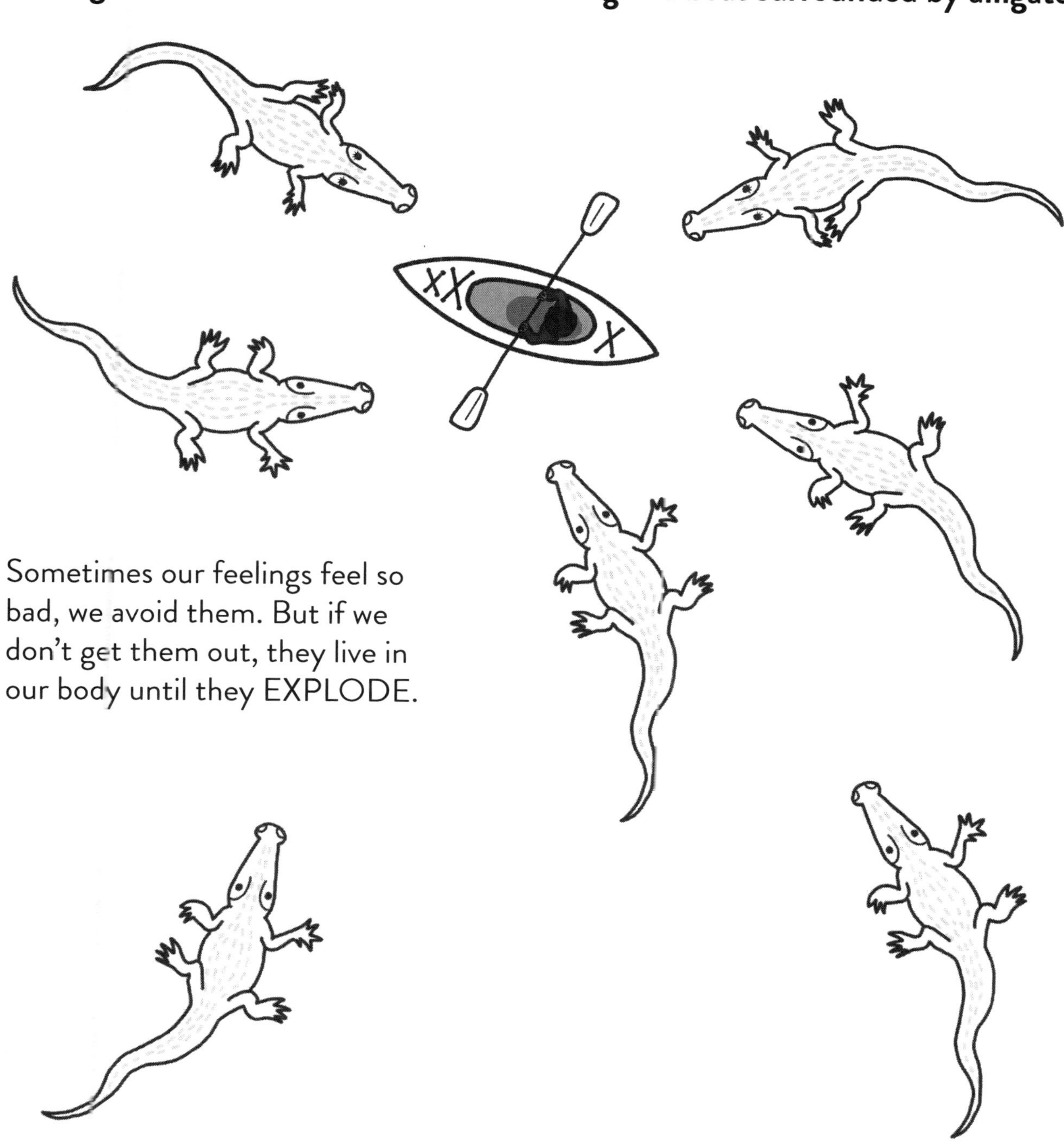

Sometimes our feelings feel so bad, we avoid them. But if we don't get them out, they live in our body until they EXPLODE.

Rate how you're feeling right now by circling a number:

1 - 2 - 3 - 4 - 5 - 6 - 7 - 8 - 9 - 10

1	5	10
totally calm	right in the middle	totally overwhelmed

Brain Dump

1. In the circle, write every single thing floating around your brain, worrying you or stressing you out.

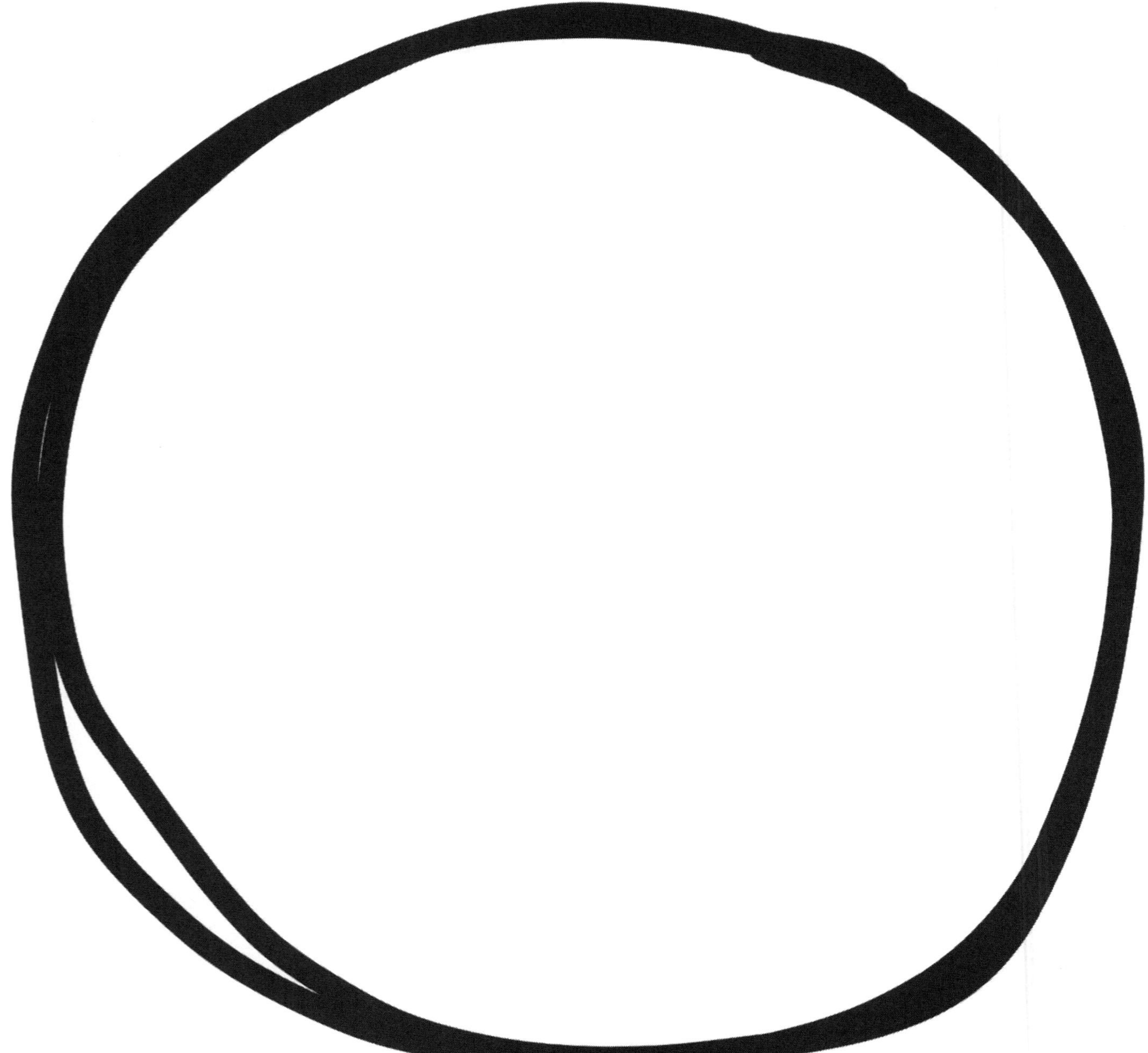

2. Circle the things that are stressing you the most.

3. Underline or highlight the things that are smaller or easier to do/solve.

List the underlined, easy things to do from the brain dump:

Rate how you're feeling right now by circling a number:

1 - 2 - 3 - 4 - 5 - 6 - 7 - 8 - 9 - 10

totally calm | right in the middle | totally overwhelmed

The circled things in your "brain dump" circle are your big and scary "alligator" worries.

Name your alligator (or multiple alligators):

Draw a crown on the alligator that feels the biggest or scariest.

That is the alligator closest to your boat.

When we are overwhelmed, it feels like we have too many problems.
The way to feel better is to deal with the alligator closest to your boat **first**.

Brainstorm some solutions for the alligator closest to your boat.

What might make this situation better? No ideas are bad ideas here. List them all in the circles below.

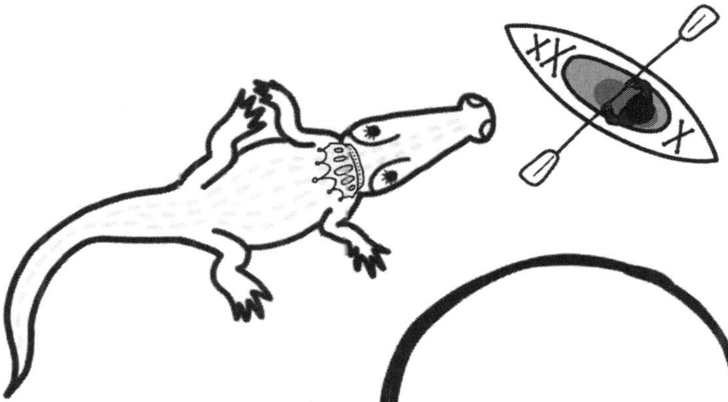

Look at each of your ideas. What might happen if you try each one? Thinking about what could happen will help you decide which solutions are better than others.

Cross out any ideas you think won't work very well.
Now decide which solution you'll try first. Put a star next to it.

There is no one "right answer." If this idea doesn't work, you will try a different one!
You got this! We can do hard things.

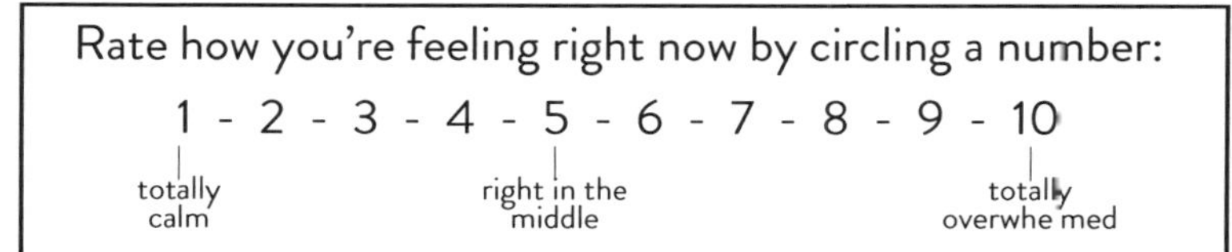

OVERWHELMED?

Being overwhelmed feels a little like being in a boat surrounded by alligators.

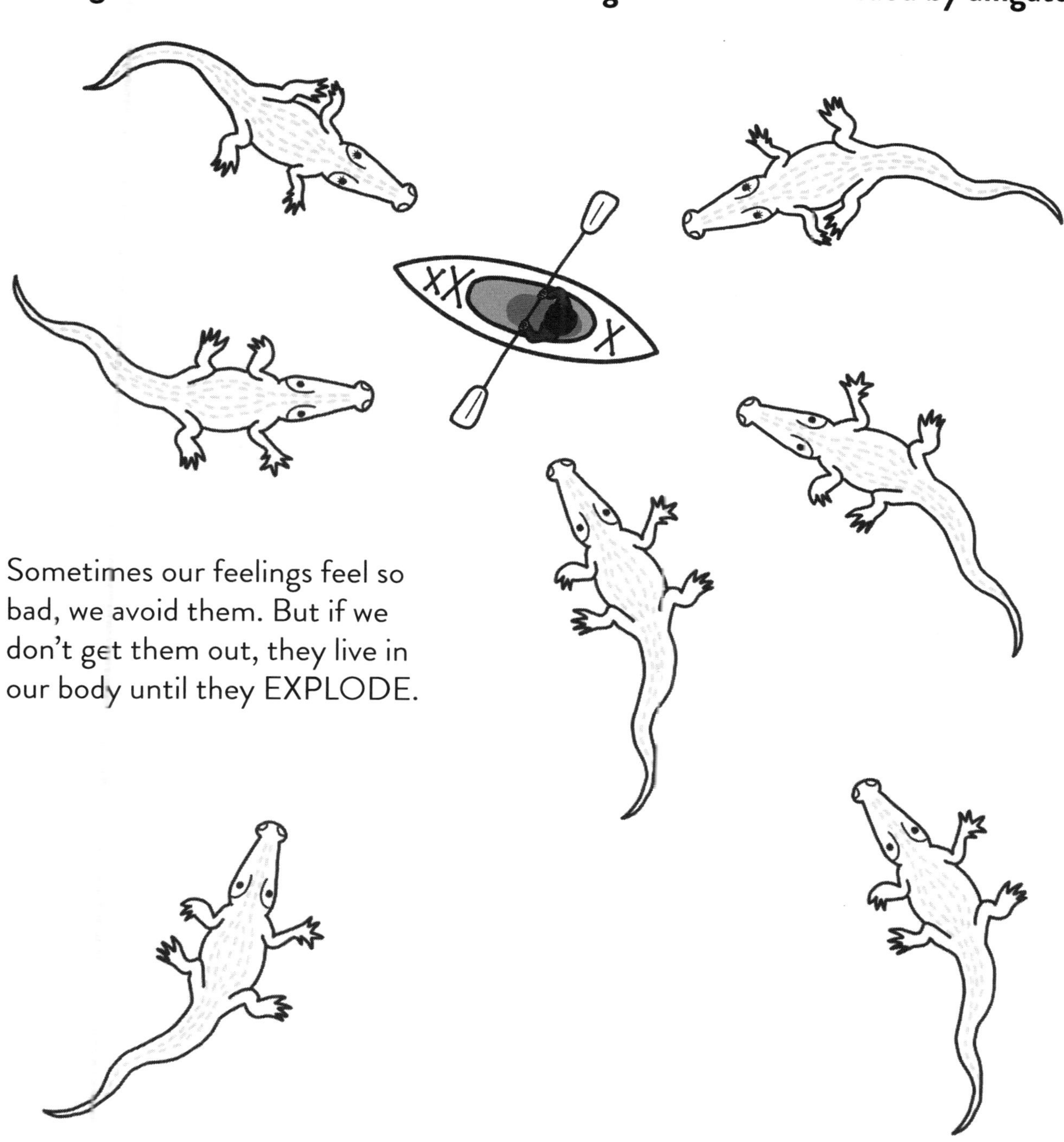

Sometimes our feelings feel so bad, we avoid them. But if we don't get them out, they live in our body until they EXPLODE.

Rate how you're feeling right now by circling a number:

1 - 2 - 3 - 4 - 5 - 6 - 7 - 8 - 9 - 10

totally calm (1) · right in the middle (5) · totally overwhelmed (10)

Brain Dump

① In the circle, write every single thing floating around your brain, worrying you or stressing you out.

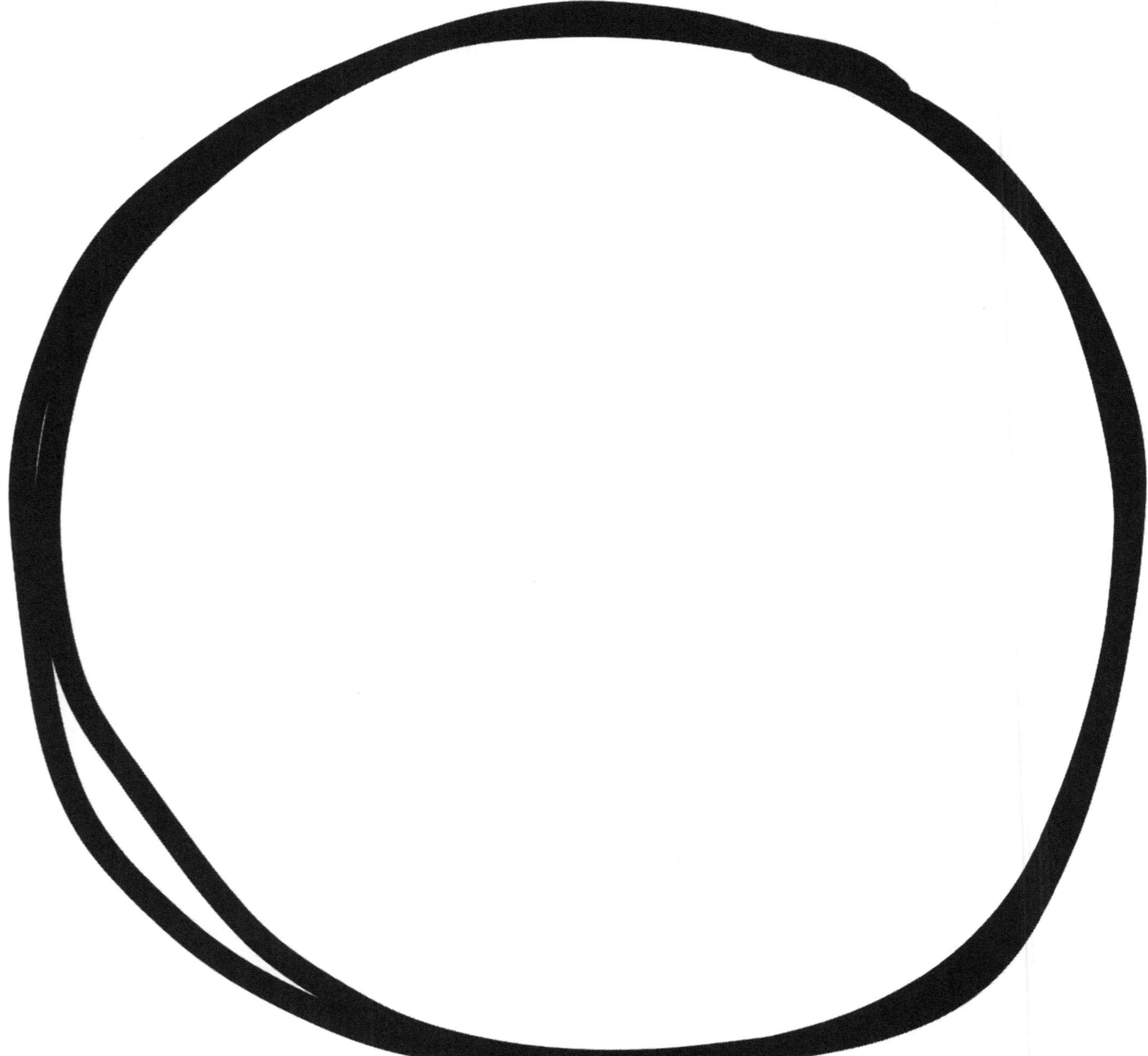

② Circle the things that are stressing you the most.

③ Underline or highlight the things that are smaller or easier to do/solve.

List the underlined, easy things to do from the brain dump:

Rate how you're feeling right now by circling a number:

1 - 2 - 3 - 4 - 5 - 6 - 7 - 8 - 9 - 10

totally calm | right in the middle | totally overwhelmed

The circled things in your "brain dump" circle are your big and scary "alligator" worries.

Name your alligator (or multiple alligators):

Draw a crown on the alligator that feels the biggest or scariest.

That is the alligator closest to your boat.

When we are overwhelmed, it feels like we have too many problems.
The way to feel better is to deal with the alligator closest to your boat **first**.

Brainstorm some solutions for the alligator closest to your boat.

What might make this situation better? No ideas are bad ideas here. List them all in the circles below.

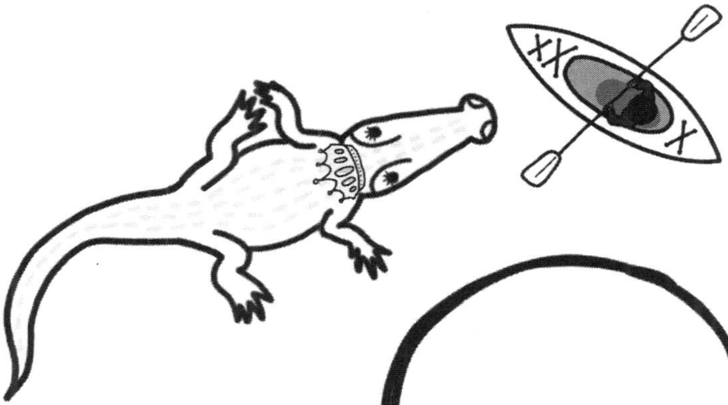

Look at each of your ideas. What might happen if you try each one? Thinking about what could happen will help you decide which solutions are better than others.

Cross out any ideas you think won't work very well.
Now decide which solution you'll try first. Put a star next to it.

There is no one "right answer." If this idea doesn't work, you will try a different one! You got this! We can do hard things.

Rate how you're feeling right now by circling a number:

1 - 2 - 3 - 4 - 5 - 6 - 7 - 8 - 9 - 10

totally calm (1) · right in the middle (5) · totally overwhelmed (10)

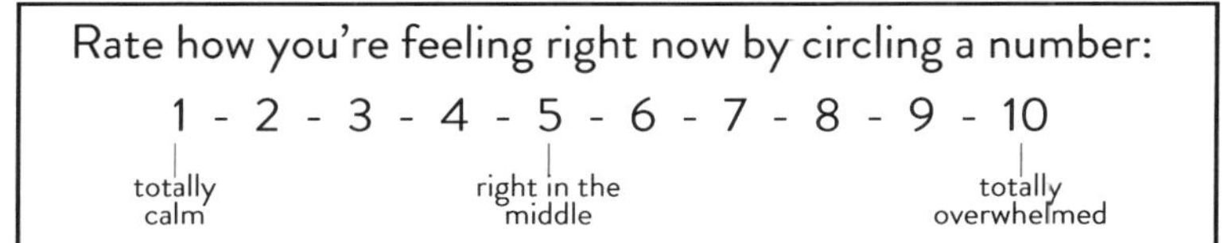

Made in the USA
Monee, IL
20 October 2023

44911557R00068